CRITICAL PERSPECTIVES ON WORK AND OR~~GANISATIONS~~

Series editors:

David Knights, Department of Management, University of Keele
Paul Thompson, Department of Business Studies, University of Edinburgh
Chris Smith, School of Management, Royal Holloway, University of London
Hugh Willmott, Manchester School of Management, UMIST

This series offers a range of titles examining the broad areas of work and organisation within a national and global arena. Each book in the series is written by leading experts and covers a topic chosen to appeal to students and academics. Originating out of the International Labour Process Conference, the series will be informative, topical and leading edge.

Published:

Alan Felstead and Nick Jewson *Global Trends in Flexible Labour*

Paul Thompson and Chris Warhurst *Workplaces of the Future*

Macmillan Critical Perspectives on Work and Organisations Series
Series Standing Order ISBN 0–333–73535–8
(outside North America only)

You can receive future titles in this series as they are published by placing a standing order. Please contact your bookseller or, in case of difficulty, write to us at the address below with your name and address, the title of the series and the ISBN quoted above.

Customer Services Department, Macmillan Distribution Ltd
Houndmills, Basingstoke, Hampshire RG21 6XS, England

Global Trends in Flexible Labour

Edited by
Alan Felstead and Nick Jewson

MACMILLAN
Business

First published 1999 by
MACMILLAN PRESS LTD
Houndmills, Basingstoke, Hampshire RG21 6XS
and London
Companies and representatives throughout the world

ISBN 0–333–72998–6 hardcover
ISBN 0–333–72999–4 paperback

A catalogue record for this book is available from the British
Library.

This book is printed on paper suitable for recycling and made
from fully managed and sustained forest sources.

10 9 8 7 6 5 4 3 2 1
08 07 06 05 04 03 02 01 00 99

Printed and bound in Great Britain by
Creative Print & Design (Wales), Ebbw Vale

Contents

List of Figures

List of Tables

Preface

Most of the chapters in this volume began life as papers delivered at the Fifteenth Annual International Labour Process Conference held in Edinburgh. We organised one of the streams on non-standard forms of employment and flexible labour, inviting a range of specialist scholars from all over the world to make contributions. Their presentations form the nucleus of this book.

We would sincerely like to thank all those who attended and participated in this enjoyable event. We would also like to acknowledge our gratitude to the conference organisers for suggesting that we put this collection of essays together, and to our Series Editor, Chris Smith. Finally we would like to thank Ian Goodchild for the excellent help he gave us in preparing the manuscript for publication.

Alan Felstead
Nick Jewson

Notes on the Contributors

NICOLA JOSÉ DE FREITAS ARMSTRONG was formerly a Lecturer in Sociology at the University of Canterbury, Christchurch, New Zealand. She published in the areas of paid and unpaid work, the state and feminist research. Tragically she died on 15 June 1998 shortly after completing her contribution to this book.

JOHN BURGESS is Senior Lecturer, Department of Economics, University of Newcastle, New South Wales, Australia. His research interests include employment restructuring, regional workplace industrial relations, employment policy and comparative public policy. Has published articles in the *Australian Bulletin of Labour*, *New Zealand Journal of Industrial Relations*, *International Journal of Employment Studies*, and *Labour and Industry*.

TONY MAN-YIU CHIU is a postgraduate student at Nuffield College, Oxford University, UK. His research interests focus on the spatial order of global cities and he has recently completed a study of the transformation of the urban structure of Hong Kong.

CHRISTINE COUSINS is Principal Lecturer in the Department of Social Sciences, University of Hertfordshire, UK. Her current research interests include work, employment and welfare in Europe and she has recently published on women in the labour market and the welfare state in Spain. She is the author of *Controlling Social Welfare: A Sociology of the Welfare State, Welfare Work and Organisations* (1987) and *Society, Work and Welfare in Europe* (1998).

ALAN FELSTEAD is Director of Research and Senior Research Fellow at the Centre for Labour Market Studies, University of Leicester, UK. His books include, with Patricia Leighton (eds), *The New Entrepreneurs: Self-Employment and Small Business in Europe* (1992), *The Corporate Paradox: Power and Control in the Business Franchise* (1993) and, with Nick Jewson, *In Work, At Home: Towards an Understanding of Homeworking* (1999).

MARK HARVEY is a Senior Research Fellow at the Centre for Research in Innovation and Competition, University of Manchester, UK. His current research interests include forms of capitalism, the role of the state, taxation policies, welfare regimes and labour markets.

NICK JEWSON is Director of the Ethnicity Research Centre in the Department of Sociology, University of Leicester, UK. He has published extensively on ethnicity, employment and equal opportunities policies. His recent publications include, with Suzanne MacGregor (eds), *Transforming Cities: Contested Governance and New Social Divisions* (1997) and, with Alan Felstead, *In Work, At Home: Towards an Understanding of Homeworking* (1999).

EIJI KYOTANI is Professor of Industrial Sociology at Nagano University, Japan. He has published articles and books on the labour process and labour-management relations in Japanese corporations, including *Flexibility towa Nanika* (*What is the Flexibility of the Japanese Labour Process?*) (1993). He is currently conducting research on changing managerial strategies and multi-national Japanese corporations.

JUNE LAPIDUS is Associate Professor of Economics at Roosevelt University, Chicago, USA. Her areas of interest include comparable worth, welfare reform and poverty. She has published in *International Contributions to Labour Studies*, *Review of Radical Political Economics*, *Feminist Economics*, and *Work and Occupations*. She is also a staff economist at the Center for Popular Economics based in Amherst, Massachusetts, USA.

TAI-LOK LUI is Associate Professor of Sociology at The Chinese University of Hong Kong. He is the author of *Waged Work at Home: The Social Organisation of Industrial Outwork in Hong Kong* (1994) and the co-author of *City-States in the Global Economy: Industrial Restructuring in Hong Kong and Singapore* (1997).

PETER ROBINSON is Senior Economist at the Institute for Public Policy Research (IPPR), London, UK. He is the editor of *New Economy*, the IPPR's journal. He is also a Research Associate at the Centre for Economic Performance at the London School of Economics, UK. His main areas of interest are macroeconomic policy, the labour market, unemployment and wages, education and training and the welfare state. He has an interest in international comparisons of economic performance and educational attainment.

SAM ROSENBERG is Professor of Economics at Roosevelt University, Chicago, USA. He is currently conducting research on labour market segmentation and low-wage labour in Chicago. He is the editor of *The State and the Labor Market* (1989). His forthcoming work includes *Growth, Decline and Rejuvenation: The American Economy Since 1940*.

GLENDA STRACHAN is Senior Lecturer, Employment Studies Group, Department of Management, University of Newcastle, New South Wales, Australia. Her research focuses on national and workplace industrial relations, employment policies and affirmative action. She also has interests in labour history, especially with respect to women's work. Her book *Labour of Love: The History of the Nurses' Association in Queensland 1860-1950* was published in 1996. She has also published in the *Journal of Industrial Relations*,

Journal of Interdisciplinary Gender Studies, Nursing History Review and *Nursing Ethics.*

SUE YEANDLE is Professor of Sociology at Sheffield Hallam University, Sheffield, UK, where her research is based in the Centre for Regional Economic and Social Research. She has written widely on employment, gender and family issues, and was co-author/contributor to *Changing Places: Women's Lives in the City* (1996).

1 Flexible Labour and Non-Standard Employment: An Agenda of Issues

Alan Felstead and Nick Jewson

Introduction

This collection of essays examines the worldwide growth of flexible labour. Flexible labour is conventionally thought of as part-time, temporary and self-employment. However, it is also often taken to include a host of other types of work, such as freelancing, subcontracting, outsourcing, homeworking, teleworking, franchising, zero-hours contracts, fixed-term contracts, seasonal working, flexi-time, consultancy work and many more. A common feature of all these types of employment is that they diverge from the pattern which became regarded in mid-twentieth century advanced capitalist economies as the 'norm'. Such 'standard' jobs and careers were defined as full-time, permanent, open-ended and secure. These rested upon a formal contract of employment, a range of legally binding terms and conditions, and other obligations placed on the employer and the state.

It is immediately apparent that the range of jobs thus identified encompasses many different and contrasting types of work and employment relationships. This diversity inevitably prompts the question: what constitutes the common feature of these types of employment? Uncertainty is heightened still further by confused and contradictory terminology which litters the literature. This nomenclature includes a plethora of terms, some with contrasting meanings and others which appear to be different but which, in practice, are similar (Atkinson and Meager, 1986; Hakim, 1987; Rodgers and Rodgers, 1989; Pollert, 1991; Polivka, 1996b; Cohany, 1996; Krahn, 1995; Akyeampong, 1997; Casey *et al.*, 1997; Kalleberg *et al.*, 1997; Purcell and Purcell, forthcoming). The phrase 'precarious employment' highlights that some workers have jobs that can be readily terminated and they are highly vulnerable to unemployment. This term is sometimes used interchangeably with 'contingent work'. The latter refers to jobs which workers themselves perceive as coming to an end in the near future. In principle, contingency might also be taken to denote jobs within the enterprise that are neither necessary nor essential. This conception of contingency implies not perceptions of future prospects but an evaluation of functions within the labour process. The concepts of 'core' and 'peripheral' workforce, in part, entail a similar distinction. The term 'insecure workforce' is often used to refer to those who fall outside the formal regulations surrounding labour markets and are therefore left unprotected. The extent of such employment must of necessity reflect the coverage and character of the regulatory framework in a society. Another term with extensive currency is 'atypical work'. This implies unusual or not average work – although in some labour markets a majority might be engaged in precarious or contingent employment. 'Flexible labour' itself has several meanings, revolving around employers' scope to make rapid short-term adjustments to the supply of labour in response to changes in demand.

The multiplication of terms to refer to an assortment of types of work is indicative of a lack of theoretical precision characteristic of research in this area. It also has practical implications for data gathering and the inter-pretation of trends. Different numerical estimates can be derived by operationalising competing concepts. Failure to distinguish adequately be-tween contrasting types of jobs results in lumping together incommensurate categories of work and relations of employment. A basic requirement for research in this field is, therefore, greater conceptual clarity. One of the aims in bringing this collection of essays together within a single volume is to confront the reader with different terms and data sets, drawn from around the world. We will use 'flexible labour' and 'non-standard forms of employment' interchangeably to designate these segments of the labour market. However, these should be regarded as a working terminology and they will be prob-lematised in the course of the text.

It should be recognised at the outset that these terms – flexible labour and non-standard forms of employment – are not value neutral. They blur differ-ent meanings and incorporate moral and political judgements. The term 'non-standard' has several layers of meaning which can easily be confused. It can denote 'exceptional' or 'unusual' employment relations. This implies that there is a concept of a normal distribution of types of work which raises questions about where to draw the line. An arbitrary and misleading di-chotomy may be imposed on what is, in reality, a graded continuum. Another usage indicates work which is 'inferior', 'deviant' or 'flawed' – in short, *sub*standard. Here the concept of standard implies to a floor below which it is unacceptable to fall. In this context, trade unions and other labour organisa-tions may regard 'keeping up standards' as essential to their aims and seek to eradicate non-standard forms. Similarly, without labouring the point, the word 'flexible' has many connotations. In general, flexibility is regarded as a virtue, implying creativity, innovation and positive response to change. While non-standard forms of employment have their trenchant critics, it is apparently difficult to mount a defence of *in*flexible employment.

The use of these terms should not be allowed to obscure the historically specific origins of standard employment. It is not our intention here to give an account of that history. Rather, we wish to register that the experience of full-time, permanent, secure employment by the mass of the workforce is a relatively recent phenomenon. It is characteristic of large-scale, highly capitalised economies undergoing long-range processes of economic growth. These were conditions which flourished in Western societies in the three or four decades after the Second World War. Even then, however, many forms of employment persisted which departed from the standard. The notions of standard and non-standard labour do not, therefore, refer to universal features of jobs in capitalist societies. They are instead social constructions generated during particular periods and within specific sets of institutional structures.

Indeed, the very notion of 'a job' – as a continuous activity within a specific occupation for one employer – evolved only relatively recently. In the eighteenth century many labourers moved from one task to another as the seasons changed and new opportunities arose. Work involved multiple activities, each with their own spatial and temporal rhythms, and a fluid movement between a range of skills (Joyce, 1987; Thompson, 1968). 'The job' referred to an activity or to raw materials being processed by the labourer, rather than to a bureaucratically defined position in an organisation. As jobs in the modern sense came into existence, they ushered in a series of new practices, institutions and discourses, that opened up the possibility of formalised systems of terms and conditions, rewards and remuneration, and modes of negotiation.

There is considerable evidence that in the 1980s and 1990s large corporations – in sectors such as banking, finance, sales and retail – switched to the employment of part-timers and workers on short-term contracts at all levels in the workforce. The rise of non-standard employment at the end of the twentieth century has sometimes been characterised as the 'decline of the job'. Its advocates see the future as belonging to 'portfolio people', offering their skills to many different clients and customers, moving between different workplaces, working from home using modern technology at some point in their lives (Handy, 1995). This optimistic vision also claims that the openness and variety of these arrangements generates access to the labour market for groups – such as women with children – that were disadvantaged by restrictions in the past. A more pessimistic interpretation of these trends expresses great concern about the fate of low-paid employees who do not enjoy employment protection and statutory benefits. Far from opening up new opportunities, the fear is that the surge of non-standard work is associated with rock-bottom wage rates, coercive management, intensified labour processes, unsocial hours and high rates of job turnover.

Setting the Agenda

These developments have increasingly attracted the attention of economists, sociologists and policy analysts. Debate about non-standard employment initially gained prominence in the 1980s, triggered by the idea of the so-called 'flexible firm' (Atkinson and Meager, 1986). According to this model, management divides workforce into core and peripheral groups – often regarded as equivalent to standard and non-standard respectively – thereby achieving enhanced levels of flexibility in hiring and firing, numbers of hours worked, job demarcations and worker remuneration. The 'flexible firm' was seen as associated with radical changes in the organisation of production, including post-Fordism, flattened managerial hierarchies, team working and technological innovations.

The concept of the 'flexible firm' came in for substantial criticism (e.g. Pollert, 1988a, 1988b and 1991), not least because it was derived from generalisations drawn from the behaviour of a small number of employing organisations. Controversy surrounded the extent to which flexibility is deliberately sought by management as part of a forward-looking plan which systematically relates labour-use patterns to corporate or business objectives. Subsequent case studies suggested that, contrary to the model, a significant trend towards such an employment *strategy* was difficult to detect (Hunter and MacInnes, 1991).

In the wake of these criticisms, some researchers turned their attention to trends in the size and structure of labour markets. This was also prompted by an awareness of the impact of changes in modes of regulation and institutional forms of employment. A number of investigators examined large national data sets, such as the Labour Force Survey in Britain (Dex and McCulloch, 1995; 1997) and the Current Population Survey in the United States (Polivka, 1996a and 1996b). These studies revealed a consistent picture of steady growth in non-standard forms of employment, but not one as dramatic and as radical as originally suggested by proponents of the 'flexible firm' thesis.

Other large-scale surveys explored the employment practices of firms. Among the most well-known in the UK are the Company Level Industrial Relations Survey (CLIRS), the Employers' Labour Use Survey (ELUS), and the Arbitration, Conciliation and Advisory Service (ACAS) survey (Marginson, 1986 and 1989; McGregor and Sproull, 1991 and 1992; Hakim, 1990; ACAS, 1988). These confirmed that employers with a conscious core-periphery employment strategy form a very small minority of those who have peripheral workers on their payroll. There is also evidence that more change may be claimed by corporate management than actually takes place at establishment level (Marginson, 1989).

Despite the reservations of those academics who have criticised the 'flexible firm' thesis, influential policy-makers have anticipated – and indeed have sought to facilitate and hasten – the growth of non-standard forms in many different societies across the globe. Flexible labour has, at various times, been heralded as the way of the future in countries across Europe, North America, Asia and Australasia. These are, however, very different societies, with contrasting institutional structures, cultural traditions and historical experiences. Each has its own ways of collecting and compiling labour market statistics, making comparisons a complex process. The concept of non-standard work covers many different types of labour in each. There is, therefore, a need to examine and compare the reputed global rise of non-standard forms within the context of the specific features of a range of contrasting types of societies. Such is the aim of this book.

The essays that follow have been selected in order to build upon earlier work, addressing a series of issues which are prominent in the literature. In addition, they seek to raise new questions and open new avenues of theoretical and empirical investigation. A number of these themes are dealt with in particular chapters; some are common to many.

Definitions and concepts

As Pollert has remarked, 'a quagmire of confused assumptions' (1988b:311) has long characterised the debate about flexibility and non-standard employment. Many definitions simply adopt a negative approach. Flexible labour becomes a residual category. Conventional ways of operationalising the definition in national data sets typically confine the non-standard workforce to temporary workers, part-timers and the self-employed. This approach has primarily been driven by practical considerations of data collection and manipulation. While it has the merits of seeking to generate comparative data, this strategy leaves the concept untheorised. It also aggregates groups whose commonality is by no means obvious. However, this statistical project has largely eclipsed more theoretical concerns. A third approach adopts legal definitions which rest on some notion of the employment contract (Deakin, 1986). The problem here is that different national legal systems imply different definitions and legal concepts are not necessarily those of social science (Hakim, 1997:23).

A fundamentally different approach is needed. One such would be to define non-standard forms of employment in terms of the social relations of production. This principle seeks their common denominator in the relationship between the seller and purchaser of labour power. One of the implications of such an approach is that many of the self-employed would not be included within the ranks of the 'non-standard workforce' since their employment relations are fundamentally different from those of wage labour. A fruitful line of enquiry might be to compare the juxtaposition of the social relations of production and reproduction within the lives of standard and non-standard workers. An approach along these lines requires a sustained theoretical analysis that has yet to be fully developed in the literature. These themes are, however, taken up in this volume (see Chapters 2 and 3).

Data and evidence

The study of large data sets on national labour markets has been the leading source of evidence for those investigating global trends in flexible labour. These include Labour Force Surveys in the UK, Canada and Australia and the Current Population Survey in the United States (Polivka, 1996b). Various time periods have been considered by different researchers. For example in the UK, Hakim (1987) reviewed the 1981–86 period and Casey (1991) examined 1979–87. More recently, Dex and McCulloch (1995; 1997) and Robinson (1994) have extended these analyses to the mid-1990s. In Canada, Krahn (1995) focused on the 1989–94 period, while Akyeampong (1997) looked at changes between 1991 and 1995. In Australia, Campbell (1996) investigated trends in casual employment from 1982–95. Blossfeld and Hakim (1997) focused on women working part-time in a range of European societies and the United States in the post-war period.

The authors of the chapters in this book have drawn heavily upon these and other such sources of evidence. They have marshalled the statistics in ways which highlight processes of change and patterns of diversity. They have also revealed the characteristics of those who engage in non-standard forms of work. A few have commented on the technicalities of data collection instruments and the degree of comparability between different sources (see Chapter 4 in this volume). The problem here is that different definitions imply the collection of different data – and different data sets group together various categories of workers. Most authors in this collection, however, have sought to keep technical issues to a minimum and have concentrated on substantive findings (see Chapters 5, 6, 7 and 8).

Another kind of evidence is that of the in-depth study typically involving interviews and the generation of qualitative material. Rarely have these attempted to make international comparisons, although there have been some notable exceptions (Gregory, 1991; O'Reilly, 1994). Some types of flexible labour, such as homeworking and 'teleworking', have attracted particular attention in recent years (Felstead and Jewson, 1996 and 1999; Phizacklea and Wolkowitz, 1995; Boris and Prügl, 1996). One of the essays in this volume follows in this tradition (see Chapter 3).

Characteristics of non-standard workers

There is a considerable amount of evidence to suggest that certain social groups are over-represented among temporary, part-time and other forms of non-standard labour. Women with dependent children have been a major source of recruitment, as have young workers, those nearing retirement and members of ethnic minorities (Dex and McCulloch, 1995; Blossfeld and Hakim, 1997). In contrast, the self-employed have largely been drawn from the male population (Felstead *et al.*, 1997). However, these divisions have not been the exclusive preserve of one group or another. In recent years, others have been absorbed into the non-standard labour force. Furthermore, jobs that once set the standard (e.g. banking and finance) have now had their terms and conditions redefined, thereby casting the net of flexibility wider.

Discussion of the characteristics of those engaged in flexible labour makes it clear that some disadvantaged groups have, over long historical periods, experienced severe limitations on their access to standard jobs. For these, standard jobs were rarely typical or average. Standard employment has stereotypically been white, male and middle class. A new feature of the labour market may be the extension of flexibility into these bastions.

From the perspective of this volume, two questions arise. To what extent are non-standard workers drawn from traditional groups? To what extent are their ranks swelled by people who in an earlier era might have been expected to command a standard job? Responses are provided in Chapters 4, 5, 6, 7, 8, 9 and 10.

Quality and choice

Opinions are divided about the quality and desirability of non-standard employment. Some argue that not only employers but also workers enjoy the benefits of flexibility. For example, respondents to a survey of part-time workers by Watson and Fothergill (1993) suggested that this form of employment offered them 'the best of both worlds', enabling them to strike a balance between work and other activities. Many of these were women with dependent children who felt that they had to fit working around school holidays and other family commitments. This has echoes with Hakim's thesis that female workers may be divided into two groups: those with a strong commitment to a full-time career; and those whose identity is rooted in the family, for whom employment is of secondary importance (Hakim, 1996). The latter may wish to increase their disposable incomes without taking on the additional routines and responsibilities associated with standard employment.

An alternative view is that non-standard forms offer only low pay, unsocial hours, poor working conditions, poor promotion prospects and minimal job training (Dex and McCulloch, 1995). As Payne and Payne (1993 and 1994) note, there is a strong association between recent unemployment and non-standard forms of work. Far from reflecting choice, they are a measure of the constraints faced by large numbers of workers who are disadvantaged in various ways. They are portrayed as the victims of inequality arising from their gender, ethnicity, age, regional location and educational qualifications.

The essays contained in this collection provide a wealth of information about the quality of jobs (see Chapters 3, 4, 6, 7, 8, 9 and 10) and some seek to estimate the extent to which non-standard work can be regarded as a 'voluntary' option (see Chapters 4 and 5).

Global trends

A tentative conclusion from the various data sources described above is that non-standard forms are on the increase worldwide – but that the pattern varies from country to country and from period to period. This collection brings together within one volume up-to-date analyses of data sets from around the world. The various chapters discuss trends in New Zealand (Chapter 3), USA (Chapter 4), Britain (Chapters 5, 6 and 8), Sweden (Chapter 6), Spain (Chapter 6), Germany (Chapters 6 and 8), Australia (Chapter 7), France (Chapter 8), Denmark (Chapter 8), Italy (Chapter 8), Hong Kong (Chapter 9), Taiwan (Chapter 9) and Japan (Chapter 10).

International comparisons raise as many questions as they answer and thereby open up further items for the agenda addressed in this book. In order to explain differences and similarities between countries it is necessary to consider the key institutional frameworks which regulate their labour markets, the managerial strategies of employers, the broader societal contexts within which these relationships are played out and long-term processes of economic change.

Labour market regulation

One of the major reasons for differences between countries in the extent and type of use of flexible labour, concerns their systems of labour market regulation, both legal and voluntary. Recent years have seen radical changes in regulations affecting labour markets (e.g. Blanchflower and Freeman, 1994). However, the relationship between deregulation and employment restructuring is far from straightforward (Dex and McCulloch, 1997; McLaughlin, 1994). Different forms of non-standard work may be subject to greater or lesser levels of formal control. Moreover, in situations where workers in full-time permanent employment with open-ended contracts themselves enjoy relatively little protection, employers who seek flexibility may not need to resort to non-standard terms and conditions.

An international collection of essays offers an opportunity to develop comparative analyses of the relationship between different forms of labour market regulation and different categories of standard and non-standard employment. The chapters contained in this volume make comparisons between Britain and France (Chapter 2); Britain, USA and other OECD countries (Chapter 5); and Germany, Spain, Sweden and the UK (Chapter 6).

Managerial strategies and issues of control

The growth of non-standard forms of employment has been linked with analogous developments in organisational structures and labour processes.

These have undermined and eroded formal, bureaucratic and rule-bound modes of recruiting, mobilising and disciplining labour. They have been associated with increased levels of outsourcing, subcontracting, networking, franchising and niche marketing (Piore and Sabel, 1984; Felstead, 1993; Amin, 1994). Many of those involved are self-employed, working on a freelance basis. By their very nature such developments weaken standard forms of employment and open up scope for the growth of non-standard work.

Post-Fordist modes of organisation have commonly been seen as responses to enhanced international competition from both the developed and less developed world. These pressures are stimulated by and contribute to new forms of global interdependency, locking societies into market-driven competitive cycles. Thus, global trends in flexible labour can be seen as a manifestation of the dynamics of international capitalism.

An enduring controversy concerns the extent to which employers and managers *deliberately* pursue a core-periphery employment strategy in order to enhance flexibility. In part, this debate centres on the meaning of the term 'strategy'. This may be taken to imply a detailed plan worked out in advance in order to achieve a specified objective, akin to a military campaign (Hunter *et al.*, 1993). Alternatively, it may be taken to refer to patterns that emerge as the outcome of a looser series of related decisions (Procter *et al.*, 1994).

The chapters which follow explore managerial strategies and issues of control in a range of national contexts and link these to competitive pressures generated by the world economy (see Chapters 4, 7, 9 and 10).

Societal contexts

Social processes *within* labour markets and workplaces are shaped and influenced by relationships *between* economic institutions and the wider social system (Lane, 1989). An understanding of the growth in non-standard forms of employment cannot, therefore, be complete without an analysis of broader societal contexts. Of particular significance are the mediating influences of welfare systems, family structures and gender relations. These provide a framework of entitlements and obligations, comprising a range of opportunities and constraints, that shape levels and forms of participation in employment. Crucial here are divisions of class, gender, ethnicity and age.

An understanding of differences in societal contexts begins to explain why particular types of non-standard employment flourish in some countries rather than in others. In addition, the impact of flexible labour on the lived experience and life chances of individuals can only be appreciated by placing their employment histories in the context of their overall social memberships. It follows that the study of global trends in flexible labour implies comparative analysis of the economic, political, social and cultural institutions of societies around the world.

This very difficult conceptual and empirical challenge is taken up in Chapter 8. Chapter 9 provides insights into these processes that form an interesting counterpoint. In addition, the theoretical analysis contained in Chapter 2 provides a definition and conceptual model of non-standard employment in terms of the relationship between work and non-work.

Economic development

A focus on global trends in flexible labour draws attention to processes of macroeconomic change. Non-standard forms of employment may be one of the ways in which late-developing industrial economies mobilise cheap labour to attain rapid economic growth. These strategies commonly entail international links between sections of the capitalist classes in the developed and less developed worlds. Such relationships are commonly forged around subcontracting chains which span the globe. In short, the growth of flexible labour is integral to the process of globalisation. Some of these issues are illustrated in the analysis of the industrialisation of Hong Kong and Taiwan provided in Chapter 9.

Outlining the Chapters

The agenda of issues identified in the previous section provides a framework that informs the various contributions to this book. In this section, the major themes of the chapters are sketched.

In Chapter 2, Mark Harvey outlines an original and closely argued theoretical perspective that provides a basis for defining and analysing standard and non-standard forms of employment. He avoids the empiricism and essentialism characteristic of definitions current in much of the literature by theorising employment *relationships* and the dynamics of their restructuring. His discussion is illustrated and informed by a comparison of the British and French construction industries.

Harvey focuses on the temporalities of work and what he calls 'the economies of time'. He is particularly interested in articulations between the sequences, rhythms and cycles of time in work and non-work. The chapter argues that the temporalities of the workplace and the household are fundamentally different and should not be regarded as equivalent. Similarly, Harvey proposes that the temporalities of standard and non-standard employment are incommensurate. He goes on to argue that standard employment is characterised by remuneration that covers not only time spent in work activities but also aspects of non-work time. For example, wages for standard jobs typically include payments for holidays, sickness and pensions (i.e. non-working time both during and after the termination of the employment relation). In contrast, workers holding non-standard jobs are paid solely for the blocks of time they spend working. There is no remuneration for non-working time.

Harvey suggests that the distinctive economies of time of standard and non-standard employment articulate with the times of the household in contrasting ways. The temporalities of the household are highly gendered. Moreover, temporal boundaries in households are relatively fluid, informal and variable. These features, he argues, facilitate intensification of work in the household as a way of accommodating the growth of non-standard forms and the restructuring of employment relations in a capitalist labour market.

In Chapter 3, Nicola José de Freitas Armstrong further explores temporal and spatial aspects of the relationship between home and work experienced by non-standard workers. Her interest lies in interactions between the micropolitics of households and the restructuring of labour markets.

Her chapter presents some of the findings from her empirical studies of 'teleworkers' in New Zealand. 'Teleworking', she argues, is of particular sociological interest because it entails the conjunction of two spheres of activity and meaning that are commonly presumed to have been separated during the early stages of capitalist industrialisation. Armstrong's research explores how men and women negotiate the identities of worker, partner, parent and household member when all these relationships occur in the same domestic space. Her contribution reports on in-depth interviews she conducted with male and female 'teleworkers', their partners and other household members. All the 'teleworkers' in the study were in professional occupations, typically involving manipulation of electronic text and participation in virtual networks.

Armstrong's analysis reveals the contested and competing nature of their identities and practices. The lived experience of 'telework' is shown to be constructed around highly gendered notions of self-discipline, physical endurance, emotional control and self-respect. These, in turn, shape the availability and subjectivities of teleworkers as parents and partners. The identities of Armstrong's respondents are expressed in the way in which they organise time and space within the home. Their use of a variety of boundary-making strategies in the household reflects the struggle between competing demands. The social construction of 'telework' is seen as emerging from often contradictory and fractured discourses surrounding autonomy, risk, control, pleasure, security and the body.

Armstrong's chapter offers a fascinating insight into what she calls the 'chaotic practices of everyday life' associated with one particular form of non-standard employment. It also identifies an agenda of issues and a series of interconnected layers of analysis. These encompass mediations that link the global to the local, institutional practices to personal feelings, and the labour market to its wider societal context.

In Chapter 4, Sam Rosenberg and June Lapidus shift the focus of attention to the host of competing terms, definitions and meanings contained in the analysis of large-scale data sets. They examine these in the context of the US debate about alternative ways of counting 'disposable workers'. Known in the US literature as 'contingent' or 'insecure workers', their employment is conditional on product demand – making their jobs uncertain and short term. Estimates of their numbers range from a low of less than 2 per cent of the US labour force to a high of around 30 per cent. Rosenberg and Lapidus demonstrate that this wide variation stems from the ways in which 'contingency' is operationalised.

To complicate the picture, Rosenberg and Lapidus note that within a few years of its initial usage some authors expanded the term 'contingent' to include all work arrangements deviating from the standard full-time job. Hence, the common association which many make – in the US and beyond – between non-standard work and insecurity. The chapter examines the veracity of this association. The results provide a strong antidote to those who suggest – consciously or otherwise – that *all* non-standard work is inevitably associated with greater levels of uncertainty. While higher levels of contingency and insecurity are felt by those in non-standard jobs than among regular full-timers, the picture is more complex when the non-standard category is unpacked. The proportions reporting that they did not expect their employment to last varied according to the type under focus. Most notably, independent contractors stand out as being the most optimistic, other groups are less sanguine. Similarly, independent contractors declare a stronger preference for their current working arrangements than workers in other non-standard situations.

A diverse pattern is also evident in the statistical portrait Rosenberg and Lapidus paint of those Americans who work in contingent and non-standard positions, and their terms and conditions. As a whole, contingent workers receive poorer pay and are less likely to receive employer-provided benefits such as health insurance and pensions. Rosenberg and Lapidus argue that it is more difficult to generalise about the characteristics of non-standard workers and their work in the US since the category includes a disparate collection of people and jobs. The implications of this analysis, therefore, are that there is a high level of slippage between definitions and considerable diversity within each category.

In Chapter 5, Peter Robinson also expresses dissatisfaction with the notion of lumping together a disparate collection of employment forms, as implied by the concept of non-standard work. He traces trends in flexible work in the UK over the 1979–1997 period by disaggregating the category into its commonly regarded constituents – part-time work, self-employment and temporary work. As a result, contrasting patterns are revealed which might not otherwise be visible. By disaggregating in this way, Robinson highlights a number of puzzles about the relationship between different types of non-standard work and levels of labour market regulation.

Robinson shows that part-time employment in the UK has been growing steadily since the Second World War, with no noticeable change of pace or direction in recent times. However, the data he presents suggest that trends in self-employment have varied more significantly. While its share remained broadly flat over the post-war period, between 1979 and 1989 self-employment leapt from 7 per cent to 13 per cent of the employed workforce, although since then it has fallen back slightly. Long-run trends in temporary working are more difficult to discern simply because the data are not available. Nevertheless, the evidence suggests that the growth in this type of non-standard work has been a relatively recent phenomenon in the UK, and has grown particularly steeply among men and those in the higher echelons of the labour market.

Robinson also uses comparative Organisation for Economic Co-operation and Development (OECD) data on types of non-standard forms of work in order to reinterpret the commonly held belief that a deregulated labour market is characterised by a high proportion of flexible labour. Interestingly, he argues that the evidence suggests the complete opposite. The most regulated labour markets – such as those in southern Europe – tend to have high rates of temporary engagements, self-employment and involuntary part-time working, while in deregulated labour markets – such as the UK and the US – temporary contracts, self-employment and involuntary part-time employment are comparatively low. Robinson's analysis, therefore, suggests that one would expect countries with high proportions of flexible labour to have relatively regulated labour markets and vice versa.

Christine Cousins, in Chapter 6, also focuses on the interconnections between labour market regulation and employment trends. She couches her explanation of the growth in non-standard employment in four European countries – Germany, Spain, Sweden and the UK – in terms of changes in regulatory frameworks. Her approach is, therefore, in sympathy with the argument advanced by Robinson in the previous chapter. She takes the approach a step further by arguing that non-standard employment will be more prevalent when *both* standard employment contracts are tightly regulated *and* non-standard work is loosely controlled.

Cousins argues that in Sweden and Germany all types of employment remain relatively well protected, and hence there is little incentive for employers to use non-standard forms of labour in preference to others. In these countries, employers seek to achieve flexibility in different ways by raising productivity levels, reducing working hours and increasing operating times. Elsewhere regulatory regimes continue to provide protection for some workers, while removing it from others. In Spain, for example, fixed-term contracts accounted for around a third of employment in 1995, more than double the proportion of ten years earlier. Cousins attributes these changes to employment legislation which permitted temporary employment agencies to operate for the first time in 1993.

More generally, Cousins argues that the consequences of working in a non-standard job vary enormously from society to society. In Sweden, women can exercise their right to go part-time on the birth of their first child without the loss of employment rights. However, part-timers in the UK, some of those in Germany and those on fixed-term contracts in Spain forfeit much more.

In Chapter 7, John Burgess and Glenda Strachan examine the growth of non-standard forms of employment in Australia in the context of managerial strategies, trade union responses and the implications for the overall labour market. They regard the recent growth in flexible labour as an integral part of a much wider process of economic restructuring. The spread of non-standard employment has decreased employment security, thereby enabling employers to extend their control over the labour process and to extract higher profits. This has, in part, been achieved by weakening trade unions and undermining the regulatory coverage of the Australian award structure. The logic of their argument has serious implications for *both* standard and non-standard workers.

Unlike other countries – such as the US and the UK – Australian law prescribes minimum legal entitlements to employees with on-going, or permanent, employment contracts. Those without such rights are excluded from receipt of benefits – such as sickness and holiday pay – as well as protections – such as prior notice of employment termination and unfair dismissal. Burgess and Strachan show that there have been substantial increases in a number of types of non-standard employment, including part-time and casual employees.

The chapter argues that employers have used the growth of non-standard employment to limit and weaken regulation of the labour market as a whole. As result, many workers have experienced a decrease in job security during a time of rising unemployment. In addition, employers have challenged and eroded the terms and conditions under which standard workers labour. This has, in part, been achieved by threats of off-shore relocation and by lobbying governments for labour market deregulation. Burgess and Strachan identify various implications of these trends for the Australian trade union movement. Attempts to halt or even reverse the process are hampered by a number of factors. Trade unions have traditionally been poor recruiters of female workers, yet they are the ones which dominate temporary and part-time work. Younger age groups are also found among the non-standard workforce, yet here, too, trade unions have found organisation difficult.

In Chapter 8, Sue Yeandle charts changes in non-standard forms of employment in five European countries – Denmark, Germany, France, Italy and the

UK – in the context of an analysis of their societal characteristics. She relates developments within national labour markets to the broader institutional structures and cultural systems of each society.

Yeandle begins by sketching the key features of the demographic, political and cultural frameworks within each of the countries selected for consideration. These are shown to have a range of implications for welfare systems, educational institutions, social policies, family structures, gender divisions and labour relations. She demonstrates that the five countries differ markedly in ways which have complex and cross-cutting implications for patterns of non-standard employment. Yeandle explores changes with respect to part-time jobs, self-employment, fixed-term contracts and family working. She maps national variations in each by age and gender. These are shown to correspond not only to differences in levels of demand by employers but also national arrangements with respect to childcare, training opportunities and welfare rights.

Overall, Yeandle discerns major long-term shifts in the social organisation of labour within European societies that are leading to greater diversity and fragmentation in employment relations, as well as new patterns of social differentiation and inequality. Changes in employment within and between societies, she suggests, are cutting across and redefining established divisions of class and gender, making a profound impact on personal identities, experiences of family life and life chances. In her view, the growth of non-standard working represents more than simply a reorganisation of employment relations among European workforces. It is also an indicator of complex social change across a raft of societal relationships.

In Chapter 9, Tai-lok Lui and Tony Man-yiu Chiu direct attention towards the role of non-standard forms of employment in long-term processes of economic growth. Their focus is on the industrialisation of Hong Kong and Taiwan. They explore themes concerning labour mobilisation, family relationships and gender inequalities highlighted by Yeandle in the previous chapter. These processes are located in the dynamics of global commodity production.

Lui and Chiu focus on interrelationships between global commodity chains, local economic organisation, family structures, gender divisions and labour supply. They argue that in both Hong Kong and Taiwan small-scale, family-centred manufacturing enterprises grew up under the stimulus of international market relationships that facilitated and stimulated export-oriented production. Buyer-driven commodity chains encouraged the growth of locally owned petty capitalist enterprises. These formed local networks of small- and medium-sized firms, characterised by a decentralised governance structure. The same global forces also discouraged businesses from becoming technologically sophisticated or from innovating in product design. Firms of this kind made extensive use of non-standard labour, including casual workers, part-timers, homeworkers, unpaid family members, contract labourers and the self-employed. This made possible cost reductions and rapid responses to changes in product demand.

Lui and Chiu argue that recruitment of non-standard labour was facilitated by gender inequalities and power differentials within patriarchal Chinese family structures. Cheap labour was often recruited from among the unmarried daughters of peasant and working-class families. These young women were obliged to accept low-grade employment in order to fulfil obligations to their families, such as supporting their brothers through education. In addition, homeworkers – predominantly working-class women with children – became a critical element of the flexible labour force. Many small manufacturers also mobilised the unpaid labour of female members of their own families. All these female workers were expected to subordinate their own desires and ambitions to the collective advancement of the family – thus making them a readily exploitable labour supply.

This chapter highlights the fragility and contingency of non-standard jobs. As competition from other newly industrialising societies with lower production costs increased, labour-intensive manufacturers in Hong Kong and Taiwan started to relocate their factories outside their own borders.

In Chapter 10, Eiji Kyotani reveals how the erosion of established employment contracts and the creation of non-standard forms of work increasingly characterise managerial strategies adopted by major international companies in Japan. In this example, large-scale businesses in an advanced capitalist economy deliberately respond to enhanced global competition by developing flexible labour policies intended to claw back the favourable employment conditions previously enjoyed by the Japanese core workforce. This chapter makes an interesting contrast, therefore, to that of Lui and Chiu which focuses upon small-scale enterprises in newly industrialising economies.

High levels of job security, lifelong employment and promotion by seniority were built into labour-management agreements in Japan after the Second World War. In the 1990s, Kyotani argues, these principles have come under attack from Japanese corporations. There has been a movement by management towards the introduction of short-term and low-security contracts, the erosion of the system of lifelong employment, and the development of promotion and payment by results. Some firms have hastened these changes by developing programmes that encourage existing employees to take early retirement, transfer jobs or switch into self-employment. Moreover, major Japanese corporations are seeking to persuade government to reduce legal regulation of the labour market. Their demands include a loosening of the regulations surrounding agency work, female employment, working hours and terms of employment.

As a result of these trends, the non-standard sector of the Japanese labour market is growing. Kyotani observes that female employees are particularly vulnerable to exclusion from the core workforce. They swell the ranks of those with flexible contracts, such as agency workers and part-timers. He also notes that these changes have implications for worker attitudes and material in-equalities. For example, evaluation by performance not only undermines expectations of predictable wage increases but also increases income differential within cohorts of workers. Japanese trade unions have, so far, responded ambiguously to these developments. They have sought to defend aspects of traditional standard employment contracts while, at the same time, making some concessions over terms and conditions. They have yet to devise a strategy that will successfully counteract the corrosive effects of these changes in the labour market on the size and solidarity of their membership.

Conclusion

A review of global trends in flexible labour thus suggests that the profound impact on those engaged in non-standard work is part of a broader transformation of the economic and social landscape. Labour markets around the world are becoming more segmented, fragmented and fractured. These changes have profound implications for material inequalities and personal identities. They also shape political ideologies, managerial discourses and the day-to-day lived experiences of workers. They pose serious challenges to the effectiveness of modes of organisation that have long served the labour movement. An understanding of these trends requires all the intellectual rigour and analytical devices that social science can muster.

The key inference of the chapters in this volume is that the starting point for this project must be a focus on social relationships in the labour market. The first task for a sociology of flexible labour is a theoretical analysis of buying and selling labour power in globalised capitalist systems of production. A comparative analysis will further reveal the complex layers of institutional and cultural mediations within each societal context. Theorising must, in turn, be informed by a quantitative perspective which operationalises – as far as possible – sociological and economic concepts in the construction and interpretation of large-scale data sets. The chapters in this volume represent lively and original contributions to the achievement of these challenging and urgent tasks. In addition – and perhaps more importantly – collectively they chart a broad research agenda which others may seek to follow.

References

ACAS (1988) *Labour Flexibility in Britain: The 1987 ACAS Survey*, London: ACAS.

Akyeampong, E. (1997) 'Work Arrangements: 1995 Overview', *Perspectives on Labour and Income*, 9: 1, 48–51.

Amin, A. (ed.) (1994) *Post-Fordism – A Reader*, Oxford: Blackwell.

Atkinson, J. and Meager, N. (1986) *Changing Working Patterns: How Companies Achieve Flexibility to Meet New Needs*, London: National Economic Development Office.

Blanchflower, D.G. and Freeman, R.B. (1994) 'Did the Thatcher Reforms Change British Labour Market Performance?', in Barrel (ed.) *The UK Labour Market: Comparative Aspects and Institutional Developments*, Cambridge: Cambridge University Press.

Blossfeld, H.-P. and Hakim, C. (eds.) (1997) *Between Equalization and Marginalization: Women Working Part-Time in Europe and the United States of America*, Oxford: Oxford University Press.

Boris, E. and Prügl, E. (1996) *Homeworkers in Global Perspective: Invisible No More*, London: Routledge.

Burchell, B. (1989) *Precarious Jobs in Labour Market Regulation: The Growth of Atypical Employment in Western Europe*, Geneva: International Institute for Labour Studies.

Campbell, I. (1996) 'The growth of casual employment in Australia: towards an explanation', in Teicher, J. (ed.) *Non-Standard Employment in Australia and New Zealand*, Melbourne: National Key Centre in Industrial Relations, Monash University.

Casey, B. (1991) 'Survey Evidence on Trends in "Non-Standard" Employment', in Pollert, A. (ed.) *Farewell to Flexibility?*, Oxford: Blackwell.

Casey, B., Metcalf, H. and Millward, N. (1997) *Employers' Use of Flexible Labour*, London: PSI.

Cohany, S.R. (1996) 'Workers in Alternative Employment Arrangements', *Monthly Labor Review*, 119: 10, 31–45.

Deakin, S. (1986) 'Labour Law and the Developing Employment Relationship in the UK', *Cambridge Journal of Economics*, 10: 3, 225–46.

Dex, S. and McCulloch, A. (1995) *Flexible Employment in Britain: A Statistical Analysis*, Manchester: Equal Opportunities Commission.

Dex, S. and McCulloch, A. (1997) *Flexible Employment: The Future of Britain's Jobs*, London: Macmillan.

Felstead, A. (1993) *The Corporate Paradox: Power and Control in the Business Franchise*, London: Routledge.

Felstead, A. and Jewson, N. (1996) *Homeworkers in Britain*, London: HMSO.

Felstead, A. and Jewson, N. (1999) *In Work, At Home: Towards an Understanding of Homeworking*, London: Routledge.

Felstead, A., Krahn, H. and Powell, M. (1997) 'Contrasting Fortunes across the Life Course: Non-Standard Work among Women and Men in Canada and the United Kingdom', *University of Leicester Centre for Labour Market Studies Working Paper*, No. 17.

Gregory, A. (1991) 'Patterns of Working Hours in Large-Scale Grocery Retailing in Britain and France: Convergence after 1992?', *Work, Employment and Society*, 5: 4, 497–514.

Hakim, C. (1987) 'Trends in the Flexible Workforce', *Employment Gazette*, 95: 11, 549–60.

Hakim, C. (1990) 'Core and Periphery in Employers' Workforce Strategies: Evidence from the 1987 ELUS Survey', *Work, Employment and Society*, 4: 2, 157–88.

Hakim, C. (1996) *Key Issues in Women's Work: Female Heterogeneity and the Polarisation of Women's Employment*, London: Athlone.

Hakim, C. (1997) 'A Sociological Perspective on Part-Time Work', in Blossfeld, H.-P. and Hakim, C. (eds.) *Between Equalization and Marginalization: Women Working Part-Time in Europe and the United States of America*, Oxford: Oxford University Press.

Handy, C. (1995) *The Future of Work*, WH Smith Contemporary Papers 8.

Hunter, L. and MacInnes, J. (1991) 'Employers' Labour-Use Strategies – Case Studies', *Employment Department Research Paper*, No. 87.

Hunter, L., McGregor, A., MacInnes, J. and Sproull, A. (1993) 'The "Flexible Firm": Strategy and Segmentation', *British Journal of Industrial Relations*, 31: 3, 383–407.

Joyce, P. (1987) *The Historical Meanings of Work*, Cambridge: Cambridge University Press.

Kalleberg, A.L., Rasell, E., Hudson, K., Webster, D., Reskin, B.F., Cassirer, N. and Appelbaum, E. (1997) *Nonstandard Work, Substandard Jobs: Flexible Work Arrangements in the US*, Washington: Economic Policy Institute/Women's Research and Education Institute.

Krahn, H. (1995) 'Non-Standard Work on the Rise', *Perspectives on labour and Income*, 7: 4, 35–42.

Lane, C. (1989) 'From "Welfare Capitalism" to "Market Capitalism": A Comparative Review of Trends towards Employment Flexibility in the Labour Markets of Three Major European Societies', *Sociology*, 23: 4, 583–610.

Marginson, P. (1986) 'How Centralised is the Management of Industrial Relations?', *Personnel Management*, 18: 10, 53–57.

Marginson, P. (1989) 'Employment Flexibility in Large Companies: Change and Continuity', *Industrial Relations Journal*, 20: 2, 101–109.

McGregor, A. and Sproull, A. (1991) 'Employer Labour Use Strategies: Analysis of a National Survey', *Employment Department Research Paper*, No. 83.

McGregor, A. and Sproull, A. (1992) 'Employers and the Flexible Workforce', *Employment Gazette*, 100: 5, 225–34.

McLaughlin, E. (1994) 'Flexibility or Polarisation?', in White, M. (ed.) *Unemployment and Public Policy in a Changing Labour Market*, London: PSI.

O'Reilly, J. (1994) 'What Flexibility do Women Offer? Comparing the Use of, and Attitudes to, Part-Time Work in Britain and France in Retail Banking', *Gender, Work and Organization*, 1: 3, 138–50.

Payne, J. and Payne, C. (1993) 'Unemployment and Peripheral Work', *Work, Employment and Society*, 7: 4, 513–34.

Payne, J. and Payne, C. (1994) 'Recession, Restructuring and the Fate of the the Unemployed: Evidence from the Underclass Debate', *Sociology*, 28: 1, 1–19.

Phizacklea, A. and Wolkowitz, C. (1995) *Homeworking Women: Gender, Racism and Class at Work*, London: Sage.

Piore, M. and Sabel, C.F. (1984) *The Second Industrial Divide: Possibilities for Success*, New York: Basic Books.

Polivka, A. (1996a) 'A Profile of Contingent Workers', *Monthly Labor Review*, 119: 10, 10–21.

Polivka, A. (1996b) 'Contingent and Alternative Work Arrangements, Defined' *Monthly Labor Review*, 119: 10, 3–9.

Pollert, A. (1988a) 'Dismantling Flexibility', *Capital and Class*, 34: 42–75.

Pollert, A. (1988b) 'The "Flexible Firm": Fixation or Fact?', *Work, Employment and Society*, 2: 3, 281–316.

Pollert, A. (ed.) (1991) *Farewell to Flexibility?*, Oxford: Blackwell.

Procter, S.J., Rowlinson, M., McArdle, L., Hassard, J. and Forrester, P. (1994) 'Flexibility, Politics and Strategy: In Defence of the Model of the Flexible Firm', *Work, Employment and Society*, 8: 2, 221–42.

Purcell, K. and Purcell, J. (forthcoming) 'Insourcing, Outsourcing and the Growth of Contingent Labour as Evidence of Flexible Employment Strategies', *European Journal of Work and Organizational Psychology*, forthcoming.

Robinson, P. (1994) 'The British Labour Market in Historical Perspective: Changes in the Structure of Employment and Unemployment', *Centre for Economic Performance Discussion Paper*, No. 202.

Rodgers, G. and Rodgers, J. (1989) (eds) *Precarions Jobs in Labour Market Regulation: The Growth of Atypical Employment in Western Europe*, Geneva: International Institute for Labour Studies.

Thompson, E.P. (1968) *The Making of the English Working Class*, Harmondsworth: Penguin.
Watson, G. (1994) 'The Flexible Workforce and Patterns of Working Hours in the UK', *Employment Gazette*, 102: 7, 239–47.
Watson, G. and Fothergill, B. (1993) 'Part-Time Employment and Attitudes to Part-Time Work', *Employment Gazette*, 101: 5, 213–20.

2 Economies of Time: A Framework for Analysing the Restructuring of Employment Relations

Mark Harvey

Introduction

Temporalities of work have been brought into new focus by the restructuring of employment relations. What is normal any more about a 'normal working day'? In many countries, the social institution of the normal working week took decades if not centuries to establish. In the now classic formula of E.P. Thompson: 'Attention to time in labour depends in large degree upon the need for the synchronization of labour' (Thompson, 1991:370). From the current perspective, this formula on time now itself appears to be one viewed through the limited optic of industrialized, factory-based, male labour. His construction of time leaves all other temporalities as 'outside time', un- or non-temporalised.

To open out a wider perspective on temporalities of work, let us consider a few examples:

(1) An academic wakes up in the middle of the night, and despite herself drafts a memo to the Head of Department. According to a standard academic contract of employment, 'There are no specified hours of work ... but the appointment is full-time and the member may not undertake continuous engagement or paid employment with other parties. Members of staff are entitled to reasonable holidays by arrangement ... with full pay.' Here there are no clear boundaries between working time and non-working time, even to the extent of establishing sharp demarcations between weeks and weekends, holidays and non-holidays. It is difficult, sometimes, for a person to tell whether they are working or not working.

(2) A parent wakes up in the middle of the night to care for a distressed infant. The work of care and social reproduction for young infants is a continuous and 24-hour activity, even if it can be distributed between a number of agents. But, depending on whether this work is paid or

unpaid, such work either falls within the temporality of 'the working day' or within the very different temporality of the sequencing and co-ordination of activity within the household.

(3)   A government may institute strong guidelines on the number of hours of school homework. In subsistence economies, or indeed in countries where children engage in commodity production for the market of various kinds, the performance of labour for self-reproduction, and repro-duction of the household unit, is clearly recognised as work, and hence working time. Factory legislation in the nineteenth century, by excluding children from paid working time, helped to create a sharper divide between paid and un-paid self-reproductive time. Now, the establish-ment of set times for educational self-reproduction is instituting a 'normal working day' for such work.

(4)   Lorry drivers are subject to legal limitations on the number of hours of continuous driving, because of a recognition of the need for sleeping time as an essential correlate of working time, to prevent accidents. In the absence of supervisory or physical constraints on continuous driving, and with strong financial or personal incentives to engage in it, the tachometer and the state impose a temporality of sleeping/resting time and working time.

Of course, examples of this kind are innumerable, and perhaps academics are becoming sensitive to them only now because their own peculiar work-temporality has become subject to stress. The purpose of giving these illustra-tions of diverse temporalities is to lay the ground for a reconceptualisation of temporality. The conceptual framework being adopted here can be summa-rised in four points.

First, Elias (1992:8, 10), and from a very different perspective Latour, have suggested, 'It is the sorting that makes the time, not the time that makes the sorting' (Latour, 1993:76).

The concept of 'economies of time' proposes that the *temporal co-ordination, sequencing, articulation of work/labour*, whether paid or unpaid, formal or infor-mal, establish *diverse regularities and cycles* and thereby constitute particular temporalities. This does not imply that the 'sorting' of work and hence the *economy* of time is the exclusive, independent or 'basic' form of 'sorting'. Indeed, turning E.P. Thompson's formula on its head, one could argue that the synchronization of leisure activities through the development of national or global television or radio schedules has supplanted the distinctive tempo-ralities of fêtes and fairs of pre-industrial periods. A moment's reflection suggests, moreover, that these 'non-work' temporalities are themselves ar-ticulated with 'work' temporalities, and as we shall see, work temporalities are often themselves characterized by the way they also institutionalize the boundary between work and non-work. But this chapter's focus is on how the restructuring of employment relations can be viewed as a restructuring of the temporalities of work.

Second, the advantage of adopting an 'economies of time' approach is that it provides a broader framework than 'economies of money', where values established through market exchanges provide a standard of measure. Thus, it enables an analysis not only of different temporalities, different regularities and cycles, but also of ways in which they articulate with each other. A primary example would be the articulation between the temporalities of the household economy with that of formal or paid employment, under diverse and continuously changing employment relations.

Third, the concept of diverse temporalities removes the privilege of the clock, or, in other words, dispenses with the single optic of what Thompson assumed (hastily) to be the identity between chronometric time and industrial employment time.[1] Chronometric time can of course provide a standard of measurement across all types of work, whether monetarily remunerated or not. The adoption of 'time use' studies to measure non-paid, and especially household activities has the considerable advantage of highlighting the significance of such work for national economies hidden by economies accounted solely in monetary terms (United Nations, 1990a; 1990b; 1991; Floro, 1995; Gershuny, 1988). '"Economic processes" of great importance to the development of society take place *outside the blue book economy*' (Gershuny, 1988:597). Equally, the use of chronometric time to reconstitute an 'hourly rate of pay' for work paid by the piece rather than by time undoubtedly serves the extremely useful purpose of emphasising the extremely low rates of return for much 'homework' production (Felstead and Jewson, 1996: Tables 11.1 to 11.3; Phizacklea and Wolkowitz, 1995:55).

Nonetheless, the use of chronometric time as a standard, and unique, measure of activities structured within diverse temporalities, runs the risk of reductionism, and of wrongly equating an hour spent under one temporal organization with an hour spent in another. What may be important is precisely the difference between temporal orderings rather than, in the optic of Thompson, everything being organized under one dominant clock. Indeed, part of the argument of this chapter will be that, *even in paid employment*, the temporality of standard employment is *incommensurable* with the temporality of non-standard employment. Central to this argument is the idea that, whereas *within* the temporality of the household economies, there may be all kinds of regularities and exchanges of time, and some notable non-reciprocities in exchange, there are no exchanges between paid and non-paid work that permit the establishment of equivalences, or standards of equivalence. The whole significance of the difference between paid and non-paid work is that there is no medium such as money which might act as a standard of measure between them. An hour of operating a washing machine for domestic washing has no relation of exchange with an hour of industrial or commercial washing by which equivalence might be established. Measurement by the clock, by substitution, cannot establish equivalence or non-equivalence, but only confirms the passage of chronometric time. In short, scales of equivalence and difference are *internal* to different temporalities, and, depending on the relations between temporalities (the degree and nature of exchanges of work or products of work between them), different standards of measure or equivalence, from exact and routine exchanges through rough-and-ready equivalencies to radical incommensurability, are established.

The fourth element of the conceptual framework refers to the fact that many people – but especially women – by necessity combine different temporalities of work, and negotiate their way between them. These combinations are sometimes 'synchronic', as when piecework at home may be combined with childcare; serial, as when part-time paid work is combined with household economic activities; or 'diachronic' in terms of a succession of different temporalities through the course of a lifespan, depending on phases of economic 'independence', childrearing, and post-childrearing.

Having set out some key features for an 'economies of time' perspective, the structure of the chapter will proceed as follows. The first section undertakes to examine and problematise the conception of 'normal working time' associated with standard employment relations, and compare these temporalities with those associated with non-standard employment relations. This is based on the empirical study of developments within the European construction industry. Thus, it will compare French standard time with UK standard time, and UK non-standard time. It will demonstrate that, even within paid employment, in the formal 'blue book' economy, there is no such thing as a single abstract labour time, such as suggested in classical and neo-classical political economy. There is a diversity of 'normal' times as well as distinctive non-standard temporalities, each entailing a different relation between work and non-work time. The second section will then extend this analysis of temporalities within paid employment to re-examine some studies of non-standard, and informal, or unpaid economies of time. From there it will go on to discuss the ways that different temporalities are articulated with each other, the formal and informal, the paid and unpaid.

Standard and Non-Standard Economies of Time

Different wage forms are linked to different economies of time through the way that they articulate relationships between the *product* of labour, the *utilization* of labour, *money* and *time*. The survey of French and UK construction workers[2] revealed an interesting variety of qualitatively different 'economies of time' as expressed through wage forms, and it is these qualitative differences which are the focus of this section. The diagram below (Figure 1) sets out five broadly defined economies of time, in terms of how they each articulate the four elements of product, utilisation of labour, money and time.

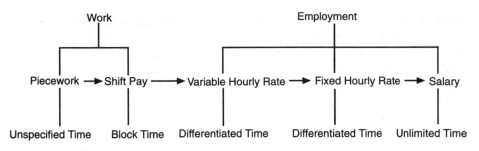

Figure 2.1   Paid economies of time

Although there were a few examples of piecework (roofers, metalworkers, and dryliners) in the sample of UK construction workers, the analysis of piecework will be left to a wider discussion of piecework in a variety of different settings. Here, the three major qualitatively different economies of time found in the survey will be explored – French standard time, UK standard time, and UK non-standard, shift pay. French standard time and UK standard time share some common characteristics and to avoid repetition, these shared features will be described first. Both fall under the variable hourly rate wage form.

What is 'normal' about normal working time?

This section begins by examining some of the common underlying characteristics of 'normal' time on both sides of the Channel, the 'variable hourly rate' in Figure 2.1. When the purchase of labour is an exchange for employment rather than either the product of labour, or work, time is *a general quantitative medium*: divisible, multiplicable, and accretional. Scales of hourly rates and coefficients of them form an integrated system of exchange (thus able to embrace variations of hourly rates for levels of productivity output, sickness or holidays). A basic hourly rate, for the first x units of time, is frequently multiplied by various coefficients for supplementary hours, exceptional hours or hours worked under abnormal conditions. Thus, whether or not a worker actually works overtime, receipt of a rate for the normal working week/month, is receipt of the basic unit of calculation *within a system of possible variations of that rate*.

Aside from the exchange taking the form of money for time, however, this wage form has one other major defining characteristic: it is paid for the duration of the employment relation, rather than only for the duration of the actual performance of labour. That is, to some degree or other, and again usually as a coefficient of the basic rate, the wage is paid for non-working periods: holidays, sickness, interruptions due to external circumstance (weather, interruptions of supply of materials or work for whatever reason).

All of these aspects of this wage form generally indicate some definition of a normal working week/month. Because the exchange is an exchange for the duration of the employment relation when this extends beyond the normal periods of performance of labour, the money exchange can be seen as exchange for *employment time*, as exclusively opposed to actual working time. Hence, within employment time, a *tripartite division of time* is constituted: normal working time, abnormal working time, and non-working time.

Critically, only when the exchange between buyers and sellers of labour is for employment is there a distinction drawn between a normal working time, abnormal working time, and non-working time. Further, non-working time is also an absolutely integral part of the purchase. Often explicit in employment contracts, working for another employer in one employer's 'non-working' time is prohibited. It is by definition 'moonlighting'. After all, an employer can have a strong interest in 'purchasing' non-working time of an employee in order to ensure the full value of productivity in working time. It is perhaps the erosion of the normal or standard employment relation by the emergence of new employment relations that now brings into full relief this aspect of the purchase of normal employment. It is integrally a purchase over both working time and non-working time. One is paid both to work *and not to work*.

For the present analytical purposes, moreover, it is important to distinguish payments for holidays and sickness (non-working time within the employment duration) which may or may not be secured through social insurance schemes rather than direct payment by employers of labour, and tax or insurance components of the wage which are not exchanged for employment (pensions) or are not exchangeable by the sellers of labour for commodity purchases (e.g. state provision of healthcare, training or education). Retirement and the provision of (some) training and healthcare are attached to the employment relation, the exchange for employment, normally via the mediation of the state.

In the majority of cases, the French and UK standard-time wages are combined with other components which are not simply purchases of time. A basic time rate is used as a calculating rate for additional productivity-over-time rate (bonus schemes), profit-sharing or other monetary incentive related to performance. In a general way, the additional elements, often expressed in terms of coefficients of the basic rate, are directly or indirectly related to output or performance over various time periods. These wage forms thus are generally composite forms in which an hourly rate is used as the basic calculating medium:

$$[x + f_1x + f_2x \ldots \ldots]$$

where $f_{1,2\ldots\ldots}$ are the coefficients used for calculation of bonus, holidays or other supplements. The significance of these composite elements is directly related to the tripartite division of time. The greater the proportion of the wage that is related to productivity, or working performance, the stronger is the tripartite division of time, in particular the division between working time and non-working time within the employment relation. If the hourly rate of pay is the same for non-working time as it is for working time, the more the exchange is broadly based on employment, rather than work.

To conclude this survey of the common characteristics of French and UK standard employment, it is worth underlining two points. First, the tripartite division of time is a radical departure from simple chronometric time, in the way that, *societally*, it divides people's lives into three differently time-valued periods, *linking working lifetime with non-working lifetime*. An hourly rate, linked to a coefficient, is used as *a general measuring instrument* for combining different wage elements and different rates, to produce a composite wage. Second, the development of this general measuring instrument presupposes a relatively stable employment relation between employer and employee over the medium or long term, with holiday and sickness entitlements accruing. As a calculus often of some complexity, it implies transaction and administration costs, an investment in stability. Moreover, as a calculus it is also used for differentiating levels of productivity. This too implies a strong employment relation. For, in order to differentiate levels of productivity, there is a need to establish some measurements, and an apparatus for allocating differentials based on output. Although measurements and allocations can vary in complexity, there is normally quite a significant cost/investment in the process. To pay one worker more than another, on the basis of such measurements, implies an *inclusion* of the worker in the productive process organized by the employer, and often a long-term cost in establishing the apparatus and the functioning of measurement. It is only worth making such a substantial investment in the expectation that the worker's performance will be affected, which in turn assumes variability in performance over time. Moreover, the development of the instruments of measurement are normally applicable, with modification, across contracts. New measurements or systems of allocation are not generally reinvented from scratch with each new contract. There is a relatively fixed, long-term investment in measurement and allocation systems. Thus workers' performances can be measured across successive contracts. In short, these wage forms strongly imply continuous employment. The form of temporality implies a form of employment relation.

French standard time

French standard temporality institutionalises the tripartite division of time cross-sectorally, and, most importantly in the present discussion across all forms of employment contract: the 'permanent' employment contract (*Contrat de durée indéterminée*); short-term and fixed contracts (*Contrat de durée déterminée*); and temporary agency labour (*Contrat de travail temporaire*). Moreover, since the late 1980s, pay has been converted into a monthly salary for all categories of employee, fixing the normal working month at 169 hours. Holidays and sick pay are statutory for all categories of employment relation, and there is a distinctive indemnification for temporary agency workers for periods of unemployment between contracts.

Furthermore, the normal working month, abnormal working time, and holiday, sickness and unemployment, are enshrined in law, forming an integral part of all legally binding collective agreements, in a triangular relation between the state, the trade unions and the employers associations. This provides great stability for the tripartite temporality across all enterprises, contracts and employment relations. 'Normal' really does mean normal: there is real justification for describing this temporality as a societal standard, an institutionalised structuring of a uniform time regime.

Even though Castel (Castel, 1995:400–410) has argued that the days of the pre-eminence of 'permanent' employment may be threatened, the growth of non-standard employment does not entail a change in time regime, and has so far left this distinctive temporality unaffected. Indeed, with the passing of the European Working Time Directive (1996), it may be more securely established than before. Confirmed by our present survey, moreover, it appears that very few workers (under 5 per cent) work significantly longer than the normal working week, with half working no overtime, and the remainder less than an hour a day in a five-day week. This finding is supported by national data on overtime in the construction, and indeed other, industrial sectors (INSEE, 1990).

If the tripartite structure of temporality thus firmly and sharply divides paid workers' lives into working and non-working time, this is further reinforced by the relatively low marking of the difference between pay for working time and pay for non-working time. Output-related pay is notably a lower proportion of total wages than found in the UK, ranging from between a bottom quartile of under 5 per cent to a top quartile of 17 per cent. Pay is thus predominantly a purchase of the employment relation, rather than of work alone (Linhart *et al.*, 1994; Tallard, 1994).

UK standard time

Cross the Channel, or even from a construction worker's point of view, dig a tunnel under it, and you enter a different temporality zone, even with UK standard time. First, there is no single standard working week. Even in construction industry collective agreements, a normal working week ranges through 35 hours to 37, 38 and 40 hours, depending on which agreement is in force (the Local Authority Building and Civil Engineering Agreement, the Engineering Construction Agreement, the Building and Civil Engineering Agreement, the Civil Engineering Agreement, to mention only some of the major ones). The variable normality of the normal working week can also be made yet more variable by local, even site-specific or contractor-specific agreement. So, within standard, direct employment relations, although there is a tripartite division of time, and a common usage of the hourly rate as a general calculating medium of the $[x + f_1x + f_2x \ldots \ldots]$ form described above, it has none of the universality found in France, largely, it could be argued, because of the historically different role of the state in employment regulation. Moreover, as we shall see, the tripartite division of time is only effective within standard employment relations, direct employment. So, unlike France, in the UK the rapid growth and now dominance of non-standard employment relations[3] in the construction industry has meant the effective disappearance of the normal working week.

Two further contrasts can be made with French standard time. First, as many directly employed construction workers, especially working in the private sector, are now but a small minority in the overall workforce dominated by the self-employed, they adjust their hours to those of the majority. Thus, in the survey the six-day week is 'normal'; over half worked at least 10 hours a week overtime (a 50-hour week) and over a third worked 60-plus hours a week. Second, the division of pay for working time and for non-working time was much more strongly marked than in France. The lowest quartile was over 10 per cent of wages; the highest quartile reached one-third of wages.

In summary, both the stability of the tripartite division of time and the meaning of 'normal' in a 'normal working week/month' are sufficiently different to support a concept of *different national temporalities*, even within standard employment relations.

Non-standard employment and temporality in the UK construction industry

A stronger contrast still is to be found *between* different UK national temporalities, arising from the growth of non-standard employment relations in the construction industry. In the survey, the dominant employment relation found on private-sector construction sites, whether commercial construction, civil or engineering construction, was illegal self-employment. The wage form associated with 'bogus' self-employment is overwhelmingly 'shift pay', payment for a shift of work.

The temporality of shift pay can be distinguished from 'hourly rated' pay associated with standard employment relations in a number of ways. First, there is no tripartite division of time. The exchange between purchasers and sellers of labour is for work and work alone, rather than for employment which embraces working and non-working time. Consequently, there is no payment for holidays, sickness, retirement, unemployment, interruptions of work due to weather or any other cause. A sharp disjuncture is effected between working time, which falls within the exchange, and non-working times of all kinds, which lie outside it. To express this differently, the non-standard employment relation is a much narrower base for the organization of social temporality than the standard employment temporality, which integrates other aspects of social life within its orbit (post-employment, etc.) To put it simply, if someone were to go to a doctor on their own or someone else's behalf, their relationship with the purchaser of their labour would then cease, often permanently.[4] The separation of working time from non-working time in this acute manner is itself an aspect of this social temporality.

Second, time in this form of temporality is quite different from the universal calculating medium found in a tripartite division of time. It can best be described as block time. A person is either employed for a block of time, or they are not employed at all. There is no normal number of hours, or working hours distinguished as over the normal. Thus, in the survey, shifts of 9 hours (on two construction sites), 10 hours (on six sites); 12 or more hours (on two sites), were found. Indeed, in one instance a gang of carpenters was found to work a continuous 70-hour shift, at flat-rate shift payments. Time is thus not conceived as a complex apparatus or general calculating medium by which different rates are paid. Time just comes in blocks.

Third, it follows from both the disjuncture between working and non-working time and the characteristically long shift hours, that this temporality is gendered much more sharply than 'normal' employment temporalities. Under this employment relation, a person's responsibility for the household economy is severely curtailed if not excluded. Conversely, the activity of undertaking the social reproduction of labour, making it available for sale on a day-by-day basis, is almost necessarily undertaken by other agents, typically women in the household economy.

Fourth, and as a further consequence, shift time does not have any implicit product over time, or productivity regime related to time. Productivity, rather, is exacted by recruitment and dismissal, recruitment of sufficient numbers, and dismissal of those considered to be insufficiently productive. An intrinsic aspect of this time-product-money relationship, therefore, is the extremely high level of turnover of labour found on sites, on the one hand, and the strategy of increasing production simply by increasing numbers of workers, on the other.

Fifth, because of the National Insurance regime under which the self-employed work, employers make no National Insurance contributions, and so workers are disbarred from state earnings-related pensions and unemployment, or any other non-means tested benefits.

In conclusion, shift pay involves a distinctive temporality which is characteristic of mass employment on a casual basis with minimum employer–employee responsibilities. It is a take-it-or-leave-it, 'no frills' form of payment, with minimum transaction costs or elaborate apparatuses for managing the wage relation. In an industry beset by extended chains of subcontracting, no employer bears the costs of maintaining or reproducing the quality of labour. The risks and costs are 'downloaded' to the individual.

To take the example of paid holidays, if a subcontractor functions only as a supplier (of labour, or labour and supervision) to a main contractor, then the subcontractor is paid by the main contractor only for that contract. Under this relation between subcontractor and main contractor, there is no reason for the main contractor to pay as if employment extended beyond the contract, and so include periods of paid non-working time; and given the subcontractor's dependent relation to the main contractor, there is hence a cost constraint not to pay for anything other than on the basis of immediate exchange for labour.[5] So, either the worker works, in which case she or he is paid; or she or he does not work, and is not paid. In interviews, the self-employed therefore indicated two options: either continuous working – and there were examples of individuals who had worked six days a week continuously for over two years – or unemployment. The possibility of paid non-working time is squeezed out.

The argument so far has attempted to demonstrate how different temporalities are related to different employment relations. Table 2.1 (below) summarizes the extent of the disparity between the three different temporalities so far considered. But there is an important consequence of this analysis, relating to normal calculations of labour costs, but also to the question posed in the introduction of the 'Thompson temporal optic'. Whereas the table demonstrates that there are both intra- and international temporalities of labour, it is perhaps only when two temporalities appear in the same labour market that the question of comparative labour costs, and commensurability, appears most acutely. For the argument that temporalities are internal to specific employment relations, whether standard or non-standard, is the flip side to an argument against the appropriateness of chronometric time standing outside employment relations as a universal measuring instrument.[6]

The example of UK standard time of a differentiated hourly rated pay and shift pay is thus particularly important in illustrating that even when both wage forms use time as a base, they are incommensurable. The exchange for employment time, where time is a general quantitative medium, justifies computation of average hourly earnings over the duration of employment (including sick pay, holiday pay, overtime, exceptional circumstance pay, etc.). There is no unit of employment time for shift pay, only for time of immediate use of labour. Thus for the shift worker a calculation of average hourly earnings would only include those hours actually worked. Everything else falls outside the exchange.

Of course, in gross terms, one form of employment relation might be deemed cheaper than another (less transaction costs, less social costs, etc.). But so is a bicycle cheaper than a BMW, and in this case too, there is an absence of pertinent common trading measures such as cost per mile, when the question can be asked: per mile of what? Per hour of work cannot be equated with per hour of employment. What needs to be explained is not

Table 2.1   Summary of French and UK construction industry economies of time

Purchase of Labour	Economies of Time		
	French Standard Time	*UK Standard Time*	*UK Non-Standard Time*
	Employment	*Employment*	*Work*
Temporality	Universal and stable tripartite division of time	Variable and unstable tripartite division of time	Work time only
	Hourly differentiated time calculus	Hourly differentiated time calculus	Block time, undifferentiated
Product/Time	Low product/time marking of working vs. non-working time	High product/time marking of working vs. non-working time	Payment for time only
Intertemporality:	Strong linkage:	Moderate and variable linkage:	No linkage:
Linkage between working and non-working lifetime	Sickness Unemployment Retirement Dependency Holidays	Sickness Unemployment Retirement Dependency Holidays	Severance of working from non-working lifetime

differences in the price of labour, but differences in the pricing mechanisms of labour, and differences in the temporalities being purchased by them. Different pricing mechanisms purchase different temporalities of labour.

Paid and Unpaid Economies of Time

In the previous section, discussion of full-time paid employment described two broad patterns of relationship between working and non-working life, the 'normal', where linkages between spheres were explicitly built into the employment relationship, and the non-standard which marked the severance between the two. But 'non-working' life was there treated as something of a black box, although the household economy was by implication seen as one of the black box's main occupants. Thus a 'normal working week' can be seen as a form of historical accommodation between a certain type of paid employment and the household economy. But the temporality of non-standard full-time employment has increasingly undermine that accommodation, by imposing a regime of long shifts and a six-day week, and excluding all forms of linkage between the two spheres. As has been pointed out, excessively long working hours, and here in combination with pay tied exclusively to work, effectively allocates the time for non-market reproduction of labour to women (Glucksmann, 1995b:68; Beynon and Austrin, 1994:163–74). It has recently been demonstrated that the UK, of all European countries, is typified by high male working hours combined with high female part-time work on low total paid working hours (Rubery *et al.*, 1995; Bulletin on Women and Employment in the EU, 1995). Gender dimensions of 'normal' male temporalities of employment are relatively hidden. But the distinctive temporalities of women's employment relations make the gender aspect transparent. It may be worth some further consideration as to how the rise of non-standard male employment, by altering the relation between temporalities of paid work to the household economy, intensifies the gender polarity.

Until quite recently, non-standard employment relations in the construction industry had been typified by piecework (Clarke, 1991; 1993), and even in the survey reported here, there were still a few pieceworkers, working at the margins of the workforce. These were floorlayers laying a standardised franchised product; dryliners limited to a narrow range of task activity; sheetmetal workers undertaking traditional craft copper-restoration roofing; and slaters, also undertaking a relatively narrow range of task work. It is evident, however, that the use of piecework (where prices are given for products of labour), involves considerable transaction costs, and an elaborate pricing mechanism, were it to be applied to the whole construction process embracing hundreds of co-ordinated tasks, and a workforce size also in the hundreds, if not thousands. Moreover, piecework in this working environment does not resolve the problem of synchronisation, or of the temporal organisation of the labour process, and indeed, could indeed impede it were hundreds of workers each to be pursuing individual price targets. In these circumstances, the wage form of shift pay replaced piecework as non-standard employment relations became dominant, as self-employment became mass self-employment.

This process usefully provides a pivot for the argument to which I now turn, where piecework can be seen as engaged with the distinctive temporalities of homeworking, and multiple individual production sites, linked to household economies of time. Before turning to the discussion of home-working and other 'economies of time', it is necessary to emphasise two points made by Glucksmann and others (Glucksmann, 1995a; 1995b; 1996; forthcoming; Beechey and Perkins, 1987). First, from the outset we are confronted with articulations between the different temporalities of paid and non-paid (household or subsistence) work, in a way that makes the gendered relations of time as visible as the gendering of standard full-time paid employment is invisible. Women have always had to juggle multiple temporalities, and negotiate their way between them. Second, if the household economy makes it possible for workers to present themselves for work every day, conversely, the external exigencies and inputs from outside the household place constraints on its economic operation: different temporalities articulate, not always harmoniously or functionally, indeed often with many stresses and strains, with each other. This can be represented diagrammatically (Figure 2.2).

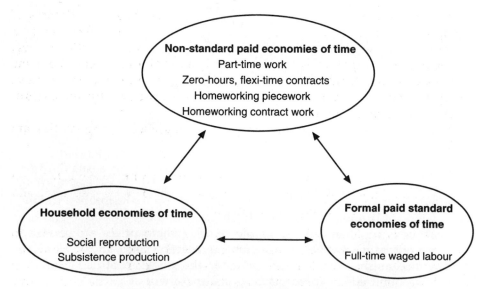

Figure 2.2   The multiple articulation of temporalities

This section will therefore examine some of the articulations between different temporalities, and in particular some aspects of the repercussions of changes in one order of temporality (in paid employment, or as a result of commodity innovation such as domestic capital goods); and another (the household economy). In so doing, however, it starts by questioning the assumption that time in one domain can in any simple or straightforward manner be traded or exchanged with time in another domain, or, indeed, that paid time can lead directly to commodity substitution of unpaid household work (Gershuny, 1988; Horrell *et al.*, 1994; Gershuny *et al.*, 1994; Horrell, 1994). The argument is that these approaches, by aggregating time as if it were a homogeneous medium, presents itself with puzzles, such as why there is 'lagged adaptation' to the higher participation rates of women in full-time, paid employment by a failure to reallocate household non-paid working time. Likewise, earlier theories of convergence of domestic working hours between households that purchased domestic service and those that provided it, to households of both classes each possessing household domestic capital goods (Gershuny, 1988), are now presented with problems of the inflexibility of household working hours, below a certain floor. These approaches, by assuming time as a common homogeneous and aggregatable medium, therefore also assume that there can be exchanges and substitutions between spheres, without considering the specificities of the temporalities of different domains.

Household economies of time

Some brief comments can be made first about the distinctive features of household economies of time, although this is by no means intended as a thorough analysis. Some interesting clues are given about the distinctiveness of household temporalities by Gershuny *et al.* (1994) comment about the methodological difficulties of reducing them to aggregate chronometric time. They argue that perceptions of household time are structured by sequences of tasks rather than quantities of hours.[7]

Here some of the structural features of household temporalities are enumerated:

(1) There are no clear boundaries between work and non-work, between working time, and non-working time, let alone between necessary and unnecessary, or 'luxury' producing, labour.

(2) There is no fixed ceiling or floor to the amount of time expended in household work, but this can vary considerably according to need, use and cultural norms. Household work 'is never done', but it has no clear lower limit either. If care of dependants requires, for whatever reason, continuous attention beyond the span of a day, work can too. Time, in

such circumstances, is under a regime of need. Whether in childcare time or cooking, the amount of time spent rarely meets the point of negative returns.

(3)   Characteristically, the temporality of work is structured by the sequencing and synchronisation of different tasks. Some of these sequences have an internal logic (washing up after cooking); others combine an externally driven logic with an internal one (cleaning after taking children to school/nursery). One of the problems of the use of chronometric time is that tasks such as clothes washing can be performed simultaneously with others (cooking plus childcare, for example) while also listening to the radio. It is certainly possible to perform chronometric measurements and calculations, but these erase what is distinctive about the possibility of combining such activities temporally within households, within a pattern of sequential tasks. The purchase of domestic capital goods from the proceeds of participation in the paid economies may enable tasks to be performed synchronously that had previously been performed successively, but these 'inputs' are then inserted within household temporalities, rather than producing simple time-substitutions, or dictating a new sequencing of tasks from outside.

(4)   There is a strong cyclical structuring of household activity over the course of a lifetime, whether this is linked to care of infants or care of the elderly.

(5)   The temporalities of household economies of time vary substantially with the size of the household, and the age and gender of its members. Thus, irrespective of the advance in domestic capital goods, the historical decline in family size, and the 'nucleation' of the family, have involved fundamental changes in household economies of time. The relation between individual 'self-reproduction' (such as washing, or a child's school homework) and social reproduction within the household as a collectivity, changes according to members' relative position in their lifespan.

(6)   Last, but not least, whether internally generated within household economies of time, or externally reinforced by the differential linkage between household activities and paid economies of time, there are highly gendered temporalities within the household economy of time.

Household economies of time and piecework

The evidence from recent studies of homeworking, whether in clothing manufacture, packaging or in teleworking (Felstead and Jewson, 1996; Allen and Wolkowitz, 1987; Phizacklea and Wolkowitz, 1995; Huws, 1984), all confirm that piece-rate working is the almost universal mode of payment, on the one hand, and on the other, that total hours worked are often considerable. As has been pointed out, the effect of piecework in the household economy is very often an extension of the working day into many hours of evening or nightwork. The articulation between paid work and non-paid household work, therefore, does rely on the use of a payment system which allows blocks of time to be intercalated with the sequencing and schedules of the household economies of time. The result is often an overall intensification of labour, especially through the setting of piece-rates, the delivery and collection of materials, and the quantities of outputs required (Phizacklea, 1995:35–36 and 108–10; Allen and Wolkowitz, 1987:115–18).

But one of the most striking illustrations to be found of the articulation between paid work and the household economy of time can be seen in the diary accounts of the ordering of paid and non-paid work, switching from childcare, to piecework, to cleaning, back to piecework, to evening meal preparation, and back to piecework, 'interrupted' by the calls again of childcare, all necessary to meet the deadline for collection of output the following morning (Allen and Wolkowitz, 1987:124–5). Finally, the use of piece-rates permits the participation, often disguised, of various members of the household collectivity (children, male partners), precisely because it is not a time-rated, or employment-related, form of paid labour. In terms of the restructuring of employment relations, the development of new forms of outworking such as the contracted-out office (Meiksins and Whalley, 1996), and teleworking, therefore, the significance of the household economies of time is that they allow this degree of intensification of work in the household, either by extension of the working day, or by the combination and sequencing of paid and non-paid tasks. The lack of clear time-boundaries in the household makes its time particularly vulnerable to invasion.

Household economies of time and part-time or flexi-time work

In this section, I will not dwell on the well-documented and well-argued relationship between the requirements of managing a household economy, gender participation rates in paid employment and part-time work (Beechey and Perkins, 1987; Horrell *et al.*, 1994; Naylor, 1994). It is also well established that there has been a substantial increase of, primarily women's, part-time employment. Instead, three examples will be chosen to illustrate the interactions between household economies of time and the restructuring of non-standard paid employment.

Neathey and Hurstfield (1995) have shown that there has been a growth in new flexi-time and zero-hours contracts in the retail, banking and financial services sectors. From a temporalities perspective there are two points to be made. First, zero-hours contracts are themselves a distinctive temporality, with people held in a contract unpaid while not working, that is without a retainer, and yet freely available 'on call' to meet the peaks and troughs of work. Flexi-hours contracts only differ slightly in that they do entail a minimum of paid, part-time working hours. But both these contractual forms are characterized by a high level of unpredictability, coupled with, in many cases, the inability of the employees to refuse calls on their time. It is well known that lack of predictability, and loss of control over part-time working hours, creates the maximum difficulty for childcare and other household arrangements, so disrupting the household economy of time.

Second, there has been a substantial shift from employment in manufacturing and industry into the service sector, where female and part-time casual working is much more dominant. From a purely distributional analysis, Froud *et al.* (1997) have demonstrated that this produces a polarization between full-time, job-rich households, and households dependent on a succession of casual and part-time work. They aptly coin the term 'household lottery' to describe this divergence. This includes a massive increase in the servicing of the job-rich families, as demonstrated by a recent Mintel survey estimate of an expenditure on cooking, gardening, cleaning and childcare services of £4 billion annually. As the authors argue, 'the institution which generates the synergistic gain and also takes the strain is the household' (Froud *et al.*, 1997:29). So major changes in the paid economy impact directly on the articulation between household and paid economies of time.

Third, in a fascinating study of the production and commodity chain which ensures that Thompson's seedless grapes are available in UK supermarkets all the year round, Barrientos and Perrons (1997) have shown that there are two different articulations between household and paid employment at either end of the chain. In Chile, women are seasonally employed for intensive picking and packaging over three months, then return to subsistence farming and household occupations for the remainder of the year. At the supermarket end of the chain, they interviewed women engaged in serial childcare through the serial part-time work of partners, and flexi-time contracts. What is important, however, is that while at each end the relationship between household and paid economies of time is embedded in local labour market conditions, the two ends are directly tied to each other, integrated in a single structure of production through to consumption. So there is a second-order articulation between different temporalities and different economies of time, spanning the globe.

Conclusion

In conclusion, the argument has run the following course. It was shown that the growth of full-time male, non-standard employment relations in the construction industry resulted in an increased dislocation between the paid work and the life outside paid work, notably within the household. The erosion of the normal working week, and the breaking of linkages between life inside work and life outside work, can thus be described in terms of an increased gender polarisation of the two spheres. The changes in temporality in one sphere fundamentally alters the relations between spheres, as a result of the restructuring of employment relations.

Consequently, in the second section, a model of the interaction between the three spheres of household economies of time, non-standard paid economies of time, and formal paid standard and non-standard economies of time was proposed, in order to grasp the multiple articulation between distinct temporalities. An outline analysis of the distinctive characteristics of household economies of time was then elaborated to allow a direct examination of the relationship between household economies of time and non-standard, non-full time, paid economies of time (Figure 2.2), especially for women homeworkers and part-time workers. It was suggested that there have been increasing tensions and strains placed on household economies of time, resulting from the restructuring of employment relations, and the emergence of new types of flexi-time working and new temporalities. It was argued that because of its distinctive characteristics, the household economy of time is particularly vulnerable to pressures from exogenous changes. But in turn, this demonstrates that the household has become once more a central and visible focus of the reproduction of the overall productive system (Rubery, 1994), rather than a peripheral relic of earlier historical economic systems. This centrality of the household economy, and the contradictions and conflicts clustering around it, are therefore more a result of the *friction between different temporalities* than of any absolute increase in aggregate (paid and non-paid) working time. An 'economies of time' perspective is thus particularly fruitful for this type of analysis, releasing the perception of 'normal working time', household time and non-standard time, from the grip of the chronometric optic.

References

Allen, S. and Wolkowitz, C. (1987) *Homeworking: Myths and Realities*, London: Macmillan.

Barrientos, S. and Perrons, D. (1997) 'Fruit of the Vine – Flexible Women Workers in the Production and Retailing of Winter Fruit', *ESRC Labour Studies Seminar, Sector Restructuring*, University of Manchester International Centre for Labour Studies, January.

Beechey, V. and Perkins, T. (1987) *A Matter of Hours: Women, Part-Time Work and the Labour Market*, Cambridge: Polity.

Beynon, H. and Austrin, T. (1994) *Masters and Servants: Class and Patronage in the Making of Labour Organisation*, London: Rivers Oram Press.

Bulletin on Women and Employment in the EU (1995) *Time is a Gender Issue*, Brussels: European Commission, October.

Castel, R. (1995) *Les Métamorphoses de la Question Sociale: Une chronique du salariat*, Paris: Fayard.

Clarke, L. (1991) 'The Significance of Wage Forms: The Example of the British Construction Industry', Thirteenth Annual Conference of the International Working Party on Labour Market Segmentation, Bremen.

Clarke, L. (1993) 'Particularities in Wage Relations in the Construction Labour Process', 11th International Annual Labour Process Conference, UMIST.

Deakin, S. and Wilkinson, F. (1995) 'Contracts, Cooperation and Trust: The Role of the Institutional Framework', *ESRC Centre for Business Research Working Papers, 10*, Cambridge: University of Cambridge.

Elias, N. (1992) *Time: An Essay*, trans. E. Jephcott, Oxford: Blackwell.

Felstead, A. and Jewson, N. (1996) *Homeworkers in Britain*, London: HMSO.

Floro, M.S. (1995) 'Economic Restructuring, Gender and the Allocation of Time', *World Development*, 23: 11, 1913–29.

Froud, J., Haslam, C., Johal, S. and Williams, K. (1997) 'From Social Settlement to Household Lottery', Fifteenth International Annual Labour Process Conference, Edinburgh.

Gershuny, J. (1988) 'Time, Technology and the Informal Economy', in Pahl, R. (ed.) *On Work: Historical, Comparative and Theoretical Perspectives*, Oxford: Blackwell.

Gershuny, J., Godwin, M. and Jones, S. (1994) 'The Domestic Labour Revolution: A Process of Lagged Adaptation', in Anderson, M., Bechhoffer, F. and Gershuny, J. (eds) *The Social and Political Economy of the Household*, Oxford: Oxford University Press.

Glucksmann, M. (1995a) 'Gendered Economies of Time: Women Workers in North-West England', *Working Chapter Series, EUF No. 95/8*, Florence: European University Institute.

Glucksmann, M. (1995b) 'Why "Work"? Gender and the "Total Social Organisation of Labour"', *Gender, Work and Organisation*, 2: 2, 63–75.

Glucksmann, M. (1996) 'What a Difference a Day Makes: Thinking about Gender and Temporality', Paper to the Sociology Department, University of Essex, mimeo.

Glucksmann, M. (forthcoming) *Cottons and Casuals*.

Harvey, M. (1995) *Towards the Insecurity Society: The Tax Trap of Self-Employment*, London: The Institute of Employment Rights.

Harvey, M. (1996a) 'Vanities of Continuity and Discontinuity of Employment. Restructuring the Employment Relations in the Construction Industry in Britain and France,' *International Labour Process Conference*, University of Astin, March 1996.

Harvey, M. (1996b) 'The Illegality and Insecurity of Employment in the Construction Industry' Paper to the Building the Future Conference, London: Building Industry Link-up.

Harvey, M. (1997) 'Taxation Regimes, Competition and the Transformation of Employment Relations', Paper to the Dynamics of Wage Relations in the New Europe International Symposium, Maastricht: European Union.

Horrell, S. (1994) 'Household Time Allocation', in Anderson, M., Bechhoffer, F. and Gershuny, J. (eds) *The Social and Political Economy of the Household*, Oxford: Oxford University Press.

Horrell, S., Rubery, J. and Burchell, B. (1994) 'Working-Time Patterns, Constraints, and Preferences', in Anderson, M., Bechhoffer, F. and Gershuny, J. (eds) *The Social and Political Economy of the Household*, Oxford: Oxford University Press.

Huws, U. (1984) *The New Homeworkers: New Technology and the Changing Location of White-Collar Work*, London: Low Pay Unit.

Latour, B. (1993) *We Have Never Been Modern*, trans. Catherine Porter, Hemel Hempstead: Harvester Wheatsheaf.

Linhart, D., Rozenblatt, P. and Voegele, S. (1994) 'Vers une nouvelle rémunération scientifique du travail', *Travail et Emploi*, 57: 30–46.

Meiksins, P. and Whalley, P. (1996) 'Expertise at Arm's Length: Controlling Technical Workers in the New Workplace', Fourteenth Annual International Labour Process Conference, Aston.

Naylor, K. (1994) 'Part-Time Working in Great Britain – an Historical Analysis', *Employment Gazette*, London, December.

Neathey, F. and Hurstfield, J. (1995) *Flexibility in Practice: Women's Employment and Pay in Retail and Finance*, London: Equal Opportunities Commission and Industrial Relations Services.

Phizacklea, A. and Wolkowitz, C. (1995) *Homeworking Women: Gender, Racism and Class at Work*, London: Sage.

Rubery, J. (1994) 'The British Production Regime: A Societal-Specific System?', *Economy and Society*, 23: 4, 335–54.

Rubery, J., Fagan, C. and Smith, M. (1995) *Changing Patterns of Work and Working-Time in the European Union and the Impact on Gender Division*, Brussels: Report for the Equal Opportunities Unit, European Commission.

Tallard, M. (1994) 'Refonte des grilles de classification, salaires et gestion de la main-d'oeuvre dans le bâtiment', *Travail et Emploi*, 59: 32–47.

Thompson, E.P. (1991) 'Time, Work-Discipline and Industrial Capitalism', in *Commons and Culture*, London: Merlin.

United Nations (1990a) 'Improving Statistics and Indicators on Women Using Household Surveys', *Studies in Methods, Series F*, 48, New York: United Nations.

United Nations (1990b) 'Methods of Measuring Womens' Participation and Production in the Informal Sector', *Studies in Methods, Series F*, 46, New York: United Nations.

United Nations (1991) 'The World's Women 1970–1990: Trends and Statistics', *Social Statistics and Indicators, Series K*, 8, New York: United Nations.

Union of Construction, Allied Trades and Technicians (1997) *Viewpoint*, London, December–January.

Wilkinson, F. and You, J-i. (1992) 'Competition and Cooperation: Towards an Understanding of Industrial Districts,' *Centre for Business Research Working Papers*, 18, University of Cambridge.

Notes

1   In his characteristically imaginative presentation it is significant that the technological development of the clock and its diffusion is given as the context for the synchronisation of labour in factory production. The clock is both the instrument of measure and of discipline. In Elias's or Latour's terms, this view tends to conflate the ordering of the measure with the ordering of the measured.

2   The research reported in this paper is part of a European project *Disparities in Wage Relations and Reproduction of Skills in the European Construction Industry*, of which the French and UK parts are now complete. The UK research has been funded by the Leverhulme Foundation, and was based in the Education, Training and Labour Market Research Group at the University of Westminster. Sixteen construction sites with workforces totalling 6000 were investigated, with interviews of 124 construction workers.

3   It should be noted that the dominance of non-standard, illegal, self-employment in the construction industry was overwhelming at the time the research was undertaken in 1995 (Harvey, 1995; 1996a; 1996b). But since then, a remarkable change has

taken place in the taxation and social insurance regulation of the industry, resulting in a shift of some 250 000 to 500 000 construction workers back into legitimate direct employment (UCATT, *Viewpoint*, December/January 1996/7).

4   A number of the interviews with construction workers on sites emphasised that they would certainly lose pay, but also risk dismissal, were they to treat their responsibility for dependents as a priority over the sale of their labour.

5   The same applies *a fortiori* to agency, and especially external agency, labour.

6   Indeed, as I have argued elsewhere (Harvey, 1997), timescales should be seen as part of institutional pricing mechanisms, and are established as such in common trading standards. Other common trading measures are also gradually established: car-power is now normally rated by cubic capacity rather than break horsepower, or horsepower; variable spin speed is used for washing machines; 386, 486, or pentium as chip-capacity for PCs, etc. Only as a result of the peculiarities of an extremely deregulated labour market were two very different timescales co-present in a single market, leading to much confusion, and 'degenerative competition' (Wilkinson and You, 1992; Deakin and Wilkinson, 1995).

7   'It is this contrast between our ignorance of our own aggregate time allocation and our knowledge of our activity sequences, that explains the use of the diary in time-budget research' (Gershuny *et al.*, 1994:158).

3 Flexible Work in the Virtual Workplace: Discourses and Implications of Teleworking

*Nicola José de Freitas Armstrong**

Introduction

The following chapter charts a particular reading of the literature concerning people who telework, that is, people who perform paid work from home at a distance from clients, and who employ information and telecommunications technologies in their businesses (e.g. computers, faxes, modems, 'smart' phones). I want to argue that rather than being an elitist, statistically insignificant aberration,[1] telework is an important *juncture* in a network of sociological concerns that circulate in the academic literature. These include the connections between the global economy and the spatial dispersal of labour, the dynamism of information and communications technologies and their applications, feminist analyses of gendered identities and practices as they are enacted in employment, partnering and parenting, and indeed, a foundational narrative of sociology itself concerning the separation of 'home' and 'work'[2] during the Industrial Revolution.

Thus, telework unfolds as a many-layered site of research where a variety of macro and micro sociological concerns coalesce and which is an unusually rich focus for 'empirical' investigation. This chapter traverses a number of these sociological concerns but focuses on the micropolitics of families and the gendered identities of teleworkers as paid workers, parents and partners and macro concerns regarding the restructuring and externalisation of professional work and the reconfiguration of the timing and spatial location of employment. In order to canvas these issues a feminist reading of the gendered nature of one particular construction of telework is pursued, namely

---

* It was with great regret that we heard, during the final preparation of this book, of the tragic death of Nicola José de Freitas Armstrong. We are, however, very pleased to be able to publish this example of her work.

43

that element in the literature which focuses on the relationship between teleworking and technology and the issue of dis/embodiment in the virtual workplace. Run against these discussions in the literature are excerpts of narratives generated in a qualitative study of parents who are self-employed teleworkers, where these individual stories are played against the 'public narratives'[3] (Somers, 1994:619) concerning technology, family and work.

The 'New' and 'Old' Stories about Home-Based Work

Given the extensive feminist literature regarding industrial homework,[4] one of the notable characteristics of the literature regarding telework, is the muffling of *feminist analyses* and the invisibility of women in the visualisations of utopian electronic futures imagined by telework enthusiasts. The telework literature is seemingly preoccupied with both technology and entrepreneurism, to the neglect of relations and exchanges outside of the market economy and the social and political context within which telework occurs. And yet it is these very analyses which are so clearly articulated in the feminist industrial homework literature.

This suggests that aspects of the literature and media representations of telework which focus on the technological and entrepreneurial aspects of this work practice are *marked as masculine* despite the clear over-representation of women in the home workforce, which in Aotearoa/New Zealand was estimated to be 70 per cent female in 1991 (Loveridge *et al.*, 1996:23). Given this shaping of a significant proportion of the literature, designing a research project to investigate the gendered identities of teleworkers appeared *strategic*, as a means to investigate how women and men negotiate the identities and practices of paid work, partnering, parenting and domestic labour when these occur in the same place and at the same time in the site of domestic dwellings.

In telework there is an unusual degree of *simultaneity* in the discursive routes through which identity and subjectivity are constituted. This stems from the lack of the usual spatial and temporal boundaries between, for example, being a parent, a partner and a paid worker. The research design sought to generate both narrative accounts of identity and relationships *and* accounts of practices concerning, for example, the management of domestic and paid tasks, space and time, in order to enrich the understanding of how teleworkers make and cross the boundaries between 'home' and 'work'. The research focused on the ways such identities and practices were experienced as contradictory (as well as complementary) and how the participants talked about their identities and practices (such as being a baby's caregiver and being a successful entrepreneur) by 'storying' themselves through particular narratives, a teleworking 'tale'.

Inquiring in Practice

It was this background and these curiosities that contributed to the design of the study which investigated – through a qualitative,[5] multimethod, longitudinal approach, the working lives of twelve families – that is, six female and six male teleworkers, their twelve heterosexual partners, their children and their personal assistants and/or childcare workers (n = 31). All of the teleworkers in this study had professional, predominantly home-based work, involving electronic text, rather than occupations which required a high degree of face-to-face contact with other adults. They were also all self-employed although all had experiences of direct employment within organisations.

In order to heighten the critical nature of the research, the study specifically investigated the *gendered* dynamics of teleworking, dividing the focus of the empirical work between families where the teleworking parent and partner was a woman and those where they were men, including two cases where the teleworking father was the most significant carer of their baby children. The research focused on two kinds of families, six of which included children who were under fifteen years old, and the other six, families with babies under two years old. Dividing the research between families with children old enough to participate in the study themselves, and families where the children were not, allowed a further set of questions to be posed regarding the differences between juggling the demands of older children with teleworking and meeting the needs of infant children whose demands are not easily deferred and potentially occur at any time of the day or night. The narrative and visual material generated in this research is suggestive of the shifting, complex identities and practices of teleworkers as they are *contested* in the two important arenas of paid work and the family, the way *competing* identities and practices were asserted in these contests, and their articulation with what we might call the macrosocial forms of history, politics and the economy.

The remainder of this chapter is devoted to a discussion of some of these narratives in relation to one of the seven themes which emerge in the literature regarding telework as a virtual workplace. This demonstrates some of the concerns alluded to above regarding the connections between the global and the local and the neglect of the social and economic context within which telework occurs, through the lens of a specifically feminist reading.

Telework and the Virtual Workplace: Invoking Dis/embodiment

One of the more interesting constructions of telework figures it as the work practice of the future, which maintains the security and familiarity of 'home', while allowing, through connection to the Internet, participation in the 'international traffic of ideas and information' (Huws, 1991:20). The notion of telework as a 'virtual' workplace; that is, an electronic mediation of localised physical presence into virtual participation, positions individuals as simultaneously within the global at the same time as it promulgates an imagery of 'village-like encounters' (Green, 1994:163). In this 'global village', social networks are envisioned beyond those facilitated by physical proximity alone, such that new collectivities of shared interests are imagined though the networking capabilities of the new or anticipated information and communication technologies, for those, at least, who could afford them.[6]

Rather than isolated and privatised, the home is refashioned in this construction as the nexus of communication of unlimited possibility. And yet the protagonist at its centre is still most frequently imagined as a man with no dependants. That is, this 'discourse'[7] constructs a subject who, through technology, is empowered to communicate in a rapid way with an incredibly vast virtual world, yet the social relations which surround this corporeal body and the sex of this body itself, are still imagined as they were in the 1960s: as a masculine, intellectual, individual body unhindered by obligations to care for others.

These 'space-age' technologies, then, are mapped onto social relations which are assumed to remain constant. As Judy Wajcman (1991:33) has suggested, technology does act as a force for change and yet there has been a remarkable stability in the social organisation of phenomena such as the gendered segregation of occupations, *despite* rapid technical changes. She suggests that rather than social change being determined by technology, technological developments build on and may even reinforce *existing* gendered, classed and 'raced' relations (1991:48).

An intriguing example of this dynamic is imagined in the paper 'Corporate Virtual Work Space' written by two software engineers, Pruitt and Barrett (1991). They construct an account of the fictional character Austin Curry, experiencing his morning routine, which is interesting because of the forms of dis/embodiment it narrates. Austin lives somewhere in the continental United States, where he rises at 6.00 a.m. 'grabs' his coffee, lets Bowser the dog out of the house, then 'shuffles down the hall' in his pyjamas to the study where he begins his working day 'immediately'. Austin dons his customised computer clothing, and notes that on this day the shower and breakfast can wait, because he has an 'idea he is anxious to explore' (1991:384). Austin's current project is to develop a data analysis application for an upcoming mission to Mars and in order to focus on this 'stimulating' work (1991:385) Austin reduces the 'visual, aural and tactile acuity' of his computerised clothing in order to ignore all but 'close range external stimuli' such as his coffee cup.

Austin's experience of entering his corporate virtual workspace is contrasted to the need to bathe and make the 'long commute to the city' that characterised his work experience 'in the old days'. In this scenario Austin is at work 'within 60 seconds of crossing the study's threshold' whereupon he 'walks' around meeting colleagues, international experts and clients, most of whom he has never 'physically' met, who live in places like 'Guam, the Bahamas' and an 'A-frame in Aspen'.

On this particular workday Austin is taking advantage of the 'enticing' opportunities for developing software offered by his virtual colleague Johann. Johann is based in Bonn and has developed a gadget called the 'concept canon' a technology which is 'about six inches long [and] . . . rolls around on two tiny wheels' which is 'fired' at the client in order to render images onto 'vertical expanse'. Johann thinks the concept canon may be a 'bit wild' for Austin, but that it would 'surely get his "creative" juices flowing'. Having appreciated the 'power' of the concept canon, Austin returns from his corporate virtual workplace at 7.30 am to take a shower and 'grab' some breakfast, finding only Bowser the dog 'more than ready' to come in from the patio.

What is interesting about this account is the discourse of dis/embodiment that it constructs. Austin ignores the body physical in favour of the virtual world of ideas which he inhabits with other men who are part of this global community. While located within this virtual world he is introduced to a technological innovation, the 'concept canon', metaphorically figured in strikingly phallic terms. Austin dims or represses the 'physical world' during this session in the corporate virtual workplace, a practice that would, for example, muffle his awareness of a baby's cry or a toddler's movements. When Austin returns suitability 'stimulated' to the 'physical' world he finds only his dog waiting for him, albeit a little impatiently. We assume there is no-one in Austin's bed when he awakes and the needs of his dog are easily dealt with or delayed while he enjoys his knowledge work in virtual space.

Such futuristic imaginings of telework construct a peculiarly male world peopled by men and premised on the assumption of little or no responsibility for the care of others. This is not the experience of teleworkers with families, especially those with small children. It is particularly not the experience of women with imputed responsibility for the home and family.

Elizabeth Grosz (1987:4) has argued that women more than men are linked to their 'fixed corporeality'; women are constructed as more object than subject, natural than cultural, more 'biologically governed'. It is this construction which, Dorothy Smith (1979:163) argues, has confined women to the bodily realm and limited their entry into the 'abstract conceptual mode' and yet for Smith, entering and being absorbed by the abstract conceptual mode is conditional upon attention to the 'local and bodily' (1979:167). Smith argues that it is the structuring of *women's work* which 'provides for the logistics of the philosopher's (or the computer expert's) bodily existence' and makes possible 'all but passing attention to the bodily location of consciousness'

(1979:168). Further evidence for this analysis is suggested in the literature concerning masculinity and entrepreneurism which examines the ways in which the women partners of entrepreneurial men support their careers by providing them with unreciprocated domestic and emotional labour and the practices through which male entrepreneurs' work activity 'invades and colonises domestic life' (Mulholland, 1996:141).

Zoë Sofia (1995:157) argues that virtual reality extends this possibility of separating the abstract/conceptual mode from the local/bodily mode in that it 'plays out masculinist fantasies of transcending the messy gravity-bound material body and becoming a luminous ethereal being in a fully programmed irreal world'.

It may not take virtual reality technologies to move toward this disembodiment as Shoshana Zuboff observed in *In the Age of the Smart Machine* (1984). Zuboff argues that 'work' has increasingly become the business of 'manipulating symbols' (1984:23) where new information technology 'lifts skill from the historical dependence upon a labouring sentient body' (1984:57).

In this process of the 'textualisation' of work, Zuboff argues, the rigid separation of mental and manual labour 'collapse' because of the increasing intellectual content of all work (1984:393). For professional workers (and here I would include teleworkers) the implications of this increasing dependence on 'mastering the electronic text' are that they 'risk a new kind of hyper rationalisation and impersonalisation' as they work at an increasing distance from employees and clients (1984:393).

In this sense this disembodiment is simply one example of the continuum of the increasing textualisation of work, of which the body-suited, virtual, corporate professional is one extreme form. These revisionings of the global and the local, the mind and body, of 'home' and 'work' are suggestive of the fascinations of researching telework and of the utility of specifically feminist analytical interventions into this debate.

On Being 'Close' to your Work

While we may imagine a disembodied male protagonist in the virtual workplace of the future, then the work of Kidder (1982) and Turkle (1984) investigates 'actual' bodies in the computing workplaces of the present. Tracey Kidder's (1982) *The Soul of the New Machine* presents an account of a group of men constructing the 'perfect' computer, stretched to the limits of their capacity, working compulsively into the small hours with little compromise being made for life outside of the organisation. In a similar vein, Sherry Turkle's *The Second Self: Computers and the Human Spirit* (1984:210) describes the 'hacker culture' of the Massachusetts Institute of Technology and its epitomisation of the male cultural values of 'mastery, individualism [and] nonsensuality'. It is a workplace culture which is profoundly alien for women. According to Turkle, 'hacker culture', is macho culture, because 'the preoccupation with winning and subjecting oneself to increasingly violent tests (such as working non-stop for days on end) make their world peculiarly male in spirit, peculiarly unfriendly to women' (1984:210).

These accounts are compelling when run against the interview material generated in the qualitative study described above. The 'violent tests' endured by the men in Turkle's account certainly paralleled the experience of men in this study, whose work patterns were characterised by 'self-denial, discipline and physical endurance' (Mulholland, 1996:144) including long hours of work during time usually allocated for sleep or leisure (Armstrong, 1997).

For example, one man in this study group who developed software for international clients, was working every day up to 115 hours per week (an average of 16- to 18-hour days) in a home office which both facilitated and reinforced this use of time. 'John' had constructed a self-contained, sound-proofed, insulated, artificially heated and lit office with its own internally screened entrance way but no external windows or natural light. This workspace allowed John to work at a 'tremendous intensity' in the middle of the night and 'around the clock' without being aware of local time and without these odd hours strongly affecting his cycadian rhythms. His wife described this space in the following manner:

> ... it's too accessible, it's only upstairs, it's a perfect environment. He works in a room with no windows, so you're not sort of tempted by the sun, or you don't hear the rain or the wind. You don't even know what time it is down there, because you're working under lights all the time. So that would be one of the disadvantages working at home, is that you're too close to it.

This narrative, like many of the others articulated during the research, captures the teleworking dilemma in a nutshell: the key advantage of telework is 'being close to work all of the time'; the key disadvantage is 'being close to the work all of the time'. Julia's mixed feelings about this arrangement were summarised by the following polarisation of opinion about John's home office; it made John in his own words 'the perfect worker' *and* it made him less available as a husband and father, a less than perfect companion and parent.

Loving the Machine for Itself

This narrative connects to Turkle's (1984) suggestion that men who partici-pate in the 'hacker culture' substitute an intimate relationship with the com-puter as a refuge from the more uncertain and complex relationships that characterise social life. Turkle suggests that for such men their addiction is not to computer programming but to the issue of control; power and domination can more easily be exercised in the unambiguous world of machinery. In this withdrawal from 'animality, the unconscious and . . . the feminine' (Pryor, 1991:589) computers acted for some as automated companions offering the illusion of companionship without the demands of friendship (Turkle, 1984).

An example of this, in the study with teleworking parents, was 'Tom's' relationship with his personal computer which he described as 'really my love'. 'Delle', Tom's wife, confirmed his 'fascination' with the machine which she associated with the breakdown of Tom's first marriage and the sense of social isolation that he had experienced as a result; as well as his enjoyment of the technology for its own sake: '[H]e described his time with the computer as a love affair in that his marriage had ended, and that he hadn't lived with his wife for about two years at the time I met him . . . and um the computer was virtually his only other interest . . . So yeah he spent a lot of time with it actually.'

Delle observed that the technology was some sort of compensation for 'relational failure'; a source of solace and satisfaction in response to the complex and uneven character of human relating. In this sense the computer took the form of a consuming passion, without the disruption and uncertainty that characterises passion in human relationships. This passion was apparent when Tom talked about the longest period away from his computer, a 10-day holiday, where he admitted that 'In fact I wanted to take [the computer]. I wasn't allowed (by Delle). Sounds like a fetish doesn't it? . . . If I had a laptop it would have gone, but I didn't. I'd love a laptop now, but it will come.'

It is interesting that Tom sustains the sexualised imagery, from figuring the computer as 'his real love' to in this case a 'fetish', suggesting a passionate relationship where the machine is encountered as a thing in itself, related to as a quasi-human entity, a position sometimes said to be favoured by computer 'nerds' (Sofia, 1995:155). Here the need to relate to this quasi-human entity is directly opposed to the need to relate to a fully human entity; or more specifically, for Tom to meet his wife's needs for him to relate to her. At stake were the complex negotiations that occurred between this couple (and each couple in this study) about how they would share time together, time to work, time with the children and time alone.

An interesting inversion of this idea was the way Tom discussed the work of parenting his baby son, for whom he was the primary carer for two years, as a 'job' including metaphorically figuring Kaz as 'just a little feeding machine' that had to be kept 'warm and fed and changed, etc'. If Tom's computer was his 'real love' then the baby was symbolically related to as a modernist massified production system orientated toward inputs and outputs. There was thus an ironic element to Tom's narrative, where the machine was metaphorically related to as a person while the baby was symbolically figured as

like a machine. Turkle's (1984) point concerning the substitution of a relationship with the computer, for the rather more complex and uneven relationships that characterise social life, is apposite in this regard; passion for the
machine is contrasted with a certain automaticity in the relationship with the
baby.

Loving the 'Work' for Itself

Although Turkle's (1984) analysis is compelling, the research with
teleworking parents also solicited narrative material about women's relationships with their computers and their work more generally, and gives pause
for thought before making a too-hasty or essentialising equation between men
and machines. One could question, for example, the assumed male exclusive-
ness of the identity of the computer enthusiast. One could ask if computer
technologies are inherently 'marked' as masculine and 'sexually coded' to
reinforce, as Cockburn (1983:203) suggests, 'the construction of men as strong,
manually able and technologically endowed, and women as physically and
technically incompetent'? Furthermore, if, as Turkle argues, 'hacker culture'
creates a workplace which is alien to women, what happens when women
perform computer work in an arena culturally marked as feminine, such as
'the home'?

Sally Pryor's (1991) work is compelling in this regard when she reflects
on *herself as a computer*. This material comes closest to the issues of
'heightened work orientation' suggested in both Turkle's and Kidder's
accounts, from the perspective of a teleworking woman, albeit a woman
without children.

Pryor describes her body as 'other', as 'almost a nuisance' that 'gets in the
way of the mesmerising interaction between the screen and mind, unreason-
ably demanding food . . . stiffening one's back . . . when one just wants to
keep working' (1991:585).

In contrast to Smith's vision of women located in the bodily realm, Pryor
clearly positions herself within the abstract conceptual mode, as *becoming* a
computer, 'jamming my finger, thinking 'UNDO' and *expecting* this reversal
to happen' (1991:586, original emphasis).

The non-maternal body Pryor possesses, is likened to 'a brain attached to a
stick figure', her body's function is to 'carry my mind around', her arms' role
'to execute my ideas' (1991:587). When Pryor suffered severe 'repetitive-stress
injury' (occupation overuse syndrome) she was forced to re-evaluate her
assumptions about her body. This had included her rejection of exercise, of
sport and of bodily adornment as part of a competitive 'Jane Fonda Syndrome' (1991:587) just as a woman in this research with teleworking parents,
rejected 'taking walks' unless she walked for someone (the dog) or for something (the milk).

When Sally Pryor reflects on her neglect of her body during 'marathon computer sessions' she candidly admits that her 'most squalid moment was being force-fed by my partner while still sitting in front of the screen' (1991:585) and worries that she will injure her left arm as she has her right. At the end of the article it is clear that compulsion to continue to work still overrides her awareness that she 'should' stop and rest and she reflects on her body's physical sensations with an unusual degree of disassociation: 'My body, when I remember to notice it, begins to feel stiff, even so I must FORCE myself to stop work for a while. But first I will type this text, then add something else, then change something else . . .' (1991:590, original emphasis).

The women in this study, as partnered women with children who were either babies or under 15 years old, were not free to engage in such practices, because the demands of their partners and children *actively* prevented them from doing so. And yet, as they spoke about their work, their compulsion to work and their sense of absorption in it were palpable. These women were positioned between a desire to focus in an uninterrupted way on their work, and the vocal and visible demands of their children and partners which prevented them from doing so.

This ambivalent positioning of the women was expressed, for example, in the location of their home offices in 'liminal' spaces (Longhurst, 1996) *between* the family and the kind of isolated working environment suggested by John's workspace above, such as a corridor or a dining room or a dedicated space close to the kitchen. All of the women in this study shared their workspaces with other (usually multiple) family members, while none of the men did. All of them negotiated means of being available to their families *and* concentrating on their businesses, by creating boundaries between the two but especially between the children and their work. For example, one of the women ran a desktop publishing business in a converted garage located less than five steps from her kitchen door, but only allowed herself to be called on the phone by the children, but not visited, in her home office.

Despite these boundary-making strategies, the struggle between wanting to keep working *and* wanting to be with their families, remained present for the women in this study. This struggle was expressed in the envy they felt for the 'straight runs' their partners' on-site work afforded them and in their own tendency to telework at all hours, interrupting meals, sleep, leisure and romance, in order to make time for their work. This research is thus suggestive of the ways in which for these women work is a key marker of their identity, where work represents to them the experience of *being in control*[8] of their lives, in contrast to the less controllable experience of marriage and family. Additionally, for both the women and the men, the experience of a *dichotomy* between home and work, or work and leisure, is a false one. It is through work that these people felt engaged, stimulated and enjoyed themselves; through work they experienced themselves as powerful, talented and masterful. For them, work was not a drudge: they did not work for the money[9] or for the weekend (where neither income nor leisure time was in large supply), rather their work was intimately entwined with issues of identity, autonomy, control, in addition to the pleasure they found in the work itself.

For example, throughout Julia's discussion of John's 'overwork' as a problem for her, there was a clear sense of her awareness of his enjoyment of the work, of his 'sharpness', his 'tremendous intensity'. John's presentation of himself was reminiscent of the 'prototypical knowledge workers' at the centre of Wajcman and Probert's (1988) study. He demonstrated both his enthusiasm for his work and his sense of himself as an innovator when he asked me what kind of interactive technologies I commonly used. When I mentioned an interactive video experience I had recently had, his response was to describe me as 'a conservative' reliant on 'old' references to face-to-face contact, positioning himself, in contrast, as someone who interacted with international databases and 'experts' where his only contact would ever be via the screen or the phone line.

The teleworkers in this study often perceived themselves as powerful, proactive and, most importantly, 'in control' in relation to their lives and their work, in response to experiences of being *unable* to control one's working life; particularly the trauma of redundancy for the men and forms of sexual discrimination within organisations for the women. Telework offered unprecedented levels of *autonomy* and *self-definition* with regard to the way 'work' (and 'home') could be organised, but within the context of the *constraints* and *vulnerabilities* associated with self-employment and raising a family, to which this chapter will return.

Deconstructing the Virtual Workplace

I would make three observations in relation to the construction of telework as a virtual workplace and as a form of dis/embodiment, with regard to teleworkers as an externalised workforce, women's identities and the marketisation of domestic labour, and the refiguring of 'other' bodies in the virtual workplace.

Teleworkers as an externalised workforce

First, the 'electronic cottage' envisaged in futuristic accounts and materialised in the lives of some teleworkers, would seem to have the potential to open up a world of global opportunities for intellectual and creative engagement. But it also has the potential to 'flatten out' identity into a singular form; that of the worker as I have suggested above. Additionally some commentators have argued that information and communications technologies may offer new opportunities for connection and participation but they may also 'intensify the worst aspects of a competitive society . . . and institute a technocracy' (Jones, 1990:254), strengthening the 'monopoly of economic activity over the social and political dimensions of our lives' (Barr, 1985:5).

Furthermore, while the 'techno-love affair' has its place in an understanding of the compulsiveness toward, and fascination with, computers, such accounts exclude an analysis of the more 'material' considerations of income, contracts of employment and demand for services which also stimulate heightened orientation toward working with computers. The fascinations of 'the machine' are only one aspect of this phenomenon; others include the very real problem of finding work, maintaining an income and meeting deadlines. The disembodied intellectual at the centre of this technologically orientated construction is curiously asocial in this regard, as well as in terms of their seeming isolation from the demands of family and coupledom. This research with teleworking parents is suggestive of the ways the casualisation of work, and the demands of payment by output, keep people in front of their screens as much, if not more than, the joys and absorptions of the work itself.

Evidence to support this line of argument is included in Stanworth and Stanworth's (1995) research concerning the publishing industry in the United Kingdom. Only half of the 185 teleworkers studied received a 'living income' due to the low number of 'billable hours' they could charge in a strict output-based payment system (1995:226). The authors reflected on the way the 'balance of power' for these self-employed people lay with employers who were able to 'bid down wages and dictate terms and conditions'. Although they 'felt' more autonomous, in reality the independence of these teleworkers was limited to the control of working hours, the spatial arrangement of work and the removal of direct supervision, all of which were themselves limited by family obligations and client deadlines. Stanworth and Stanworth conclude that such self-employment was a form of casualisation with negative effects for the workers involved; presenting them as autonomous, flexible entrepreneurs, obscuring their unenviable position as an externalised workforce.

German sociologist Ulrich Beck (1992) provides some insight into this trend toward 'vulnerable' forms of self-employment, as part of wider changes in the social organisation of work. Beck examines the way that unemployment and the economic crisis has set in motion new opportunities for an 'individualization process with society', especially in relation to the flexibility of labour market relations and the regulation of working hours (1992:99). These in turn, Beck suggests, lead to social arrangements based not on class society but an *individualized society of employees* defined in terms of *labour law and by means of socio-political categories* (1992:100, original emphasis). That is, by categories such as contractual obligations, status, power and gender.

Beck argues that in this 'individualization process', standardised full-time employment has begun to 'soften and fray at the margins into flexibilisations of its three supporting pillars: labour law, work site and working hours' (1992:142).

As this occurs, individuals simultaneously experience fluidity in the boundaries between what Beck calls 'work and non work'[10] and the movement toward forms of 'risk-fraught . . . flexible, pluralised, decentralised underemployment' (1992: see also Di Martino and Wirth, 1990:529). In this process of the *'temporal and spatial decoupling* of labour and production', Beck argues, 'the much discussed "electronic cottage industry" represents only *one* extreme example' (1992:147, original emphasis). Thus while telework may be more discussed than it is actually taken up by workers, it is nevertheless according to Beck, *indicative* of wider changes in both employment relations *and* social formations.

Women's identities and the marketisation of domestic labour

The second issue the above argument canvases, that is worth further consideration, is Smith's (1979) notion of women's location in the bodily realm and their imputed responsibility for home and family. This raises the question, what happens when much or at least some of this domestic work is relocated within market relations? When domestic labour and childcare is 'outsourced' (e.g. childcare centres, laundries, prepared foods/restaurants/fast foods) or workers are bought into the home and the tasks delegated to others, does this continue to confine women to the bodily realm or are they freed to participate in the abstract conceptual mode on the same terms as men?

Rather than assume an inviolable connection between being a heterosexually partnered woman and mother and assuming the majority of the domestic and caring labour, what happens for women when they uncouple the latter from the former? Social changes such as these, while admittedly limited to a small minority of privileged women, do challenge theorists to offer analyses of gendered identities that resist essentialising generalisations in favour of conceptual narratives which emphasise the *'social, historical* and *relational* constitution of (female) identities in (particular) times and places' (Somers, 1994:612, original emphasis). This research regarding teleworking parents is suggestive of the ways in which, even with relatively modest and unstable personal incomes, women delegate, avoid, resist and/or reduce 'their' domestic labour and childcare responsibilities, by using what money they do generate to hire other women to perform this labour, in order to concentrate on their work. It is also suggestive of the relative stability of men's modest contributions to domestic labour in so far as the women in this study rarely negotiated a new or more egalitarian division of domestic and caring labour with their (male) partners as the solution to the increased paid and unpaid workload they experienced when they established businesses at home.

'Other' bodies in the virtual workplace

A third comment that could be made, regards the discourse of disembodiment discussed above, in that the virtual workplace allows for the refiguring of 'new' bodies in employment, not just in triumph of the 'computer nerd'. For example, the 'disabled body' is potentially empowered through the 'electronic cottage' to experience mobility and kinetic pleasure beyond the capacity of physical embodiment. Benedikt (1991) describes, for example, conducting a tour of Virtual Seattle with Rich Walsh, a man paralysed from his neck down and reliant on Benedikt to 'guide' him with his hands, through this virtual, spatial exploration. Benedikt (1991:381) describes the 'emotional rush, this seamless functional bonding with a stranger during several minutes of elated virtual world exploration . . . One day, Rich will steer himself through cyberspace with the same joystick he now uses to control his wheelchair.'

Additionally and perhaps more significantly, disabled teleworkers may gain an opportunity, through the virtual workplace, to engage in paid employment which allows them to avoid the discrimination and harassment they may otherwise face in employment. The Greater London Council's commissioned research report *Home Sweet Work Station* (1985:22) explicitly addressed this point with reference to disabled bodies marked by other forms of difference (ethnic/gender/'racial') and note that 'For Black people with disabilities . . . there is also a continuing risk that they face not just prejudice and mockery on the grounds of their disability but also racial harassment from workmates and superiors . . . These factors may in some cases add up to an extra incentive [for] such home-based work rather than face hostility and resentment in the outside world.'

Although the authors note that most disabled people are not willing to give into this kind of intimidation, telework in the virtual workplace may represent a refuge from a hostile employment environment.

In this sense the virtual workplace may be a more egalitarian, diverse workplace, peopled by bodies not frequently found within organisations, such as highly pregnant, lactating, ethnically diverse and/or disabled bodies. It offers a transcendence of corporeality as *re/entry* into the public and indeed global world, rather than the presentation of virtuality as a retreat from the complexities and emotionality of human relationships.

The Dangers and Pleasures of the Virtual Workplace

If the discourse of dis/embodiment refigures 'new' bodies in the virtual workspace, it also offers teleworkers work experiences both pleasurable and dangerous. That is, this construction of the virtual workplace and the dis/embodied self it imagines may create new 'dangers', as some of the above arguments about income insecurity and overwork have suggested, but also new *pleasures*. Such pleasures are signalled by the sense of exhilaration and engagement detailed by Pruitt and Barrett (1991) and Pryor (1991), pleasures likened by one software programmer (Wajcman and Probert, 1988:61) to taking heroin:

> I would say quite honestly that the prime consideration in my life is my work . . . and that has caused all sorts of problems, personal problems and I am the first to admit that I don't spend enough time doing the normal things that people do. I tend to think, live and breathe my work, um [notices something come up on computer screen] . . . I mean, to stay away from the computer for any length of time is like withdrawing from heroin.

The narrator in this account invokes drug addiction as the same kind of 'risky pleasure' as computer addiction: compelling, mind altering, compulsive. This quote is compelling not only because of the intriguingly addictive behaviour it suggests, but also because of the response made to this narrative by the programmer's partner. She said: 'I am not kidding, you can be having one of the most important discussions with him and if you are anywhere within visual sight of that thing [indicates the computer] he will be keeping one eye on it the whole time . . . we can be talking about a life and death situation and [he] has got one eye on the screen' (1988:61).

It is these 'risky' pleasures and (perhaps) the linked notion of seductive dangers which are a fascinating component of the construction of telework as a virtual workplace, and the linked envisioning of forms of dis/embodiment. Yet as Marilyn Strathern warns: 'however active the mind that socialises with the keyboard, the body is tied to the chair. One might ask, therefore, what kind of persons people are making of themselves out of these things?' (1992:x).

Conclusion: Telework as a 'Saturated Symbol'

As Ursula Huws (1991:20) has suggested, teleworking conjures up powerful images which embody both fears and desires about the worlds of 'home' and 'work':

> to the plate-glass and steel of the city centre skyscraper it counterposes a rural cottage; to the bustling, humming life of a crowded office, it counterposes domestic tranquillity; to the daily body crush on a rush hour commuter train, it counterposes a disembodied, abstract, almost ethereal form of communication . . . it promises the best of both worlds: full participation in the international traffic of ideas and information and enclosure in the protective sanctuary of home.

This chapter makes a specifically sociological contribution to this debate by focusing on the micropolitics of families, the gendered identities of teleworkers, the restructuring and externalisation of professional work and the reconfiguration of the timing and spatial location of employment. In doing so this argument has suggested that telework is a form of work organisation which resists unitary or monodimensional analyses, particularly ones that suggest that technology alone is determining this phenomenon.

Telework is neither a pathway to progress nor the road to Armageddon but rather like 'nailing jelly': as the 'action begins to bite, everything moves' (Green, 1994:xxix). However *unlike* nailing jelly there is a point to identifying the ways in which telework is constructed in the literature, and in individual narrative accounts, in that doing so reveals the *interests served* by the focus on *particular* problems and potentials this work practice holds.

In part these reflect the interests and positions of the research participants and researchers themselves, whose theoretical and political lenses shape their accounts of telework in a spectrum of opinion. Two ends of this spectrum could be described as envisioning telework as a means of promoting economic well-being, freedom of choice and balanced lifestyles, to seeing it as an intensification of the worst aspects of competitive capitalism, increasing inequality and encouraging work 'obsession'. Telework can be read as liberatory or enslaving, or indeed as elements of 'both/and' (Lather, 1991) relative to the framework through which it is constructed.

The issue of *heightened work orientation* (work 'addiction' or 'obsession') is a good demonstration of the contested and relativistic nature of these constructions. For example, heightened work orientation can appear in the guise of the disembodied computer artist in thrall to the fascinations of the machine; in the stressed teleworking mother attempting to reconcile the demands of her paid work with the needs of her family, and in the teleworking entrepreneur taking every offer that comes their way and making money by the fistful.

It is this multiplicity of readings of the literature and experiential narratives concerning telework and the conflicting, often contradictory, accounts and subject positions they offer, which make reading this material so fascinating and frustrating. Each monodimensional surface reveals beneath it a plethora of competing interpretations, just as the media representations of teleworkers submerge beneath their glossy images of perfect homes, careers and families – the chaotic practices of daily life.

References

Allen, S. and Wolkowitz, C. (1986) 'The Control of Women's Labour: The Case of Homeworking', *Feminist Review*, 22: 25–55.
Allen, S. and Wolkowitz, C. (1987) *Homeworking: Myths and Realities*, London: Macmillan.

Armstrong, N. (1997) *Negotiating Home and Work Selves: A Case Study of Teleworking in New Zealand*, PhD thesis, Massey University, Palmerston North (unpublished manuscript).

Barr, T. (1985) *The Electronic Estate: New Communications Media and Australia*, Ringwood, Victoria: Penguin.

Beck, U. (1992) *Risk Society: Towards a New Modernity*, London: Sage.

Benedikt, M. (ed.) (1991) *Cyberspace: First Steps*, Cambridge, MA: MIT Press.

Butler, J. (1995) 'For a Careful Reading', in Benhabib, S., Butler, J., Cornell, D. and Fraser, N. (eds.) *Feminist Contentions: A Philosophical Exchange*, New York and London: Routledge.

Cockburn, C. (1983) *Brothers: Male Dominance and Technological Change*, London: Pluto Press.

Di Martino, V. and Wirth, L. (1990) 'Telework: A New Way of Working and Living', *International Labour Review*, 129: 5, 529–54.

Greater London Council Equal Opportunities Group (1985) *Home Sweet Work Station: Homeworking and the Employment Needs of People with Severe Disabilities*, London: Ashmead Press.

Green, L. (1994) 'Introduction' and 'Missing the Post(modern): Cores, Peripheries and Globalisation', in Green, L. and Guinery, R. (eds) *Framing Technology, Society, Choice and Change*, St Leonards, NSW: Allen and Unwin.

Grosz, E. (1987) 'Notes Towards a Corporeal Feminism', *Australian Feminist Studies*, Summer, 5: 1–17.

Hamelink, C. (1990) 'Information Imbalance: Core and Periphery', in Dowling, J., Mohamaddi, A. and Sreberny-Mohammadi, A. (eds) *Questioning the Media: A Critical Introduction*, London: Sage.

Hollway, W. (1983) 'Heterosexual Sex: Power and Desire for the Other', in Carteledge, S. and Ryan, J. (eds) *Sex and Love: New Thoughts and Old Contradictions*, London: Women's Press.

Huws, U. (1991) 'Telework: Projections', *Futures*, January–February: 19–31.

Jones, B. (1990) *Sleepers, Wake!* Melbourne: Oxford University Press.

Judkins, P., West, D. and Drew, J. (1985) *Networking in Organisations*, London: Gower.

Kidder, T. (1982) *The Soul of the New Machine*, Harmondsworth: Penguin.

Lather, P. (1991) *Getting Smart: Feminist Research and Pedagogy With/in the Postmodern*, New York and London: Routledge.

Longhurst, R. (1996) 'Getting Dirty and I Don't Mean Fieldwork', Seminar presented to the Geography Department, Massey University, 9 May 1996, unpublished manuscript.

Loveridge, A., Graham, P. and Schoeffel, P. (1996) 'The Impact of Tele-Work on Working at Home in New Zealand', *New Zealand Sociology*, 11: 1, 1–37.

Mitter, S. (1986) *Common Fate, Common Bond: Women in the Global Economy*, London: Pluto Press.

Mulholland, K. (1996) 'Entrepreneurialism, Masculinities and the Self-Made Man', in Collinson, D. and Hearn, J. (eds) *Men as Managers, Managers As Men: Critical Perspectives on Men, Masculinities and Managements*, London: Sage.

Novitz, R. (1987) 'Bridging the Gap: Paid and Unpaid Work', in Cox, S. (ed.) *Public and Private Worlds: Women in Contemporary New Zealand*, Wellington: Allen and Unwin/Port Nicholson Press.

Phizacklea, A. and Wolkowitz, C. (1995) *Homeworking Women: Gender, Racism and Class at Work*, London: Sage.

Pruitt, S. and Tom, B. (1991) 'Corporate Virtual Workspace', in Benedikt, M. (ed.) *Cyberspace: First Steps*, Cambridge, MA: MIT Press.

Pryor, S. (1991) 'Thinking of Oneself as a Computer', *Leonardo* 24: 5, 585–90.

Smith, D. (1979) 'A Sociology of Women', in Sherman, J. and Teston Beck, E. (eds) *The Prism of Sex: Essays in the Sociology of Knowledge*, Wisconsin: University of Wisconsin Press.

Sofia, Z. (1995) 'Of Spanners and Cyborgs: "De-homogenising" Feminist Thinking on Technology', in Caine, B. and Pringle, R. (eds) *Transitions: New Australian Feminisms*, St Leonards, NSW: Allen and Unwin.

Somers, M. (1994) 'The Narrative Constitution of Identity: A Relational and Network Approach', *Theory and Society*, 23: 5, 605–49.

Stanworth, C. and Stanworth, J. (1995) 'The Self-Employed without Employees – Autonomous or Atypical?', *Industrial Relations Journal*, 26: 3, 221–29.

Statham, A., Miller, E. and Mauksch, H. (eds) (1988) *The Worth of Women's Work: A Qualitative Synthesis*, Albany, New York: SUNY Press.

Strathern, M. (1992) 'The Mirror of Technology', in Silverstone, R. and Hirsch, E. (eds) *Consuming Technologies: Media and Information in Domestic Spaces*, New York and London: Routledge.

Turkle, S. (1984) *The Second Self: Computers and the Human Spirit*, London: Granada.

Wajcman, J. (1991) *Feminism Confronts Technology*, North Sydney: Allen and Unwin.

Wajcman, J. and Probert, B. (1988) 'New Technology Outwork', in Willis, E. (ed.) *Technology and the Labour Process*, Sydney: Allen and Unwin.

West Yorkshire Homeworking Group (1990) *A Penny A Bag: Campaigning on Homework*, Batley: Yorkshire and Humberside Low Pay Unit.

Zuboff, S. (1984) *In the Age of the Smart Machine*, New York: Basic Books.

Notes

1   Relatively few people in Aotearoa/New Zealand actually or potentially telework; only 2.1 per cent of the non-farm labour force, a group of 10 089 according to the 1991 census (Loveridge *et al.*, 1996:21).

2   These words are placed in inverted commas in order to indicate that they are never two discrete spheres but always feed off and interpenetrate one another (Novitz, 1987) as demonstrated by the practice of teleworking itself.

3   Somers (1994:619) defines public narratives as 'those narratives attached to cultural and institutional formations larger than the single individual, to intersubjective networks or institutions, however local or grand . . . these stories have drama, plot, explanation and selective criteria'.

4   See, for example, Allen and Wolkowitz, 1986; 1987; Mitter, 1986; West Yorkshire Homeworking Group, 1990; and Phizacklea and Wolkowtiz, 1995.

5   I am attracted to qualitative methodologies because 'they bring into central focus the points of view of those studied and their active participation in constructing worlds that are sometimes quite different from the worlds they are thought to live in by those in power' (Statham *et al.*, 1988:311).

6   Within these invocations of global communications networks there is an *absent* discussion of infrastructural and other costs. People who live on those nations described as 'developing' have much less information and less access to information technologies. For example, of the world's 700 million, 75 per cent can be found in the 9 richest countries; in the most rural areas there is less than one telephone for every 1000 people. Similarly, in the United States a daily newspaper enjoys a circulation of 268 copies per 1000 people; in Japan the comparable figure is 562, while in African countries the average is 16.6 copies per 1000 (Hamelink, 1990:219).

7   I would define discourse as 'systems of statements which adhere around common meanings and values ... [that] are a product of social factors, of powers and practices, rather than an individual's set of ideas' (Hollway, 1983:231). In this sense I am employing a specifically Foucauldian use of the concept of discourse which emphasises not only language, forms of meaning construction and representation, but the discourse 'on subjects' (for example, the discourse on sexuality) as it constitutes the '*lived* and *actual* experience' of subjects (Butler, 1995:143).

8   This word appears an extraordinary number of times in teleworkers' transcripts as a desire, ambition and/or value they have.

9   For example, teleworkers in Aotearoa/New Zealand generated relatively modest incomes in 1991. Full-time professional home-working women (excluding clerical workers who would tend to earn less) earned on average $20403 in 1991, which was lower than the median income for all women workers of $21461. Male professional homeworkers earned $28024, more than the average male median wage at that time of $27270 (Loveridge *et al.*, 1996:25).

10 I would note Beck's problematic assignment of domestic labour and childcare as 'non-work' underscoring invisibility of women's contributions in the home within his account.

4 Contingent and Non-Standard Work in the United States: Towards a More Poorly Compensated, Insecure Workforce

Sam Rosenberg and June Lapidus

Introduction

In the United States we hear much about 'family friendly' workplace initiatives. There are more dual-earner couples and female-headed households bringing to the fore work/family conflicts. Employers are said to be responding with more 'family friendly' working time arrangements. As jobs become more flexible and work schedules more diverse, it is alleged that the 'factory clock' is in the process of becoming more aligned with the cycles of workers' personal lives. Moreover, it is argued that workers have not had to pay for these more desirable work arrangements through lower compensation or poorer benefit packages.

For some workers and companies this characterisation may be accurate, but for most it is not. Rather, there is a dark side to labour flexibility as practised in the United States. In general, employers have been the driving force behind the push for more flexible employment. As 'just-in-time' organisation of inventory and production has spread, so has 'just-in-time' personnel management. Long-term employment relationships between employers and workers are eroding and the 'disposable employee' is more common. Even while the economy has been strong and the unemployment rate low by historical standards, workers have been feeling more insecure about their jobs. The more flexible job is often a more precarious job, one providing lower wages, fewer benefits and less security than the previously more typical full-time, long-term position.

In this chapter, we evaluate the role of flexible employment in the United States. This chapter is divided into five main sections. The first defines and describes different forms of contingent and non-standard work and presents alternative estimates of the extent of these forms of employment in the United States. The second section analyses whether contingent labour and non-standard work have become more prevalent. Following this overview, the third section investigates the social characteristics of those engaged in contingent and non-standard work, where they work and the quality of their jobs. With this information as background, the fourth section analyses the sources of growth of contingent labour and alternative employment arrangements from both the demand and supply sides, with particular attention to what flexibility means for both sides of the labour market. The fifth, and final, section develops the public policy implications of non-standard employment relations in the United States.

Contingent and Non-Standard Employment Arrangements in the United States

There are no official definitions of contingent and non-standard employment. Furthermore, there is no official definition of what constitutes standard employment. This is reflective of the fact that in the United States there are minimal federal governmental regulations of working time for those 16 years of age and older. The existing laws do not specify the number of hours to be worked daily, weekly or annually, the hours in the day when work can occur, the number of days per week to be worked, the specific days on which work can occur, or the amount of vacation time that must be provided to workers. Rather, the major piece of federal legislation regulating working time – the *Fair Labor Standards Act* of 1938 – only states that covered employees, mainly non-supervisory personnel in the private sector, be paid a minimum of one-and-a-half times the regular hourly rate for all hours worked after 40 hours per week. Employees do not have a legal right to be able to retain their jobs, once hired. Generally, a private employer, unless limited by statute, contract or collective bargaining agreement, is free to hire and fire any employee at will.

In the absence of a clear legal definition, a standard employment arrangement is the commonly perceived norm of a full-time wage and salary job. For many that norm also includes a long-term relationship between workers and employers. It is true that such long-term employment relationships do exist. In 1991, 32.2 per cent of workers aged 25 and above had been with their current employer for 10 years or longer (US Department of Labor, 1995:15). Nevertheless, very few full-time workers are guaranteed lifetime employment or even long-term employment. Therefore, the definition of a 'contingent' employee is somewhat arbitrary and the term 'contingent work' has taken on a wide variety of meanings. It was initially coined by Audrey Freedman, then of the Conference Board of New York, at a 1985 conference on employment security. It referred to a conditional employment relationship initiated by an immediate need for labour, perhaps due to an increased demand for a particular product or service. The employment relationship was conceived as short-term, to be terminated when the product or service demand was satisfied. Within a few years of its initial usage, the definition of contingent employment was expanded to include 'virtually any work arrangement that might differ from the commonly perceived norm of a full-time wage and salary job' (Polivka, 1996a:3).

Not surprisingly, given the varying definitions, the estimates of the share of the workforce employed in contingent positions range from a low of 1.9 per cent of total employed (US Department of Labor, Bureau of Labor Statistics, 1997) to a high of about 30 per cent of the labour force (Belous, 1989:16). That analysts would not agree on the size of the contingent labour force and, as will be shown shortly, on the number of workers in alternative employment arrangements is to be expected. Yet what is at stake in the debate is ultimately of more importance than merely 'getting the numbers right'. Underlying the wide range of estimates is a disagreement over whether a fundamental restructuring of the workforce is ongoing in the United States. A relatively small contingent labour force would imply that this is not happening. A growing share of the labour force working in contingent or non-standard jobs would likely signify a restructuring of primary sector labour markets and the transferring of some labour functions to an expanding secondary labour market. Given increased product market competition, continually changing technology, and the growth of educational institutions able to train workers, employers may be less interested in maintaining a loyal, company-trained workforce with low rates of turnover and more interested in being able to retrench quickly. They may be minimising the permanent ('core') workforce and expanding the contingent ('peripheral') workforce (Appelbaum, 1987). This may be occurring either within the 'lean' large corporation itself or by outsourcing work to small business suppliers and contractors employing low-wage contingent workers (Harrison, 1994). To the extent that a core/peripheral model is actually being instituted, primary sector jobs are being eliminated – along with their relatively high wages, decent benefits and some job security – and being replaced by secondary sector jobs paying low wages, providing minimal benefits, and no job security.

There are competing definitions and interpretations of contingent and non-standard employment in the United States. The ones utilised by the Bureau of Labor Statistics (BLS) are the most restrictive. Contingent workers are those individuals who do not perceive themselves as having an explicit or implicit contract for ongoing employment. Using this definition, the BLS estimates the size of the contingent labour force utilising the February 1997 supplement to the Current Population Survey, a household survey conducted monthly by the Census Bureau.

The BLS estimates of the contingent workforce vary from 1.9 per cent to 4.4 per cent of the employed workforce, or between 2.4 and 5.6 million people. The lowest estimate includes only wage and salary workers who have been in their jobs for one year or less and expect their jobs to last for an additional year or less. In the case of temporary workers and contract workers, contingency is based on tenure and expected duration of their employment with the temporary help or contract firm, not with regard to the specific client to whom they were assigned.[1] Thus, a worker who was employed by a temporary agency for more than a year, but had many short-term jobs in that period of time, would not be considered a contingent worker under this definition. This is a notion of contingency as seen from the perspective of the worker and does not speak to the extent of restructuring which may be occurring in the labour market as a whole.

The second BLS definition adds the self-employed and independent contractors who had worked at their jobs (or been self-employed) for one year or less and expected their employment to last for an additional year or less.[2] Furthermore, the employment tenure and expected duration of employment of temporary and contract workers are now defined in terms of their relationship with the client to whom they were assigned, not their temporary help or contract firm.

The third and broadest BLS definition of contingent work includes all wage and salary workers who do not expect their jobs to last, even if they have held their existing jobs for more than one year and anticipate holding them for at least another year. However, the one-year job tenure and expected duration requirements remain for independent contractors and the self-employed (US Department of Labor, Bureau of Labor Statistics, 1997).

Gordon (1996) is satisfied with the instability-based definition of contingency of the BLS but he broadens their conception to take account of workers involuntarily pushed into part-time and alternative employment arrangements. Beginning with the least restrictive definition of contingent employment adopted by the BLS, Gordon estimates the proportion of 'disposable workers' among private non-farm wage and salary workers. After eliminating agricultural and governmental contingent workers and the self-employed, he adds to the BLS-defined contingent workers, those working part-time involuntarily not already counted as contingent workers, and those working involuntarily as independent contractors, on-call and day workers, and temporary help workers, also not previously counted as contingent workers.[3] He then estimates that in February 1995, 9.9 per cent of private, non-farm wage and salary employees were 'disposable workers' (Gordon, 1996:227).

A joint Economic Policy Institute and Women's Research and Education Institute report also argues that the BLS has underestimated the number of workers in 'insecure jobs'.[4] Unlike Gordon (1996), they find the job tenure and expected duration of employment criteria utilised by the BLS to be too restrictive, since even the broadest definition of contingency adopted by the BLS retains these criteria for self-employed independent contractors and other self-employed workers. Rather, they consider a job to be insecure if workers report any one of the following: (1) the job is temporary; (2) they cannot work for their employer as long as they wish; (3) they are not sure about criteria (1) and (2); or (4) the job is expected to last for only one year or less. They find that 9.8 per cent of women and 8.5 per cent of men had insecure jobs in February 1995 (Kalleberg *et al.*, 1997:39).

The broadest view of contingent work and one of the earliest was advanced by Richard Belous in the late 1980s. His definition is based on the notion of non-standard employment arrangements and includes temporary workers, part-time workers, business service workers and the self-employed in the contingent labour force. Belous (1989:16) finds that approximately 30 per cent of the workforce would have been contingent workers in 1988.

As with contingent labour, there is not a consensus over what constitutes a non-standard employment relationship. In the broadest sense, an alternative employment relationship is one that departs from the traditional full-time career job. The BLS definition of alternative employment arrangements includes the following: (1) independent contractors; (2) on-call workers; (3) temporary help agency workers and (4) workers provided by contract firms. The BLS estimates that in February 1997, 9.9 per cent of the total employed were working in an alternative employment arrangement. Most of these people were independent contractors who were 6.7 per cent of total employed, or approximately 8.5 million people. Fewer were on-call workers (2 million or 1.6 per cent of employed workers), temporary help agency workers (1.3 million or 1 per cent of the total employed), or workers provided by contract firms (760 000 or 0.6 per cent of the workforce) (US Department of Labor, Bureau of Labor Statistics, 1997).

Not all workers in non-standard employment relationships are contingent workers and not all contingent workers are employed in alternative employment arrangements. While temporary help agency workers were more likely to be contingent workers according to the BLS than were workers in the other alternative employment arrangements, a large share of temporary workers were classified as non-contingent workers. According to the broadest estimate of contingency generated by the BLS, 56.8 per cent of employees of temporary help firms were in contingent jobs. A substantial proportion of on-call workers were contingent (26.7 per cent). However, only 16.7 per cent of contract company workers and 3.5 per cent of independent contractors were contingent (US Department of Labor, Bureau of Labor Statistics, 1997). The relatively small share of workers in alternative employment arrangements considered contingent might reflect the fact that instead of developing a stable relationship with the firms for which they are providing services, the individuals might be developing a stable relationship with the contract company or the occupation inherent in their employment relationship (Polivka, 1996a).

The joint report of the Economic Policy Institute and the Women's Research and Education Institute defines non-standard work arrangements more broadly than the BLS. To the four different types of alternative arrangements identified by the BLS, they add regular part-time work and all self-employment. Overall, in February 1995, they estimate insecure jobs to be over three times more likely to be found in non-standard work arrangements than among regular full-time work. More specifically, among all workers in non-standard jobs, 17.9 per cent of women and 18.2 per cent of men worked in insecure jobs. In contrast, only 5.4 per cent of men and women in regular full-time employment said they did not expect their jobs to last.

Furthermore, the Economic Policy Institute and the Women's Research and Education Institute were generally more likely to find insecure jobs within specific non-standard work arrangements than the BLS. For example, they defined all on-call workers and day labourers as having insecure jobs, while only 38.1 per cent of those workers were defined as contingent by the BLS in February 1995. Similarly, with temporary workers, where the BLS estimated that 66.5 per cent were in contingent positions, the Economic Policy Institute and the Women's Research and Education Institute consider more than 75 per cent to be holding insecure jobs in February 1995 (Kalleberg *et al.*, 1997:39; US Department of Labor, Bureau of Labor Statistics, August, 1995).

Additional information on the extent of contingent labour can be obtained by examining employers' use of flexible staffing arrangements. An analysis of a stratified random sample of firms in the United States by the W.E. Upjohn Institute for Employment Research found that non-standard staffing arrangements were widespread among establishments of all sizes and in all industries. Forty-six per cent of firms used workers from temporary help agencies, 38 per cent used short-term hires, 72 per cent used regular part-time workers, 27 per cent used on-call workers, and 4 per cent used independent contract workers. Excluding part-time workers, 78 per cent of establishments in the survey used at least one form of non-standard staffing. However, the intensity of use among firms was low. In 1995, agency temporaries added 1.5 per cent to regular employment and short-term hires added 2.3 per cent to regular employment among firms in the survey.[5] Given that temporary jobs are short-lived, the number of workers holding such positions at any point in time is likely to be much smaller than the number of contingent jobs in existence over the course of a year. In fact, in a year, companies created between seven and eight times the number of jobs for temporary agency workers, and between five and six times the number of jobs for short-term hires, as would be found at any point in time. As a result, it is quite likely that many more people hold contingent positions at some time during a year than are working at such jobs at any point in time (Houseman, 1997).

The Growth of Contingent and Non-Standard Work Arrangements

Just as there are no consistent definitions of contingent and non-standard work arrangements in the United states, there are no consistent longitudinal data sources. Thus, it is difficult to measure trends in contingent and non-standard work over time. Nevertheless, it does appear that growth has taken place.

The most reliable data are for employees in temporary help firms and part-time workers. Employment in the temporary help supply industry has grown at a faster rate than total non-agricultural employment. In 1982, this industry accounted for 0.5 per cent of total non-agricultural employment. By 1995, that figure had risen to 1.9 per cent (Kalleberg *et al.*, 1997:75).[6] Assuming that the share of workers in this industry who should be deemed contingent is constant over time, then the growing share of employed non-agricultural employees working in this industry would be evidence of the increasing importance of contingent labour and non-standard work.

Part-time work has also become more prevalent. Since the 1950s, the proportion of employed persons working part-time has grown gradually from 13 per cent in 1957 to 18.4 per cent in 1995. The usage of part-timers grew most rapidly during the 1970s when the share of the employed working part-time increased from 15 per cent in 1968 to 17.6 per cent in 1979 (Tilly, 1996:13–14; Kalleberg *et al.*, 1997:75). The share of total jobs officially considered part-time did not rise much during the 1980s and the first half of the 1990s.

However, these statistics on part-time work do not count the actual number of part-time jobs, but rather the number of persons whose total weekly work hours fall below the full-time threshold. The existence of moonlighting – holding two or more jobs – leads to the undercounting of the actual number of part-time jobs. Approximately 55 per cent of multiple jobholders work at one full-time job and one part-time job, yet they are only counted as full-time workers (Stinson, 1997:6). Others work part-time on two or more jobs and accumulate more than 35 hours per week. They, too, are counted as full-time workers. The undercounting of part-time jobs worsened in the 1980s since the rate of moonlighting increased rapidly in this decade. This followed a period of stability in the 1970s when the multiple jobholding rate held around 5 per cent. By 1989, the rate of moonlighting reached 6.2 per cent. It has remained at approximately that level since then (Stinson, 1997:4). Thus, there has been a growth of part-time jobs without a corresponding increase in official part-time employment figures.

If all part-time jobs are considered to be non-standard work, the increase in the share of the workforce employed part-time represents a growth in non-standard work. Part-time jobs may not be equivalent to contingent jobs. The BLS found only 10 per cent of all part-time workers were contingent while for the Economic Policy Institute and the Women's Research and Education Institute the corresponding figure was approximately 15 per cent (US Department of Labor, Bureau of Labor Statistics, 1997; Kalleberg *et al.*, 1997:39). Nevertheless, the increase in the share of the workforce employed part-time likely represents a growth in contingent employment. Until about 1970, the growth in part-time jobs was driven mostly by expanding voluntary part-time employment. However, since that time, there has been a significant secular rise in the percentage of employees who work part-time, but would prefer full-time employment. Of the 3.3 percentage point increase in the part-time employment rate between 1969 and 1993, 3 percentage points are accounted for by the growth in involuntary part-time work (Tilly, 1996:15; Ehrenberg, Rosenberg and Li, 1988; Ichniowski and Preston, 1986).

While there are no consistent longitudinal data on employer staffing patterns, the data that do exist point to a growing use of flexible staffing patterns. A Bureau of National Affairs survey of more than 400 firms reported marked increases, in the period 1980 to 1985, in the number of enterprises making use of agency temporaries, short-term hires, on-call workers, administrative/business support contracts and production subcontracting (Abraham, 1990:92). BLS survey data on contracting out behaviour of manufacturing firms showed that between 1979 and 1986 firms reported an increasing propensity to contract out at least some janitorial work, machine maintenance work, engineering and drafting work, accounting services work and computer services work (Abraham and Taylor, 1996). In general, overall trends in employment, occupations, output and input from 1972–96 provide evidence that firms have increased the purchase of business services and engineering and management services relative to directly hiring labour (Clinton, 1997).

This evidence of flexible staffing is also suggestive of a growth in contingent labour. While not all employees of firms providing services to firms work under contingent arrangements, the likelihood of contingent work is much higher among workers with alternative employment arrangements than workers with traditional arrangements (US Department of Labor, Bureau of Labor Statistics, 1997).

Contingent Workers and Non-Standard Workers: A Statistical Portrait

Not surprisingly, different definitions of contingent and non-standard work lend themselves to different interpretations of who is working under contingent and non-standard arrangements, where they are working and the quality of their jobs.

As we have argued, we believe the BLS underestimates the prevalence of these arrangements in the United States. Nevertheless, it does provide the most recent data on contingent and alternative employment. Accordingly, we will utilise BLS definitions of both contingent work and alternative employment arrangements in creating the statistical portrait below.

In February 1997, contingent workers were more likely to be young, female and Hispanic than were other workers. Thirty per cent of contingent workers were under the age of 25 compared with approximately 13 per cent of non-contingent workers. Slightly more than half of all contingent workers were

Table 4.1   Employed contingent and non-contingent workers by selected characteristics, February 1997

Characteristic	Contingent Workers	Non-Contingent Workers
Gender		
Male	49.3	53.8
Female	50.7	46.2
'Racial' and ethnic origins		
White	81.9	85.3
African-American	11.1	10.6
Hispanic origin	12.4	9.4
Full or part-time status		
Full-time workers	57.5	82.2
Part-time workers	42.5	17.8

The sum of the percentages on race and Hispanic origin exceed 100% since Hispanics are included in both the white and African-American population groups. *Source*: This table is based on information provided in US Department of Labor, Bureau of Labor Statistics (1997), Table 2.

women compared with 46 per cent of non-contingent workers (see Table 4.1). Workers of Hispanic origin were somewhat over-represented among contingent employees while whites were somewhat under-represented. African-Americans accounted for about 11 per cent of both contingent and noncontingent workers.

Contingent workers were employed in a wide variety of jobs. They were over-represented in professional, administrative support (including clerical) and service positions. They were less likely to be in managerial and sales jobs (see Table 4.2). For example, 21.2 per cent of contingent workers were employed in professional specialty occupations, in contrast to 15.3 per cent of non-contingent workers. Teachers are included within the professional specialty category and there was a high rate of contingency among teachers, particularly teachers in institutions of higher learning. In February 1995, 25 per cent of college and university teachers held temporary positions with short-term contracts. Other professional occupations with high rates of contingency were editors and reporters, photographers, actors and directors, and athletes (Polivka, 1996b).

The stereotypical contingent worker in the United States is a female clerical worker, not a professional. The stereotype is not without justification. About

Table 4.2   Contingent and non-contingent workers in the United States by occupation and industry (percentages), February 1997

Characteristic Occupation	Contingent Workers	Non-Contingent Workers
Executive, administrative and managerial	7.3	14.6
Professional speciality	21.2	15.3
Technicians and related support	3.5	3.3
Sales occupations	5.8	12.1
Administrative support, clerical	19.7	14.3
Services	15.2	13.2
Precision product, craft, and repair	10.2	10.9
Operators, fabricators and labourers	14.1	14.0
Farming, forestry and fishing	3.1	2.3
Total	100.1 (a)	100.00
Industry		
Agriculture	2.8	2.3
Mining	0.4	0.5
Construction	10.1	6.0
Manufacturing	8.0	16.8
Transport and public utilities	4.1	7.1
Wholesale trade	1.8	4.0
Retail trade	9.5	16.7
Finance, insurance and real estate	3.1	6.6
Services	55.9	35.6
Public administration	4.2	4.4
Total	99.9 (a)	100.00

(a) varies from 100% due to rounding.
Source: This table is based on information provided in US Department of Labor, Bureau of Labor Statistics (1997), Table 4.

20 per cent of contingent workers were administrative support personnel, in contrast to approximately 14 per cent of non-contingent workers. In February 1995, secretaries, stenographers, typists and file clerks had above-average rates of contingency (Polivka, 1996b).

Contingent workers were also disproportionately represented in service occupations (15.2 per cent) compared with only 13.2 per cent of non-contingent workers. In February 1995, within service occupations, the highest rates of contingency were found in food service occupations which include waiters and waitresses, cooks and bartenders. Childcare workers in private households and janitors and cleaners also had above-average rates of contingency (Polivka, 1996b).

While contingent workers were found in all industries, they were much more likely to be concentrated in the services industry than were non-contingent workers. In February 1997, approximately 56 per cent of contingent workers were employed in the services industry compared with only 35.6 per cent of non-contingent workers. Business services and educational services account for a large proportion of contingent workers in services. The construction industry was the other industry with an over-representation of contingent workers. Approximately 10 per cent of contingent workers were in construction in contrast to 6.0 per cent of non-contingent workers.

Contingent workers were more than twice as likely to be working part-time than non-contingent workers. Over 40 per cent (42.5 per cent) of contingent workers were part-time workers compared with just 17.8 per cent of full-time workers. Thus, it is not surprising that contingent workers generally earn less than non-contingent workers. However, this is not the primary reason for the lower earnings since full-time contingent workers earn less than full-time non-contingent workers and part-time contingent workers earn less than part-time non-contingent workers. In February 1997, the median weekly earnings of full-time contingent workers was $417 compared with $510 for non-contingent workers. The median weekly earnings of part-time workers in contingent positions was $111, well below the median weekly earnings of $146 of noncontingent workers (US Department of Labor, Bureau of Labor Statistics, 1997). Even after controlling for age, education, industry of employment and hours worked, the earnings of contingent workers were generally still below those of non-contingent workers (Hipple and Stewart, 1996).

Not only do contingent workers earn less than non-contingent workers, they also are less likely to receive health insurance and pension benefits from their employers. In February 1997, only 1 in 5 contingent workers had employer-provided health insurance coverage, compared with 1 in 2 non-contingent workers. Only about one-fourth of contingent workers were eligible for employer-provided pension plans compared with nearly one-half of non-contingent workers. Those in contingent jobs were also less likely to participate in an employer-provided pension plan (15 per cent compared to 44 per cent) (US Department of Labor, Bureau of Labor Statistics, 1997).

The popular view that a contingent job is one which pays low wages and provides few benefits turns out to be accurate. It is more difficult, however, to generalise about jobs with alternative employment arrangements. The broad category of non-standard work includes widely disparate jobs and workers. Furthermore, non-standard work is highly gender differentiated.

The typical independent contractor was a white male, middle-aged or older, with a college degree (see Table 4.3). Male independent contractors earned slightly more than male employees working under traditional arrangements (US Department of Labor, Bureau of Labor Statistics, 1997). They were most likely to be found in managerial, skilled craft and sales positions (Cohany, 1996). Women were under-represented among independent contractors. Only one-third of independent contractors were women (see Table 4.3). In contrast with men's experience, women working as independent contractors earned less than did women workers with traditional arrangements. (US Department of Labor, Bureau of Labor Statistics, 1997). This is due to the fact that women independent contractors worked in different fields than did men. For women independent contractors, the heaviest concentration was in services (mainly cleaners, childcare providers and hairdressers), sales, and professional specialty occupations (Cohany, 1996).

Workers provided by contract firms were also predominantly male. In February 1997, approximately 70 per cent of workers supplied by contract firms were men. As with independent contractors, male workers employed by contract companies had higher weekly earnings than male workers in traditional arrangements. This was not the case for women. Women workers provided by contract firms earned slightly less than women in traditional employment arrangements (US Department of Labor, Bureau of Labor Statistics, 1997). Male contract workers were likely to be employed in the construction and computer and data processing industries while women contract workers were more likely to be found in the general area of health services and in hospitals (Kalleberg *et al.*, 1997).

Temporary help agency workers were disproportionately young, female and members of minority groups. More than half (55.3 per cent) were women, compared with 47.3 per cent of traditional workers. African-Americans made up 21.3 per cent of the temporary help workforce, more than double their share of traditional employment. Hispanics comprised 12.3 per cent of temps, but only 9.6 per cent of traditional employees. Workers provided by temporary help supply firms had received less formal education than workers in traditional arrangements. They were heavily concentrated in two broad occupational categories – administrative support (including clerical) and operators, fabricators and labourers. In February 1995, these two broad occupational categories accounted for more than two-thirds of all temporary help agency workers. Female temps tended to be clerical workers while male temps worked as operators, fabricators and labourers (Cohany, 1996). Both male and female temps working full-time earned less than their full-time counterparts in traditional employment arrangements (US Department of Labor, Bureau of Labor Statistics, 1997).

Table 4.3 Workers with alternative and traditional work arrangements in the United States by selected characteristics, February 1997

Characteristic	Independent Contractor	On-Call Worker	Temps, Agency Workers	Workers Provided by Contract Firm	Workers with Traditional Arrangements
Gender					
Male	66.6	49.0	44.7	69.8	52.7
Female	33.4	51.0	55.3	30.2	47.3
'Racial' and ethnic origin					
White	90.7	89.3	75.1	81.5	84.8
African-American	5.3	7.8	21.3	12.9	10.9
Hispanic origin	7.3	13.3	12.3	6.3	9.6
Full- or part-time status					
Full-time worker	73.6	47.4	80.3	82.8	82.3
Part-time worker	26.4	52.6	19.7	17.2	17.7
Educational attainment					
Less than a high school diploma	8.7	13.4	11.2	7.2	9.7
High school graduate, diploma only	30.3	28.7	30.7	36.8	32.8
Less than a bachelor's degree	26.8	32.0	36.3	23.4	28.0
College graduate	34.1	25.9	21.8	32.7	29.5

The sum of the percentages on 'racial' and ethnic origin exceeds 100% since Hispanics are included in both the white and African-American population groups.
Source: This table is based on information provided in the US Department of Labor, Bureau of Labor Statistics (1997), Tables 6 and 7.

On-call workers were somewhat more likely to be white or of Hispanic origin than those in traditional employment arrangements. More than half (52.6) per cent worked part-time compared with just 17.7 per cent of traditional workers. Women on-call workers had an extremely high incidence of part-time work, much higher than either male on-call workers or women working in traditional arrangements. Many on-call employees worked part-time involuntarily; in February 1995, about one-half of the men and one-quarter of the women who worked part-time would have preferred full-time work (Cohany, 1996). Both full-time and part-time on-call workers earned less than their counterparts in traditional employment relationships.

Overall, on-call workers were somewhat less educated than other workers. However, their educational attainment varied dramatically by gender. In February 1995, only 11 per cent of the men had a college degree compared with 31 per cent of the women (Cohany, 1996). The differential educational attainment of men and women was reflected in their job profiles. The men tended to work as truck drivers, freight and stock handlers, labourers, farm workers, and craftworkers such as carpenters, electricians and plumbers. There were also some men employed as substitute teachers in elementary and secondary schools. Many more women were working as substitute teachers. Women also worked on an on-call basis as registered nurses, nursing aides, childcare and teachers' assistants, office clerks, sales clerks, cashiers, waitresses and cooks (Cohany, 1996).

As was the case with contingent workers, individuals in alternative employment arrangements were less likely to receive health insurance or pension coverage from their employer than those in traditional employment arrangements. In February 1997, nearly three-fifths (57.5 per cent) of workers in traditional work arrangements received health insurance from their employer. Of all workers in alternative employment arrangements, contract company employees were most likely to be provided with health insurance by the employer. Approximately half of them had employer-provided health insurance. Only 7 per cent of workers employed by temporary help supply companies and 19.6 per cent of on-call workers received their health insurance from their employer (US Department of Labor, Bureau of Labor Statistics, 1997).

Workers in non-standard employment arrangements were less likely to be eligible for and less likely to participate in employer-provided pension plans than other workers. In terms of eligibility for an employer-provided pension, contract company employees were most likely to be offered pensions. In February 1997, the proportion eligible for pension coverage was 47.6 per cent compared with 27.0 per cent of on-call workers and 10.4 per cent of temporary workers. In contrast, more than half (52.5 per cent) of workers in traditional employment arrangements were eligible for a pension. Temporary workers had the lowest proportion with employer-provided pensions (3.7 per cent) while contract company employees had the highest (35.7 per cent). Approximately 1 in 5 on-call workers were included in employer-provided pension plans. The corresponding figure for workers in traditional employment arrangements was 46.9 per cent (US Department of Labor, Bureau of Labor Statistics, 1997).

Explanations for the Growth of Contingent and Non-Standard Employment in the United States

Factors driving the use of contingent and non-standard employment arrangements can be found on both the demand and supply sides of the labour market. On the demand side, employers may seek more flexible employment relations in order to raise productivity, lower labour costs and transfer more of the risk of economic downturns and uncertainty to employees. On the supply side, employees may desire flexibility to meet personal and family needs, or to remain independent and not beholden to any particular employer.

For supply side factors to be the dominant force behind the creation of contingent positions, workers would need to prefer such jobs. However, in February 1997, the majority of contingent workers in the United states (56 per cent) would have preferred non-contingent jobs. Only slightly more than one-third (35.8 per cent) desired their arrangement. The remainder did not have a clear preference one way or the other (US Department of Labor, Bureau of Labor Statistics, December 1997).

Similarly, if an employee-driven scenario is most appropriate for understanding non-standard work, employees should clearly favour such arrangements. Here the evidence is more mixed than it is for contingent work, reflecting the different character of the various forms of non-standard work. Independent contractors have a stronger preference for their situation than workers in other non-standard arrangements, with 83.6 per cent favouring this arrangement over a traditional job. One-half of all on-call workers wanted a traditional arrangement. Only 40 per cent of all on-call workers were satisfied with this employment relationship. Only one-third of temporary help agency workers were satisfied with this arrangement; nearly 60 per cent would have preferred a traditional job (US Department of Labor, Bureau of Labor Statistics, 1997).[7]

Thus, it seems clear that the creation of contingent work mainly reflects employer, not employee, preference. The same holds for temporary work and, perhaps to a somewhat lesser degree, on-call work. In addition, virtually by definition, employers are the driving force behind involuntary part-time work.

Employers use these forms of flexible staffing arrangements for several reasons. First, they reduce labour costs, particularly benefit costs. As noted above, workers in non-standard jobs are less likely to receive employer-provided benefits than regular full-time workers. In fact, those firms which provide better benefit packages to their full-time, more permanent workers are more likely to rely on flexible staffing arrangements. This circumvents the legal regulations against discriminating among full-time workers in the provision of benefits. Given that employers cannot offer costly benefits to some but not others of their full-time employees, they choose to segment their workforce in another way. They hire some workers through flexible staffing arrangements and are not legally bound to provide them with benefits (Houseman, 1997).

Not only can flexible staffing arrangements lower labour costs, they can also lessen the cost of adjustment to fluctuations in product demand. Even though employers can, generally, hire and fire employees at will, they may choose to move toward flexible staffing arrangements particularly in times of uncertain product demand. Hiring, training, and firing full-time, more permanent employees is costly both in time and money. Furthermore, when large-scale downsizing occurs, there are additional costs in terms of worker morale. When workers are provided by labour market intermediaries such as temporary help and contract firms, the costs of recruitment and training are borne by the company providing the workers. They can spread these costs over longer periods of time than the client firm since the temporary or contract worker may work several jobs for the agency (Segal and Sullivan, 1995). There is some suggestive evidence that industries with large fluctuations in employment over time had higher rates of contingency (Polivka, 1996b). Similarly, Abraham (1988) and Mangum, Mayall and Nelson (1985) found that the use of temporary workers was positively related to the variability of product demand.

In addition to lowering the costs of adjustment for client firms, temporary help and contract firms may also lessen the trade-off between labour flexibility and productivity which employers may face. There is evidence of a positive correlation between job tenure and labour productivity (Solow, 1980). For example, since the wages paid to employees of temporary help firms are less than the fee paid by the firm, part of what the ultimate user is purchasing is a measure of supervision and therefore increased productivity. Consider the potential difference in the performance of the following two workers. The first is employed by a firm for a finite period, say one month, to help during a peak work period. The worker knows that it is unlikely she or he will ever see the employer again. The second is employed by a temporary help supply firm and dispatched to the same company as above. This time, however, the worker knows that the supervisor will submit a report to the temporary help supply company; a report that will influence whether and what type of assignment the worker can next expect. Both supply flexible labour to the firm; however, the productivity of the worker in the latter scenario is likely to be higher (Lapidus, 1990).[8]

Contract firms also provide other benefits to client firms. Companies utilising temporary help supply firms do not do so because of the specialised expertise of the temporary workers. Most of the tasks done by temps could easily have been performed by more long-term, in-house employees. However, contract firms perform specialised services which could not be done economically in-house. While companies contract for low-skilled janitorial services as a way to reduce labour costs, they contract for more highly skilled tasks such as machine maintenance, engineering and drafting services, accounting services and computer services in order to benefit from the economies of scale achieved by contract firms or the specialised expertise they offer (Abraham and Taylor, 1996; Carnoy, Castells and Benner, 1997).

It is apparent that employers can benefit from the utilisation of contingent and non-standard employment arrangements. In addition, there is evidence that contingent and non-standard work has become increasingly prevalent. One argument often made for seeing the growth of contingent and non-standard forms of employment as supply driven is based on the increased labour force participation of married women with young children. Women with family responsibilities self-select into temporary and part-time employment to enable them to balance the competing demands of work and family, according to this view. If that were true, married women with young children would be expected to be over-represented in temporary employment. However, this hypothesis is not supported by the empirical evidence. Lapidus (1993) found that family responsibilities could not predict whether or not a woman would become a temporary worker. Regarding part-time work, Tilly (1996) concluded that the growth in the part-time workforce from 1969 to 1993 could not be explained by the increased labour force participation of women with children seeking voluntary part-time employment.

Rather than being supply driven, the rise in contingent and non-standard work was demand driven. During the 1970s, United States corporations faced increased domestic and international competition. Imports penetrated many key markets in the United States. Furthermore, United States corporations found it impossible to maintain their relative standing in world markets. A stalemate emerged between employers and workers over who would bear the brunt of the relative decline of the United States in the world economy. Unions had enough bargaining power to push up nominal wages, gain better benefit packages and widen the pay gap between union and non-union workers. Nevertheless, while nominal wages rose, real wages did not. Employers were able to maintain profit rates but were not able to raise them to levels existing before the 'profit squeeze' of the late 1960s.

By the end of the 1970s, employers became more confrontational in collective bargaining. The rising wage premium of unionised labour, together with increased foreign and domestic competition, had a stronger impact during the serious recession of the early 1980s. These provided the economic incentives for employers to demand concessions from their workers. The macroeconomic, employment and social policies of the Reagan Administration designed to 'knock the props' out from under workers served to weaken the bargaining power of union and non-union workers alike. Government industrial relations policies setting a union-busting tone did the same.[9] Unemployment rates exceeding 9 per cent further weakened the bargaining power of employed workers. Although unemployment rose throughout the economy, it was centered in mining, construction and manufacturing, those areas where unions have traditionally been the strongest. A labour movement on the defensive increased the opportunities for employers to gain their demands at the bargaining table.

In an era of increasing competition and pressure on profits, employers wished to lower wage and benefit costs, change work rules and gain flexibility in scheduling daily and weekly working hours. Initially, in 1981–82, the wage and benefit concessions began in a narrow range of companies facing severe economic difficulties. By 1984–85, however, the situation had changed. Concessions were now being granted in virtually every industry with a unionised labour force. Even profitable firms were getting on the bandwagon and pressing their workers for 'givebacks' (Mitchell, 1985). Even as the economy strengthened in the second half of the 1980s, the labour movement remained on the defensive.

The 1980s – a period of an employer and government offensive against unions – were also a time of growth in contingent and alternative employment relations. It is very difficult to provide a direct measurement of the role played by political and institutional forces in the growth of contingent and non-standard work. However, there is strong suggestive evidence that they played an important role. Golden and Appelbaum (1992) found a positive relationship between employment growth in the temporary help supply industry and union decline. Lapidus (1990) found a positive correlation between temporary help supply industry growth and the change in the political climate after Ronald Reagan took office in 1981. The increase in involuntary part-time employment during the 1980s also points to the ability of employers to determine the terms of the employment relationship. Taken together, the evidence points to the crucial role played by political and institutional factors in converting an employer preference for 'non-standard employment' into an effective demand.

Not only did employers wish to lower wage and benefit costs, they also wanted to have workers bear more of the burden of economic uncertainty. While employers were still relatively free to adjust the size of their regular workforce, it did become somewhat more costly to hire and fire workers with more long-term employment relationships. Employers who carried out mass layoffs ran the risk of being sued by former employees on the grounds of sex, race or age discrimination. In the 1980s, particularly, the number of court cases alleging age discrimination in layoffs rose dramatically. Also, while employees still have very limited 'property rights' in their jobs, judicial decisions in the 1970s and 1980s moved toward granting employees rights based on implicit contracts and the contents of employee handbooks. According to Edwards (1993), many state courts accepted the argument that under certain circumstances employee handbooks and similar statements could impose binding obligations on employers. This may well have strengthened employer demand for non-standard workers.

Conclusion: Public Policy Implications

A large and growing number of workers are employed in contingent and non-standard work arrangements. Some of these are good jobs. In fact, many well-educated, highly skilled independent contractors indicate they would not trade their non-standard job for a more traditional position. They earn more, have more varied work opportunities and greater independence than similar workers in traditional employment arrangements.

However, the well educated, highly skilled, independent contractor is not the typical worker in a flexible staffing arrangement and his or her overall job satisfaction is not typical of workers doing non-standard work. Many non-standard jobs are also substandard with lower pay and worse benefits than could be found in similar jobs under more traditional arrangements. This raises two policy issues. First, there is a need for legislation prohibiting discrimination in pay based on work arrangements or the number of hours worked per week (e.g. full-time/part-time status). Second, in the United States, most health and pension benefits are distributed through the labour market. The right to benefits is associated with holding a particular job, generally a full-time, more permanent job. The existence and growth of alternative employment arrangements lessens the effectiveness of this delivery system and reinforces the need for more universal benefit policies.

Another reason for concern is that workers in flexible staffing arrangements often have little job security and are more likely to experience unemployment. For example, workers in the temporary help industry were much more likely to experience unemployment than other workers (Segal and Sullivan, 1995). Yet, they are not very likely to be eligible for unemployment insurance benefits. The unemployment insurance system is designed with the full-time, more long-term worker in mind. Due to the low wages and often less than full-time hours, many holding non-standard positions have difficulty qualifying for unemployment insurance. The unemployment insurance system needs to be reformed to protect the large and growing number of people in alternative work arrangements.

While the insecurity of contingent and non-standard work is a concern, it would be less of a concern if such positions were bridges to more permanent, full-time jobs paying higher wages and providing better benefits to those who want them. Yet, it is not clear whether contingent or non-standard work is linked with continued employment instability or whether a contingent or non-standard position is one step along the road to more permanent employment. This issue is of crucial importance to workers who find themselves involuntarily working in contingent or non-standard jobs.

This chapter has demonstrated some of the difficulties and pitfalls entailed in measuring the extent and growth of contingent and non-standard employment in the United States. These should not, however, blind us to the crucial changes which have overtaken a large segment of the American workforce – particularly workers who are young, female and of minority ethnic origins. There is every reason to believe that millions of Americans face more poorly compensated and insecure forms of employment than those available to an earlier generation.

References

Abraham, K.G. (1988) 'Flexible Staffing Arrangements and Employers' Short-Term Adjustment Strategies', in Hart, R.A. (ed.) *Employment, Unemployment and Labor Utilization*, London: Unwin Hyman.

Abraham, K.G. (1990) 'Restructuring the Employment Relationship: The Growth of Market-mediated Work Arrangements', in Abraham, K.G. and McKersie, R.B. (eds.) *New Developments in the Labor Market: Toward a New Institutional Paradigm*, Cambridge, MA: MIT Press.

Abraham, K.G. and Taylor, S.K. (1996) 'Firms' Use of Outside Contractors: Theory and Evidence', *Journal of Labor Economics*, 14: 3, 394–424.

Appelbaum, E. (1987) 'Restructuring Work: Temporary, Part-Time, and At-Home Employment', in Hartmann, H.I. (ed.) *Computer Chips and Paper Clips: Technology and Women's Employment*, II, Washington, DC: National Academy Press.

Belous, R.S. (1989) *The Contingent Economy: The Growth of the Temporary, Part-Time and Subcontract Workforce*, Washington, DC: National Planning Association.

Carnoy, M., Castells, M. and Benner, C. (1997) 'Labour Markets and Employment Practices in the Age of Flexibility: A Case Study of Silicon Valley', *International Labour Review*, 136: 1, 27–48.

Clinton, A. (1997) 'Flexible Labor: Restructuring the American Work Force', *Monthly Labor Review*, 120: 8, 3–17.

Cohany, S.R. (1996) 'Workers in Alternative Employment Arrangements', *Monthly Labor Review*, 119: 10, 31–45.

Edwards, R. (1993) *Rights at Work: Employment Relations in the Post-Union Era*, Washington, DC: The Brookings Institution.

Ehrenberg, R.G., Rosenberg, P. and Li, J. (1988) 'Part-Time Employment in the United States', in Hart, R.A. (ed.) *Employment, Unemployment and Labor Utilization*, London: Unwin Hyman.

Golden, L. and Appelbaum, E. (1992) 'What was Driving the 1982–88 Boom in Temporary Employment? Preferences of Workers or Decisions and Power of Employers', *American Journal of Economics and Sociology*, 51: 4, 473–93.

Gordon, D.M. (1996) *Fat and Mean: The Corporate Squeeze of Working Americans and the Myth of Managerial 'Downsizing'*, New York: Free Press.

Harrison, B. (1994) *Lean and Mean: The Changing Landscape of Corporate Power in the Age of Flexibility*, New York: Basic Books.

Hipple, S. and Stewart, J. (1996) 'Earnings and Benefits of Contingent and Non-contingent Workers', *Monthly Labor Review*, 119: 10, 22–30.

Houseman, S.N. (1997) 'New Institute Survey on Flexible Staffing Arrangements', *Employment Research*, Spring, W.E. Upjohn Institute for Employment Research.

Ichniowski, B.E. and Preston, A.E. (1986) 'New Trends in Part-Time Employment', in *Proceedings of the Thirty-Eighth Annual Meeting*, Industrial Relations Research Association.

Kalleberg, A.L., Rasell, E., Hudson, K., Webster, D., Reskin, B.F., Cassirer, N. and Appelbaum, E. (1997) *Nonstandard Work, Substandard Jobs: Flexible Work Arrangements in the US*, Washington, DC: Economic Policy Institute.

Lapidus, J. (1990) *The Temporary Help Supply Industry and the Operation of the Labor Market*, unpublished PhD thesis, Amherst, MA: University of Massachusetts.

Lapidus, J. (1993) 'Family Structure, Flexible Employment and Labor Market Segmentation: Evidence from a Study of the Temporary Help Industry', *International Contributions to Labour Studies*, 3: 91–100.

Mangum, G., Mayall, D. and Nelson, K. (1985) 'The Temporary Help Industry: A Response to the Dual Internal Labor Market', *Industrial and Labor Relations Review*, 38: 4, 599–611.

Mitchell, D.J.B. (1985) 'Shifting Norms in Wage Determination', *Brookings Papers on Economic Activity*, 2: 575–99.

Polivka, A.E. (1996a) 'Contingent and Alternative Work Arrangements Defined', *Monthly Labor Review*, 119: 10, 3–9.

Polivka, A.E. (1996b) 'A Profile of Contingent Workers', *Monthly Labor Review*, 119: 10, 10–21.

Rosenberg, S. (1983) 'Reagan Social Policy and Labour Force Restructuring', *Cambridge Journal of Economics*, 7: 2, 179–96.

Rosenberg, S. (1989) 'The Restructuring of the Labor Market, the Labor Force, and the Nature of Employment Relations in the United States in the 1980s,' in Rosenberg, S. (ed.) *The State and the Labor Market*, New York: Plenum Press.

Rosenberg, S. (1994) 'The More Decentralized Mode of Labor Market Regulation in the United States', *Economies et Sociétés*, 18: 8, 35–58.

Segal, L.M. and Sullivan, D.G. (1995) 'The Temporary Labor Force', *Economic Perspectives*, 19: 2, 2–19.

Solow, R. (1980) 'On Theories of Unemployment', *American Economic Review*, 70: 1, 1–11.

Stinson, J.F. (1997) 'New Data on Multiple Jobholding Available from the CPS', *Monthly Labor Review*, 120: 3, 3–8.

Tilly, C. (1996) *Half a Job: Bad and Good Part-Time Jobs in a Changing Labor Market*, Philadelphia: Temple University Press.

US Department of Labor (1995) *Report on the American Workforce*, Washington, DC: US Government Printing Office.

US Department of Labor, Bureau of Labor Statistics (1995) 'Contingent and Alternative Employment Arrangements', Report 900, August, Washington, DC: US Government Printing Office.

US Department of Labor, Bureau of Labor Statistics (1997) 'Contingent and Alternative Employment Arrangements, February 1997', December 2, Washington, DC: US Government Printing Office.

Notes

1   Temporary workers are defined as those who were paid by a temporary help agency, whether or not their job was temporary. Contract workers are those

employed by a contract firm who provides them to others under contract. They are usually assigned to only one customer and usually work at the customer's worksite.

2 Independent contractors are workers who were identified as independent contractors, independent consultants, or freelance workers, whether they were self-employed or wage and salary workers.

3 On-call workers are workers who are called to work only as needed, although they can be scheduled to work for several days or weeks in a row. The BLS definition of part-time workers includes everybody working fewer than 35 hours per week, except for those who usually work full-time but who have lost hours for non-economic reasons. Involuntary part-time workers are those who are working part time because of slack work, plant downtime, or an inability to find a full-time job.

4 The authors of the joint report chose not to use the term 'contingent' in describing jobs or workers since they believe it has acquired too many different meanings in recent literature on the subject.

5 These figures are consistent with estimates from governmental data.

6 These figures underestimate the number of temporary jobs since they only count those people supplied by temporary help agencies. 'Direct hire' temps are not included.

7 Data were not provided on the work preferences of workers provided by contract firms.

8 The services of temporary help supply firms may extend beyond mere supervision of temporary workers. In Silicon Valley, temporary help supply agencies are not simply providing temporary personnel but are also performing a variety of human resource services for their client firms (Carnoy, Castells and Benner, 1997).

9 See Rosenberg (1983), Rosenberg (1989) and Rosenberg (1994) for a more detailed discussion of the economic, social and industrial relations policies of the Reagan Administration during the 1980s.

5 Explaining the Relationship between Flexible Employment and Labour Market Regulation

Peter Robinson

Introduction

This chapter sets out to explore empirically three themes. First, to what extent has there been growth in flexible or non-standard forms of employment since 1979 in the UK, distinguishing carefully between part-time, temporary and self-employment? Second, to what extent are people working in non-standard forms of employment voluntarily and what can be said about the 'quality' of different forms of employment? Third, is non-standard employment more prevalent in the UK, with its relatively less regulated labour market, compared with other advanced industrial countries? Are there any links between the prevalence of non-standard employment and the degree of regulation of the labour market?

Describing part-time, temporary and self-employment as non-standard is an attempt to find a less loaded term than 'flexible'. It is also a little more precise as the term 'flexible' can be used to describe any number of other features of the labour market. The term 'flexible' is too often confused with the term 'deregulated'. A relatively deregulated labour market is one where state regulation and labour market institutions play less of a role. There is some common agreement that this is a useful way of distinguishing the UK and the US from many continental European countries. However, as the chapter shows, it is not the case that deregulated labour markets necessarily have a higher incidence of flexible forms of employment. The two terms cannot be used interchangeably.

The chapter argues that flexible forms of employment are to be welcomed if they reflect the preferences of labour market participants, as well as employers, and are associated with better aggregate labour market outcomes. Only if these forms of employment do not match the preferences of labour market participants or are associated with poorer aggregate labour market outcomes might we be legitimately concerned at their growth.

The Changing Composition of Employment in the UK since 1979

The proportion of the employed workforce in the UK who are full-time, permanent employees has declined significantly since 1979 (Table 5.1). Data on the incidence of temporary employment are not available before 1984, but in 1979 we can infer that around 74–75 per cent of all those in employment were full-time permanent employees. By 1997 this had fallen to 62 per cent. Over the period 1979–97, the share of part-time employment rose by 8 percentage points, the share of self-employment by 5 percentage points, and temporary employment by 2 percentage points (but with all these categories overlapping to some degree, a point often forgotten).

There are two features of Table 5.1 to highlight. Between 1979 and 1984 the share of employment of full-time permanent employees fell by about 7 percentage points. Between 1984 and 1990 it fell by 2.6 percentage points. Between 1990 and 1997 it fell by 3 percentage points. So the sharpest decline in the share of full-time permanent employees occurred during the recession of the early 1980s. Since then the decline has slowed down markedly. Any notion that shifts in the structure of employment are accelerating is not borne out by the evidence. It also makes the point that the decline in the share of full-time permanent employment in the first half of the 1990s was not significantly out of line with the experience of the second half of the 1980s. It is not clear from these employment data why commentators refer to the 'nervous' 90s',

Table 5.1   The changing composition of all employment in the UK 1979–1997

	Percentage of All in Employment			
	1979	*1984*	*1990*	*1997*
Full-time employees	76.7	69.7	67.1	65.2
Full-time permanent	n.a.	67.4	64.8	61.7
Full-time temporary	n.a.	2.3	2.3	3.5
Part-time employees	16.1	18.8	19.4	22.2
Part-time permanent	n.a.	16.5	17.2	19.2
Part-time temporary	n.a.	2.3	2.2	3.0
Full-time self-employed	6.5	9.4	11.3	9.9
Part-time self-employed	0.7	1.9	2.1	2.6

Note: Excluding those on Government schemes and unpaid family workers.
Source: Labour Force Survey, Spring.

while the late 1980s are considered to have been a boom period with few apparent concerns about the nature of employment creation.

Table 5.1 also shows that the trends in part-time, temporary and self-employment have all been very different. The share of part-time employment has been growing over the whole period – indeed as discussed below it has been growing over the whole post-war period. There was no growth at all in the share of temporary employment between 1984 and 1990. A growing share of temporary employment is a very recent phenomenon. The share of self-employment grew significantly in the 1980s. Since 1990 this growth has come to a complete halt. The fact that the trends are so different for these three forms of non-standard employment suggests treating each separately rather than lumping them together.

Part-time employment

This category is perhaps the easiest to deal with. The share of part-time employment has been growing steadily over the whole post-war period, with no sign of any break in trend after 1979, or more recently. In 1951 the share of part-time employment stood at just 4 per cent of total employment. By 1961 this had risen to 9 per cent, by 1971 to 16 per cent and by 1981 to 19 per cent. This growth has mirrored and has facilitated the increased entry of women into the labour market. The fastest rate of growth in part-time employment occurred in the 1960s when its share in total employment rose by 7 percentage points. Between 1984 and 1997 the share of part-time employment increased by about 4 percentage points (Table 5.1 and Figure 5.1). So there is no indication that the increase in the share of part-time employment in recent years has been faster than in previous decades.

Figure 5.1 shows that between 1984 and 1997 the proportion of all women working part-time did not change significantly. However, the proportion of all men working part-time more than doubled, with most of this occurring since 1991. Overall then, the increase in the share of part-time employment between 1984 and 1997 is a function of more women entering employment, but with no change in the propensity of women to work part-time, and a rising incidence of part-time working among men. Over one-third of male part-timers are students, and over half of the growth in male part-time employment since 1993 reflects higher educational enrolment rates matched by a rising incidence of part-time working among students.

Looking at the incidence of part-time employment by industry over the period 1984–97, there is a much higher incidence in the growing service sectors when compared with manufacturing and other traditional industries. There is a rising incidence of part-time employment within most industries, with manufacturing an exception. The shift in employment towards the service industries accounts for only one-quarter of the overall increase in part-time employment over this period. The increased share of part-time

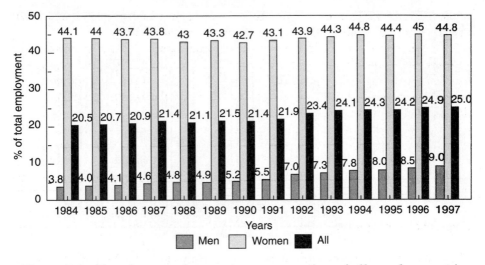

Figure 5.1   Part-time employment as a proportion of all employment in the UK, 1984–97

Source: Labour Force Survey, Spring.

employment within each industry accounts for three-quarters of the growth in the overall share of part-time employment.

Self-employment

The only sharp break in trend in the structure of employment in Britain after 1979 was the sharp increase in the share of self-employment (Figure 5.2). This share had been broadly flat over the post-war period, but between 1979 and 1984 the share of self-employment rose from just over 7 per cent of total employment to 11 per cent. This share had increased further to 13 per cent by 1989. However, in the early 1990s recession the share of self-employment fell slightly and it has been flat since. So the only break in trend which we can identity after 1979 actually appeared to come to a halt at the end of the 1980s. Does 1990 represent another break in trend?

Looking at the incidence of self-employment by industry over the period 1984–90, the incidence rose in every industry, except for the distribution, hotels and restaurants sector (probably reflecting the decline in the numbers of small shopkeepers). Almost none of the rise in the overall share of self-employment from 1984 to 1990 was due to a shift in employment towards those industries with relatively high levels of self-employment. Most of the rise was due to the increased share of self-employment within most industries. Only 10 per cent of the rise in the share of self-employment between 1979 and 1984 was due to shifts in the industrial structure (away from manufacturing with its relatively low incidence of self-employment).

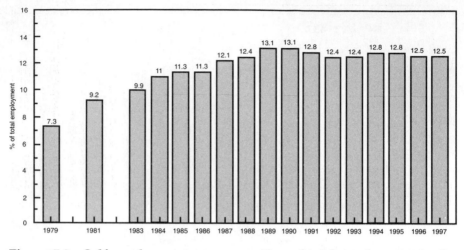

Figure 5.2   Self-employment as a proportion of total employment in the UK, 1979–97

Source: Labour Force Survey, Spring.

Since 1990 it is noticeable that the rise in the incidence of self-employment has come to a halt within nearly all industries. As the growth in self-employment in the 1980s was driven primarily by the increased share of self-employment *within* each industry, the fact that after 1990 this came to a halt in most industries suggests strongly that 1990 does indeed represent another break in trend.

Temporary employment

Between 1984 and 1991 there was no increase in the proportion of employees in temporary jobs (Figure 5.3). Between 1991 and 1997 there was an increase in the share of temporary employment, from just over 5 per cent of all employees to over 7 per cent. There is no information on temporary employment before 1984 from the Labour Force Survey, so that it is not possible to know whether there was a similar increase in the share of temporary employment in the early 1980s. It is also not possible to know whether this trend will continue or is a one off.

The increase since 1991 has been particularly sharp among men (Figure 5.3), where the share of temporary employment has increased from around 4 per cent of all employees in 1991 to over 6 per cent in 1997. The growth in temporary employment for female employees came later and has been more muted. As a result, whereas in 1991 there was a much higher incidence of temporary employment among women employees, by 1996 the gender gap was much narrower.

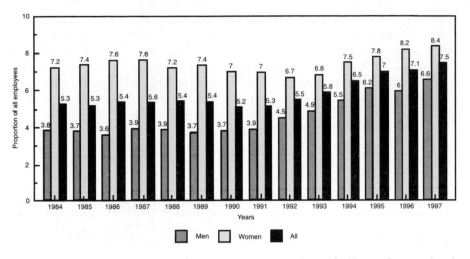

Figure 5.3   Temporary employees as a proportion of all employees in the UK, 1984–97

Source: Labour Force Survey, Spring.

Since 1991 the incidence of temporary employment has increased in most industries. In terms of overall numbers the growth of temporary employment has been especially rapid in the financial and business services, and especially the public services, sectors of the economy. The growth in the share of temporary employment in manufacturing has been muted (and came to a halt in 1995). Over this short time period almost none of the growth in temporary employment has occurred because of a shift in employment towards industries with a high incidence of temporary employment. It is almost entirely due to the increase in incidence within industries.

Looking at the incidence of temporary employment by occupation, by far the highest incidence is among professionals, and the professional occupations show the fastest growth. Indeed, the top three occupations covering managerial, professional and technical employment account for over three-fifths of the net growth in temporary employment since 1991. Most of the growth has been for workers on fixed contracts, though there has also been a significant expansion in the use of agency temps, from a low base. Fixed contract workers make up over half of all temporary workers and account for three-fifths of the rise in temporary employment since 1992.

These figures on the make-up of temporary employment are worth stressing because in the public debate temporary employment is often equated with low-paid, low-skill, 'casualised' employment. However, the 'typical' temporary worker in the UK is much more likely to be a well-paid professional, employed on a fixed-term contract within the public sector, which gives some clues as to why we have witnessed this recent expansion in temporary employment. Within the public sector, schools and health service trusts have been given greater freedom to determine their own recruitment practices at a time of budget constraints. Many seem to have responded by expanding their use of fixed-term contracts. Within the business services sector the increase reflects the greater use of agencies to provide clerical and other support staff. However, the more dramatic assertions about the arrival of a 'core-periphery' model in employment relationships finds relatively little backing in the data, particularly for manufacturing, the sector around which much of this discussion tends to revolve.

It is not clear that the rise in the share of temporary employment since 1991 represents a clear break in trend. The absence of data before 1984 presents a problem as we do not know whether temporary employment increased its share during the early 1980s recession and its immediate aftermath. The slowing in the growth in temporary employment after 1995 is interesting and any structural break might be as much to do with the public sector as with private industry.

A summing up

The increase in the incidence of self-employment within industries in the 1980s in the UK remains a relatively ill-understood phenomenon (see OECD, 1992). The halt in the rise in self-employment after 1990 is also ill-understood, though it is interesting that rising unemployment in the early 1990s was not associated with a further increase in self-employment in the way that rising unemployment in the early 1980s was.

Whether the relatively recent increase in the incidence of temporary employment will continue or not is unclear. Only the ongoing shift towards part-time employment which has occurred over the whole post-war period seems more straightforward to explain, as it is well correlated with increased female labour force participation and more recently higher educational enrolment. We can expect the share of part-time employment to continue rising. This is not a difficult forecast to make as it has been rising for nearly 50 years. The rise in self-employment may have come to a halt. As a relatively recent phenomenon, it would seem unwise to make predictions about the trend in temporary employment.

However, one critical point to re-emphasise is that the decline in the share of employment of full-time, permanent employees was significantly faster in the early 1980s, and since 1984 the pace of overall change has slowed down. In the 1980s growth came mainly in the share of part-time and self-employment. In the 1990s it is growth in the share of part-time and temporary employment. Between 1986 and 1996 there was a decline in the share of permanent full-time employees of around 4.5 percentage points. Between 1961 and 1971 the share of part-time employment alone rose by 7 percentage points (at a time when the share of self- and presumably temporary employment was relatively steady). So when compared with both the immediate past and the experience of previous decades, the UK labour market in the last decade or so has not seen employment shifts which are dramatically out of line with historical experience.

Do People Choose to Work in Non-Standard Jobs or Are They Forced into Them?

Part-time and temporary jobs tend to turn over at a faster rate than full-time and permanent jobs. As a result they are significantly over-represented among the job openings available to the unemployed. Table 5.2 shows that in 1994 only 35 per cent of those individuals leaving the status of being ILO unemployed and who entered into jobs went into full-time permanent jobs as employees. Just over half went into part-time or temporary jobs or onto Government schemes. However, this picture is little changed from 1985. In this year only 38 per cent of those who left International Labour Office unemployment and entered jobs went into full-time permanent jobs as employees and just over half into part-time and temporary jobs and Government schemes. Comparisons with 1979 are more limited due to absence of data.

Table 5.2   The changing composition of employment entered by formerly unemployed people in the UK, 1979–1994

	Percentage of Those Entering Employment		
	1979	*1985*	*1994*
Full-time employees	53.5	49.2	47.0
Full-time permanent	n.a	38.4	35.1
Full-time temporary	n.a	7.9	9.1
Full-time on Govt. schemes	n.a	1.8	2.4
Part-time employees	41.2	40.7	40.9
Part-time permanent	n.a	26.1	26.7
Part-time temporary	n.a	10.6	8.7
Part-time on Govt. schemes	n.a	3.6	5.0
Full-time self-employed	2.5	6.2	7.9
Part-time self-employed	1.2	3.6	4.2

Source: Gregg and Wadsworth (1996).

Overall the changes in 'entry jobs' since 1979 seem less dramatic than the changes in the stock of employment (Table 5.1). The decline in the proportion of the unemployed entering full-time permanent employment has been largely taken up by increased entry into self-employment.

In the 1980s there was some debate about how far the increase in self-employment reflected a genuine desire on the part of individuals to work for themselves, or whether high-aggregate unemployment pushed people into self-employment as a second best alternative. This debate was never satisfactorily resolved. In particular, the role of higher unemployment in 'pushing' people into self-employment was a source of controversy (see Bevan *et al.*, 1988), as was the role of aspects of deregulation such as the contracting out of services in the public and private sectors (see Hakim, 1988; Rubery, 1989).

The Labour Force Survey (LFS) asks those who are in part-time/temporary employment why they are working in such jobs. One of the replies is 'because I cannot find a full-time/permanent job'. The LFS thus offers a chance to explore whether entry into these jobs is 'voluntary' or not. If people have taken these jobs because of a lack of alternatives then we might legitimately worry that the employment patterns we observe are not optimal.

In 1997 only 12 per cent of part-timers were working in a part-time job 'involuntarily', though this had increased from 9 per cent in the mid-1980s. As a proportion of total employment this represented an increase from just under 2 per cent to 3 per cent.

The incidence of 'involuntary' temporary employment is much higher, with 39 per cent in 1997 saying that they were working in temporary jobs because they could not find permanent employment. This had increased from 32 per cent in 1984. As a proportion of all employees the increase in involuntary temporary employment between 1984 and 1997 was from 1.7 per cent to 3 per cent.

Looking at a time series for involuntary part-time and temporary employment suggests that they are cyclical but lagging indicators. The incidence of involuntary part-time and temporary employment fell during the late 1980s boom, though it is not really until the end of that boom (1988–90) that we saw these indicators fall. In 1996 to 1997 the incidence of involuntary part-time and temporary employment began to fall again as the aggregate labour market tightened. This suggests that a further tightening in the labour market in the second half of the 1990s would bring about a significant fall in these indices.

A key factor in assessing the problem of involuntary part-time or temporary employment is to consider where these forms of employment lead. If they are stepping stones to more acceptable forms of employment, voluntarily entered into, then this makes their existence less troublesome than if individuals fail to escape this status and remain in forms of employment which they do not consider optimal, or indeed proceed from part-time or temporary jobs back into unemployment. The OECD has suggested on the basis of research in other countries that involuntary part-time employment is often a stepping stone to more acceptable forms of employment (OECD, 1995). Research on these issues in the UK is still at an early stage. However, the OECD has reported data from the British Household Panel Survey which suggests that of those employed on a temporary basis in 1991, by 1993 only 29 per cent were still in temporary jobs while 39 per cent had moved into permanent jobs (OECD, 1996).

Is Non-Standard Employment More Prevalent in the UK Compared with Other Advanced Countries?

Do countries with less-regulated labour markets have a higher proportion of their workforce in non-standard forms of employment? Critics of flexibility allege that this is so. It is thought that the relatively deregulated UK labour market has resulted in the generation of jobs other than full-time permanent ones.

Comparing the incidence of various forms of employment across countries is difficult because there are no agreed methods for defining different types of employment. For example, in some countries, including the UK, part-time employment is self-defined by the respondent in the Labour Force Survey. In other countries an hours cut-off is used to define part-time employment and this cut-off can vary across countries. Moreover, definitions can change across time which makes a comparison of trends especially problematic. Bearing in mind the need to view the international evidence with some caution, is it true that the UK has a higher incidence of non-standard forms of employment?

Figure 5.4 looks at the incidence of self-employment (excluding agriculture) in the OECD in 1990. At this point, when the expansion in self-employment had come to a halt in the UK, Britain had a relatively high level of self-employment compared with many other northern European countries and the United States and Canada, but on a par with Australia and below the levels in the southern European economies. In 1979, by contrast, the UK had an especially low incidence of self-employment, which makes the point that the expansion of self-employment in the UK in the 1980s was generally out of line with the experience of most comparable countries. This makes the relative lack of understanding of why this phenomenon occurred more troublesome.

Since 1990 in some EU countries there has been some expansion in the share of self-employment, at the same time as this expansion appears to have come to a halt in Britain. Looking at the whole period since 1979, and bearing in mind some breaks have occurred in the time series data for some countries, Sweden, Ireland, Belgium and Spain have seen some expansion in the share of

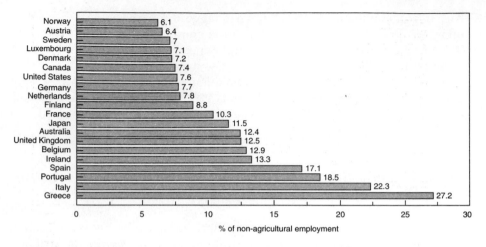

Figure 5.4   Incidence of self-employment in the OECD countries, 1990
Note: Greece 1989.
Source: *OECD Employment Outlook 1992*, Table 4.1.

self-employment, but all below the kind of expansion which the UK witnessed in the 1980s.

In 1995 the UK had an above-average incidence of part-time employment (Figure 5.5), though on a par with Australia and Sweden and below Norway, Switzerland and especially the Netherlands. However, the UK already had a higher incidence of part-time employment in 1979. It would be incorrect to say that labour market deregulation since 1979 has fostered a significantly faster rate of growth in part-time employment in Britain compared with other countries, in the same way as it is incorrect to say that part-time employment has been growing faster in Britain since 1979 when compared with previous decades.

Figure 5.6 shows that Britain has one of the lowest incidences of temporary employment. Only four other countries have a lower proportion of their employees employed on a temporary basis, with the United States having the lowest incidence of all. Germany, France, the Scandinavian countries and especially Australia and Spain, all have a significantly higher incidence of temporary employment. Moreover, a comparison with the incidence of temporary employment in the 1980s makes it clear that the modest increase in the incidence of temporary employment in the UK has been outweighed by much greater increases in a number of other countries, and especially in Australia, the Netherlands, France and Spain.

How far is the incidence of flexible forms of employment linked with the degree of regulation of the labour market? The United States has a low incidence of self-employment, an average incidence of part-time employment and the lowest incidence of temporary employment. We might conclude from

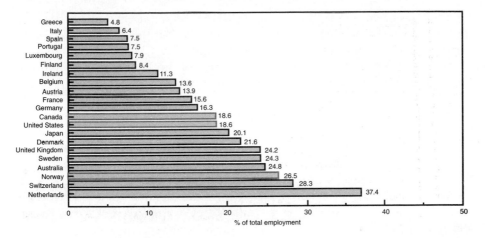

Figure 5.5   Incidence of part-time employment in the OECD countries, 1995

Note: Ireland 1994.
Source: *OECD Employment Outlook 1996*, Table E.

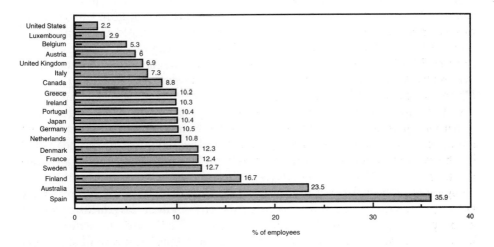

Figure 5.6   Incidence of temporary employment in the OECD countries, 1995

Note: Luxembourg, Canada, Japan, Australia 1994.
Sources: OECD/Eurostat.

this that the United States had a low overall incidence of flexible forms of employment. That is to say, a much higher proportion of employed Americans are full-time permanent employees than in many other countries. Yet there is common agreement that the US has one of the most deregulated labour markets. The Scandinavian countries generally have high levels of part-time and temporary (though not self-) employment. So they have a very high incidence of flexible forms of employment. Yet they are not generally regarded as paragons of labour market deregulation. Clearly then there is no obvious link between the degree of *regulation* of the labour market and the amount of flexible employment offered in those labour markets. The two terms cannot be used interchangeably.

In particular it is worth focusing on the apparent paradox that the United States and the UK, with their relatively deregulated labour markets, have especially low incidences of temporary employment. In the most recent public debates in the UK the growth in temporary employment is seen as one of the most important adverse consequences of deregulation. On the continent it is often assumed that the UK and the US have gone much further down the road towards more 'casualised' forms of employment, when in fact the opposite is true.

Temporary employment contracts have never been the subject of specific legislation in either the UK or the US. The only legal advantage acquired in the UK by offering employment on a temporary or fixed-term contract basis is that the employee waives their rights in relation to unfair dismissal and redundancy payments. As these rights for permanent workers have in the UK been circumscribed since 1979, and as there is little evidence that in 1979 they represented a significant barrier to employment in the UK anyway (discussed in Robinson, 1997), this explains the paradox that in the relatively deregulated UK labour market the incidence of temporary employment is quite low. Firms only have an incentive to employ workers on non-standard contracts if the regulations covering standard contracts are perceived as burdensome. So it is precisely because the regulation of standard forms of employment in the UK and the US is relatively modest that we observe a low incidence of temporary employment. And it is because the regulation of standard forms of employment is relatively tight in many European countries, that we observe that when the law allows employment on a temporary basis, firms have every incentive to exploit those provisions. Hence the rapid expansion of temporary employment in countries such as France and Spain.

So the relationship between regulation and the incidence of temporary employment is exactly the opposite way round from what might be expected. Indeed, a high and rising incidence of temporary employment could be taken as a worrying sign that regulation of standard employment contracts is seen as burdensome and may be distorting the labour market. The flip side to this is that the relatively low incidence of temporary employment in the UK is evidence that employment protection legislation is not burdensome.

High and/or rising levels of self-employment might also be taken as a possible indication that the regulations governing the employment by firms of standard contract labour are burdensome. Figure 5.4 suggests that the southern European economies which are generally regarded as the most heavily regulated also have the highest shares of self-employment. However, Figure 5.4 also suggests a relationship between the level of per capita GDP and self-employment, in that the more affluent OECD countries have a lower incidence of self-employment.

Is there any relationship between regulation and the incidence of part-time employment? Some clues can be gleaned by comparing the incidence of 'involuntary' part-time employment across countries. The relationship between the overall incidence of part-time employment and the incidence of involuntary part-time employment is generally the opposite from what might be expected. Countries such as the Netherlands and the UK with high proportions of the workforce in part-time employment have some of the lowest incidences of 'involuntary' part-time employment. Countries with very low shares of part-time employment, particularly the southern European countries, tend to have very high proportions of those part-timers saying that they are working part-time because they cannot find full-time work. So, although the UK has 4–5 times the proportion of part-time workers as Italy or Greece, involuntary part-time employment as a proportion of all employment differs little between these countries.

For the OECD countries the level, and the change in the incidence, of part-time employment are correlated with the level of, and the change in, female labour force participation. The southern European economies are usually regarded as having relatively high levels of labour market regulation. They also have low levels of part-time employment, but a high incidence of involuntary part-time employment. They also have very low female labour force participation rates. By contrast the UK and the US have relatively less regulated labour markets, relatively high levels of part-time employment, a low incidence of 'involuntary' part-time employment and high levels of female labour force participation. They are joined in this respect by a number of smaller north European economies. So relatively less regulated labour markets seem associated with higher levels of part-time employment and higher levels of female labour force participation, but with a low incidence of involuntary part-time employment.

The apparent relationship between the degree of labour market regulation and the incidence of flexible forms of employment is not then straightforward. High and rising levels of temporary (and perhaps self-) employment may be a sign that labour market regulation is too burdensome. High and rising levels of part-time employment on the other hand seem more associated with relatively lower levels of labour market regulation, and with rising levels of female labour force participation. Moreover, low levels of labour market regulation seem associated with a low incidence of 'involuntary' part-time employment.

Conclusions

The terms 'deregulation' and 'flexibility' are not readily interchangeable. The United States has one of the least regulated labour markets. It also has a relatively low proportion of its workforce in flexible forms of employment, including the lowest incidence of temporary employment and a low incidence of 'involuntary' part-time employment. Relatively more regulated labour markets such as those in southern Europe tend to have high levels of temporary employment, and although they tend to have low levels of part-time employment, a higher proportion of their part-time working is 'involuntary'. These economies also have very high levels of self-employment.

The UK has a relatively low incidence of temporary employment and although it has a high incidence of part-time employment, a higher proportion of that part-time working is 'voluntary'. This fits the picture of the UK having relatively low levels of regulation for all types of employment. And all of these things were already true in 1979. The UK has always had a less regulated labour market and has always had relatively high levels of part-time employment and the high levels of female labour force participation which seem to correlate with a high incidence of part-time employment. The exception is self-employment, the share of which grew significantly in the UK in the 1980s, an ill-understood trend which was out of line with the experience of most other countries.

In the field of individual employment rights there has been no overall shift to greater deregulation in the UK since 1979 (Robinson, 1997). Dickens and Hall (1995) make the point that in the mid-1990s the list of individual statutory employment rights in the UK was little different from that which applied in 1979. The relationship between the individual employee and the employer was relatively less regulated in the UK in 1979 (a comparison of individual employment rights across the EU is made in Barnard *et al.*, 1995), but with a strong trend towards codifying rights. This trend continued after 1979, often in response to EU Directives and the Courts' interpretations of EU Treaties. The only significant act of deregulation in this field was the lengthening in the required period of employment from six months to two years before individuals could qualify for rights to redundancy pay and compensation against unfair dismissal.

On the other hand, as a result of the House of Lords interpretation of the provisions relating to indirect discrimination contained in the Treaty of Rome, part-timers are now covered to the same degree as full-timers by employment protection legislation. Discrimination against part-timers in access to occupational pension schemes also now constitutes unlawful indirect discrimination. Many part-timers will not have access to statutory sick pay or maternity pay as such access is only available to those with wages above the earnings threshold for payment of National Insurance contributions. But generally the legal rights of full-timers and part-timers now differ little. Temporary staff waive their rights with respect to unfair dismissal and redundancy pay. However, in every other way a professional worker on a fixed-term contract will look indistinguishable from their permanent colleagues as they will be on the same pay scale, will contribute to the same occupational pension fund, attend the same training courses, and so on.

The UK labour market is relatively less regulated and always has been, but the regulations which do exist tend now to apply evenly in most respects to most types of workers. By contrast it is in other European countries that the legal distinctions between different forms of employment are more clearly delineated. In terms of individual employment rights the UK labour market has *not* become significantly more deregulated since 1979. Nor is it clear that non-standard forms of employment have grown more rapidly in the UK since 1979, either compared to previous decades or compared to other countries. The only exception was the growth in the share of self-employment in the 1980s, which anyway appeared to come to a halt after 1990. The association of deregulation with flexible forms of employment is not strongly supported by the evidence.

References

Barnard, C., Clark, J. and Lewis, R. (1995) 'The Exercise of Individual Employment Rights in the Member States of the European Community', *Employment Department Research Series No. 49.*

Beatson, M. (1995) 'Labour Market Flexibility', *Employment Department Research Series No. 48.*

Bevan, J., Clark, G., Banerji, N. and Hakim, C. (1988) 'Barriers to Business Start-up', *Employment Department Research Paper No. 71.*

Dickens, L. and Hall, M. (1995) 'The State: Labour Law and Industrial Relations', in Edwards, P. (ed.) *Industrial Relations Theory and Practice in Britain*, Oxford: Blackwell.

Gregg, P. and Wadsworth, J. (1996) 'Mind the Gap, Please? The Changing Nature of Entry Jobs in Britain', *Working Paper No. 796, Centre for Economic Performance, London School of Economics*, April 1996.

Hakim, C. (1988) 'Self-Employment in Britain: Recent Trends and Current Issues', *Work, Employment and Society* 2: 4, 421–50.

OECD (1992) 'Recent Developments in Self-Employment', in *OECD Employment Outlook*, Paris: OECD.

OECD (1995) 'Supplementary Measures of Labour Market Slack: An Analysis of Discouraged Workers and Involuntary Part-Time Workers', in *OECD Employment Outlook*, Paris: OECD.

OECD (1996) 'Temporary Jobs', in *OECD Employment Outlook*, Paris: OECD.

Robinson, P. (1997) 'Labour Market Studies: United Kingdom', European Commission, Directorate-General for Employment, Industrial Relations and Social Affairs.

Rubery, J. (1989) 'Precarious Forms of Work in the United Kingdom', in Rodgers, G. and Rodgers, J. (eds) *Precarious Jobs and Labour Market Regulation*, International Labour Office, Geneva.

6 Changing Regulatory Frameworks and Non-Standard Employment: A Comparison of Germany, Spain, Sweden and the UK

Christine Cousins

Introduction

This chapter examines recent trends in non-standard employment in Europe with particular reference to the nature of the regulatory framework surrounding the employment relationship in different European countries. The focus is on four European countries, namely the UK, Sweden, Germany and Spain, which represent four divergent approaches to employment regulation and social protection. The literature on typologies of employment and welfare regimes usually suggests that we can identify three distinct regimes in Europe: Scandinavian or social democratic; neo-liberal; and continental or conservative-corporatist European (for example, Due *et al.*, 1991; Esping-Andersen, 1990; 1996). However, it is argued here that Spain can be distinguished as a separate regime, with many features in common with other southern European countries.

Writers have explained differences in non-standard work in Europe in terms of a variety of factors including the nature of the regulatory framework of the employment relation in each country, sectoral composition and size of firms, employer policies and competitive strategies, labour market flows especially between unemployment and employment, tax and social security systems, labour supply characteristics and policies and provisions for combining paid work and family life (for example, Hakim, 1990; Rubery and Fagan, 1994; Gregory and O'Reilly, 1996). A comprehensive analysis of the 15 European Union (EU) countries would be difficult to undertake – which is why just four countries are compared here, with a focus on their societal contexts. In a single chapter it would be difficult to include an in-depth analysis of all these factors. The main emphasis is, therefore, on the policies and politics associated with the regulatory framework surrounding the employment relationship. It also considers how these may shape the nature and extent of non-standard work in each country.

The chapter first discusses trends in non-standard employment[1] in Europe in the 1990s and then examines differences in the nature and extent of non-standard employment in the four countries. The second part of the chapter examines the regulatory framework in the four countries and the politics of recent labour market reforms. Finally, there is an overall evaluation of developments in flexible work in each country.

Trends in Non-Standard Work in Europe in the 1990s

Between 1991 and 1994 employment in the EU declined by 1.5 per cent a year. Two-thirds of those losing their jobs were men and virtually all of the decline occurred in full-time employment. Most of the jobs created in this period were part-time. In 1995, for the first time since 1991, there was an increase in employment of 0.8 per cent, although in Germany, Italy and Portugal, the decline continued. At the same time as the increase in employment, however, the fall in participation rates established in the early 1990s continued. Two-thirds of new jobs created in 1995 were taken by those previously unemployed rather than those previously inactive, reversing the trend of the 1980s. However, the trend for new jobs to be taken by women continued – with women accounting for 62 per cent of the rise in the number employed. Moreover, in Germany and Austria, women accounted for all the employment growth (see European Commission, 1996).

In 1995, 71 per cent of new jobs taken by men and 85 per cent of those taken by women were part-time. In Germany, part-time employment comprised the entire increase for both men and women. In the UK, part-time jobs accounted for half of the new jobs taken by men and a third of those taken by women. In Spain, about half of the increase in employment for women was due to the creation of part-time jobs. Furthermore, a high proportion of jobs created in 1995 were also temporary rather than permanent. In the period 1991–94 across the member states, virtually all the increase in men's employment was in temporary work (with the exception of Greece). In the UK, temporary work comprised more than half the increase in men's jobs and in Spain virtually all the increase in employment took the form of temporary contracts. The pattern was similar for women. It should also be noted that growth in temporary and part-time work occurred among those of prime working age. Self-employment was another important source of employment growth for men in Germany and the UK as well as for women in Germany, Spain and France.

The trend towards flexible and non-standard forms of employment, therefore, has clearly been accelerating in the context of high and long-term unemployment in Europe, although there are still large differences in the nature and type of non-standard employment in the member states. Table 6.1 shows the proportions in part-time jobs, fixed-term contracts and self- employment

Table 6.1   Trends in non-standard employment: Germany, Spain, Sweden and UK, 1985–1995

	Part-Time		Fixed-Term Contracts		Self-Employment	
	1985	*1995*	*1985*	*1995*	*1985*	*1995*
			Percentages of Employees			
Germany						
Female	29.6	33.8	11.1	11.1	5.4	5.8
Male	2.0	3.6	9.2	9.9	11.7	11.9
Spain						
Female	13.9	16.6	18.4	38.3	19.4	17.0
Male	2.4	2.7	14.4	33.2	25.2	24.2
Sweden	[1987]					
Female	46.0	43.0	14.2	14.4	4.8	5.9
Male	6.9	10.3	9.6	10.5	13.1	16.3
UK						
Female	44.8	44.3	8.8	7.8	6.9	7.0
Male	4.4	7.7	5.7	6.2	14.7	17.8

Note: In this and all following Tables statistics for Germany before 1991 refer to West Germany, and after 1991 include the New Länder.
Source: Eurostat, 1996.

in 1995 as well as trends in these forms of employment since 1985 in the four case study countries.

In Germany, part-timers accounted for 33.8 per cent of the female labour force in 1995. Some 87.4 per cent of part-timers were women, the vast majority of whom were married (71 per cent). The pattern of women's participation in the labour market in Germany resembles that of Britain; that is, there is a tendency for women to leave the labour force at the birth of a child and to start working part-time when they return to employment. The social policy regime is one which favours a male breadwinner and mother/housewife family model. For example, the system of joint taxation encourages women to work part-time and the low income replacement level of the parental leave scheme ensures that typically, the leave-taker is the mother and that she has an employed partner to support the family.

In the New Länder only a quarter of employed mothers with a child under ten work part-time compared to nearly two-thirds of those in the former West

Table 6.2   Hours of female part-time workers

Usual hours worked per week	Germany %	Spain %	Sweden %	UK %
1–10	18.0	19.9	11.1	24.4
11–20	45.9	54.1	23.8	40.7
21–24	8.2	8.5	8.6	11.8
25–30	24.2	16.9	37.7	16.8
31+	3.7	0.6	18.8	6.2

Source: Eurostat, 1996.

Germany (Moss, 1996). Although in the New Länder women have suffered major job losses since unification and have had to accept West German social policies, there are continuing differences in the labour market position of women in the two Germanies.

Some observers consider that part-time female workers in Germany have benefited from the high degree of labour market regulation and 'the tradition of basing pay upon skills, qualifications and job content' (Rubery, 1992:617; Lane, 1993). Those working under 18 hours per week, however, are excluded from unemployment insurance and those working under 15 hours per week from sickness and pensions insurance. This group of 'marginal' workers comprises just under half of part-time workers (Marullo, 1995; see also Table 6.2).

Evidence from Germany with respect to fixed-term contracts appears inconclusive. Table 6.1 shows a remarkable stability in their numbers since 1985, at about one-tenth of both male and female employees of the workforce (including the New Länder). Some studies, though, report a slowdown in fixed-term hirings following the Employment Promotion Act 1985, especially in sectors dominated by collective bargaining. Other studies have shown an increase in the hirings of young employees with blue collar workers earning 10 per cent less than permanent workers (Rogowski and Schömann, 1996). Meulders *et al.* (1994) report that fixed-term contracts have become especially important in the civil service, professions and universities, especially for those starting their careers, and for women returning to the labour force. Some 70 per cent of men and 74 per cent of women entering employment from education or training were engaged on fixed-term contracts (European Commission, 1996).

In Spain, more than a third of the workforce are on fixed-term contracts, particularly women, young people and virtually all new entrants to the job market (see Table 6.1). In 1996, for example, only 4 per cent of new contracts were permanent (IDS, 1997). Fixed-term contracts are also much more prevalent in the private sector.[2] Married women's increased participation in the labour market in the late 1980s coincided with the widespread use of fixed-term contracts and the restructuring of work (Cousins, 1994). Such high levels of temporary work have led to concerns about the training and pay implications of the new employment. Employers may ignore training and skill requirements and use the growth in these types of work as a means of lowering wages (Perez Amoros and Rojo, 1991). Although Spanish legislation prohibits different wage rates for permanent and fixed-term contracts, Jimeno and Toharia (1994) report that, in practice, fixed-term workers receive 8–11 per cent less than permanent workers.

Part-time work in Spain has been low in comparison to levels in northern Europe for reasons which we discuss below. However, in 1994 legislation was introduced to remove the legal impediments to part-time employment and such employment has increased from 11.2 per cent of female employment in 1991 to 16.6 per cent in 1995 (see Table 6.1). About 60 per cent of these jobs are fixed-term contracts (European Commission, 1996; Milner *et al.*, 1995).

A further segmentation of the labour market in Spain is the submerged or informal economy. Estimates of the submerged economy range from 22 to 30 per cent of total employment in 1986 (Perez-Diaz and Rodriguez, 1995; Cousins, 1994). This sector is characterised by low pay, absence of social security payments and minimal protection from dismissal. There are, nevertheless, strong incentives for both employers and employees to continue with high levels of informal working. Since married women have access to health insurance through their husbands they have less incentive to seek jobs in which social security taxes are paid. On the demand side, social security payments for employers are high at almost 30 per cent of wage costs. Firms which utilise married women workers often prefer to go underground, and face the risk of being detected and penalised, rather than pay the high taxes. The Spanish labour market is therefore highly segmented into at least four different parts: workers in the protected core labour market; temporary fixed-term workers; workers in the submerged economy; and those who are unemployed, representing 22.9 per cent of the workforce in 1995 (see also Perez-Diaz and Rodriguez, 1995).

In Sweden in 1995, 43 per cent of women worked part-time, the majority working three-quarters time. Lewis and Astrom (1992) note that because unpaid work is still performed mainly by women, at the birth of their first child they tend to become part-timers taking jobs with good benefits and exercising their right to reduce their daily hours from 8 to 6. Nätti's (1995) findings also suggest that part-time work for women in Sweden is much less precarious than in many other countries, with part-timers having high levels of unionisation (80 per cent), job continuity (83 per cent), and working more than 20 hours per week (see Table 6.2). In this respect women's part-time work is different from part-time work in elsewhere in the EU, although similar to that in Norway. Fixed-term contracts, three-fifths of which are also held by women, have increased in the 1990s due to changes in legislation and the effects of the recession.[3] Mahon (1996) reports, however, that most temporary jobs have employment protection and remain unionised. There has also been an increase in self-employment associated with employment programmes and small business start-ups. For men, self-employment increased from 13.1 per cent in 1985 to 16.3 per cent in 1995 (see Table 6.1).

In the UK, the trend towards a flexible workforce, especially part-time work, began before the deregulation polices of the Conservative government. Numbers of part-time jobs began increasing in the 1940s and 1950s and accelerated during the 1970s. The UK has one of the lowest provisions of childcare facilities in Europe, with the exception of higher paid women who can afford expensive private childcare. This is undoubtedly one of the reasons for high levels of part-time working among mothers. The UK (together with the Netherlands) has the highest maternal part-time working in the EU. In both countries, some two-thirds of mothers with dependent children work part-time. However, the UK has the lowest average hours of part-time working – 16.5 hours per week compared to an average 19.2 for the EU (Moss, 1996; see also Table 6.2). The use of a threshold for National Insurance contributions is also linked with the high incidence of part-time work in the UK. In 1993 about half of all female part-time employees earned less than the lower earning limit for National Insurance (Marullo, 1995).

The increased participation of women in the labour market in the past decade has been associated with an increase in full-time as well as part-time work (10 per cent in each case) (Sly, 1996). Women's part-time work appears to have stabilised during the 1990s (see Table 6.1). The UK Labour Force Survey (LFS) reports a 3 per cent increase between 1990 and 1995 compared with a 29 per cent increase in the period 1979–1990 (Sly, 1996). Dex and McCulloch (1995) report that employers are now seeking increased flexibility from employees which part-time women workers with children are not in a position to offer. Men's part-time employment increased from 4.4 per cent to 7.7 per cent between 1985 and 1995 (see Table 6.1; for LFS figures see Sly, 1996). Men and women's self employment and temporary working[4] have also increased especially in the 1990s. Albeit from a low base, men's temporary work increased by 71 per cent. Women's increased by 21 per cent (Sly, 1996). Overall, Dex and McCulloch (1995) found that a quarter of men and one-half of women were in non-standard jobs in 1994. Moreover, if flows into the labour market are taken into account, in 1993 two-thirds of all newly filled posts were part-time or temporary (Gregg and Wadsworth, 1995).

The reasons for the high level of part-time work in the UK have been linked to cost advantages to employers (especially if workers earn less than the threshold for National Insurance contributions), lack of employment protection, numerical flexibility, uneven patterns of demand, tasks that require a limited number of hours to complete, and developments in technology (Rubery and Tarling, 1988). The increase in self-employment in the UK, which has been higher than most EU countries (see Table 6.1), has been linked to sectoral changes, technological advances, fragmentation of large firms, the economic cycle, demographic changes, increases in the availability of start-up capital and government policies to promote self employment (Dex and McCulloch, 1995).

The Regulatory Framework of the Employment Relationship

The regulatory framework includes both rules set by collective bargaining between trade unions and employers and rules derived from 'law, custom and mutual acceptance which determine the rights and obligations, or rather, powers, of each party' (Rhodes, 1989:229). The regulatory framework differs in each country reflecting 'divergent state and legal traditions, national character of trade unions and employers associations and historically determined differences in the balance of industrial power' (Rhodes, 1989:229). However, governments in most European countries during the 1980s and 1990s experimented with policies and legislation which aimed to make the labour market more flexible. The character of these policies has been shaped by the nature of the regulatory framework existing in each country, in particular by the respective employment protection systems and dismissal norms.

In West Germany, legislation and the legal enforcement of sectoral collective bargaining have traditionally played an important role in shaping the employment relationship. Throughout the 1980s and 1990s, however, governments and employers have argued for greater flexibility in the labour market and reduction in social costs associated with labour. The decline in the collective rights of employees has been more limited in Germany than the UK, although most of the deregulation legislation has affected individual labour in both countries. There have been some legislative attempts in Germany to weaken collective rights of employees to representation at plant level and in the case of strikes and lockouts (Deakin and Mückenberger, 1992).

The main piece of legislation was the Employment Promotion Act 1985, extended twice and currently in force until the year 2000. This has enabled employers to relax the rules governing fixed-term contract work, more easily to employ part-time workers and exempted firms of five or less workers from legislation which provides workers with protection from dismissal. The 1985 law lengthened the duration of fixed-term contracts from 6 to 8 months (24 months for new small businesses). Prior to the 1985 Act fixed-term contracts were strictly regulated so that employers had to show good reason for hiring such employees. Since the Act employers do not have to give a reason for hiring an employee on a fixed-term contract. The Act did however, also require that part-time workers should have the same rights as full-time workers.

Employers and trade unions have also pursued flexibility in other ways. Employers have sought to increase productivity and flexibility of working time. Unions have pursued strategies that are more 'skill oriented' and training based together with demands for a reduced working week (Mahnkopf, 1992). In the ten years since the 1985 Act, working time reductions, flexible work and extended operating hours at work have continued to be important collective bargaining issues. In the 1990s agreements were reached on reductions in working hours so that Germany now has one of the shortest contractual working weeks in the world.

Rogowski and Schömann have remarked that 'Labour law in Germany is still dominated by the view that the use of atypical employment contracts must be the exception and permanent contracts the norm' (1996:635). As the authors note, the deregulation approach, therefore, leads to tensions with the traditional doctrinal view of labour law in Germany. Streeck has also remarked that although Germany appears to be an advanced case of 'Eurosclerosis', these 'institutional rigidities' have 'forced, induced and enabled managements to embark on adjustment strategies which have paradoxically and "in spite of" has made Germany one of the world's two or three most successful economies' (1992:51).

Nevertheless, debate on Germany's competitiveness now dominates public discussion, intensified by the reunification process. Policies oriented to more liberal market measures have been proposed several times during the 1990s. In early 1996, for example, tripartite talks between the government, employers and trade unions led to an agreement on a 50-point Action Programme to revive the economy and reduce unemployment. The plan involves reductions in public expenditure and social security contributions as well as a reduction of job protection in small firms. The latter proposal raises from five to ten the number of workers a company may employ before rules protecting against dismissal take effect. The agreement broke down in April 1996 because the trade unions were unable to accept the plans on job protection and reductions in sick pay. The government has decided to push ahead with the reforms although the processes of coalition politics, lobbying and the checks and balances of the upper and lower houses of parliament may mitigate neo-liberal solutions.

In Spain, during the Franco regime, in the context of a ban on trade unions, political parties and strikes, employment security was granted to workers by Franco to provide a modicum of political legitimacy for the regime. This protected core of the labour market still exists, containing about two-thirds of the official employed workforce but only 37 per cent of total workforce (Table 6.3). The rigid rules for exit and entry to the labour market have been applied for about five decades without interruption, so that employment in Spain is still highly regulated. Temporary agencies were not permitted until the December 1993 labour market reform Act. Temporary, fixed-term and part-time work are regulated. Furthermore, Spain is today, along with Greece and

Table 6.3   **Employment status of the economically active in Spain, 1995**

1995	All %	Male %	Female %
Permanent core employees	37.4	40.1	32.8
Fixed-term contracts	20.0	19.9	20.0
Unemployed	22.9	18.2	30.6
Employer	3.7	5.0	1.7
Independent workers	12.2	13.9	9.6
Members of co-ops	0.7	0.9	0.5
Family helps	2.9	1.9	4.6
Other	0.2	0.2	0.2
Total	100.00	100.00	100.00

Source: Boletín Mensuel de Estadística (1996).

the Netherlands, one of the few EU countries to require administrative authority for terminating or suspending the employment contract (or for changes in the hours of work (Perez Amoros and Rojo, 1991). Dismissal costs are high in comparison with other countries. Compensation, depending on the size of the firm, is equivalent to from 20 to 45 days pay for each year of service. Given the low turnover of permanent staff, compensation may represent up to two years' salary.

Since 1977 employers have pressed for reforms in industrial relations which would enable then to hire and fire freely, and to utilise new forms of fixed-term contracts and, more recently, part-time workers. Joining the European Community in 1986, and especially the advent of the Single Market in 1992 produced a shift from a highly protected national economy to one exposed to competition from other European countries and from industrial and agricultural producers in other parts of the world. In the 1990s it is no longer possible, as in the past, for firms to compete on the basis of low wages and tariffs – especially as the wages of core workers have risen faster than inflation (one of the contradictory consequences of labour market reform as we discuss below). Employers' calls for greater flexibility in labour markets and work organisation have, therefore, accelerated.

The politics of labour market reform have, nevertheless, been complex, piecemeal and contradictory, as Martinez-Lucio and Blyton (1995) have documented. The main focus has been on issues of labour dismissal and its costs. The trade unions have been seen as acting defensively in seeking to protect the privileged position of core workers, thereby excluding other types of workers from access to the labour market. According to Martinez-Lucio and

Blyton (1995) there are complex political processes at work. What are now considered to be 'rigidities' in the labour market were once functional, both during the dictatorship and the political transition, in guaranteeing an element of labour acquiescence and stability. Unions have been concerned to protect the position of core workers and their families in the context of limited unemployment coverage and exposure to a large submerged economy. In the view of Martinez-Lucio and Blyton (1995), the breakdown of neo-corporatist agreements since the mid-1980s has resulted in union exclusion from state strategies of labour reform as well as a redefining and weakening of worker rights through temporary fixed-term contracts. For example, in the face of union opposition the Partido Socialista Obrevo España (PSOE) government imposed its own labour market reforms in 1994.[5] Since May 1996, however, unions have been engaged in a 'social dialogue' with employers' organisations about further labour market reforms. Agreement was reached in April 1997, the first bipartite agreement since 1984, with both parties accepting a reduction in dismissal costs in exchange for greater job security for some workers on temporary training contracts.[6]

The main pieces of legislation to promote the use of non-standard forms of employment have been the Workers' Statute Act of 1980, 1984 and 1994. Some writers have argued that, strictly speaking, experiments with atypical work do not constitute deregulation but reflect the existing employment protection system and are an amendment to it (Rogowski and Schömann, 1996). Nevertheless, labour market reform has seriously eroded the principle of job security. The legislation of 1984 introduced fixed-term contracts, renewable for six-month periods up to a maximum of three years. New employees may be contracted for a few months and then work informally before returning to legally contracted work (Miguelez Lobo, 1988). Employers, especially small firms are reluctant to transform temporary contracts into permanent ones: 'They prefer to lose trained workers rather than risk one day paying the high redundancy payments' (OECD, 1991/2:68).

The current low levels of part-time working in Spain appear to reflect long-established traditions. Restrictions were placed on such contracts prior to the Workers Charter of 1976 in which the workers and employers were required to pay social security contributions as if the job were full-time (Perez Amoros and Rojo, 1991). The labour laws of 1980 and 1984 instutionalised the principles of equality and proportionality between full-time and part-time work in rights conferred by the social security system and brought into being a written 'contrato de trabajo a tiempo parcial' (Kravaritou-Manitakis, 1988). However, in 1994 legislation was introduced to remove the legal impediments to part-time-employment and, as we have seen above, such employment has increased for women from 11.2 per cent in 1991 to 16.6 per cent in 1995 (Table 6.1). The rights of some part-timers were reduced by the legislation; for example, workers who were employed for less than 12 hours per week forfeited all rights to unemployment benefit or transitory illness payments, although this has subsequently been amended by the April 1997 agreement which introduced equal treatment between full-time and part-time workers who work fewer than 12 hours per week.

In Sweden, labour radicalisation in the late 1960s led to an extensive programme of labour legislation in the 1970s, to the extent that, in Kjellberg's (1992) opinion the model of industrial relations changed from one of self-regulation to state intervention. This legalisation included the Protection of Employment Act 1974. Other measures concerned union workplace representation, co-determination, day care for children and parental leave provisions. These reforms took place in the context of the well-known features of the Swedish model, that is, the pursuit of full employment, centralised wage bargaining and solidaristic wages policies. As a result, as women's participation in paid work, especially part-time work, increased from the 1970s onwards, female workers have been provided with a level of employment protection not available in a country such as Britain. Mahon (1996) has argued that, because these jobs were not precarious, unions did not have to face the issue of the character of atypical work.

From the 1970s the women's movement, especially the Social Democratic Party (SDP) section, has campaigned for a reduction in the working day from 8 to 6 hours, 'particularly important if women's work is not to be defined as "atypical" (Mahon, 1996:571). However, this was continuously resisted by the Landorganisationen i Sverige (LO) and social democratic governments. A compromise was reached in 1978 in which parents of young children could reduce their working day to 6 hours albeit without compensation for the loss of pay. Since it has been predominantly mothers who reduce their working day, the male typical pattern remains that of continuous and full working time. The compromise has, therefore, been a one and three-quarters income for many two-adult households. More recently, some unions have come round to supporting calls for a reduction in the working day but have adopted this approach in response to high levels of unemployment.

Reforms introduced by the conservative coalition government of 1991 to 1994 included amendments to the Security of Employment Act 1974. These entailed a relaxation of hiring and firing rules for employers and a removal of the prohibition on private labour exchanges. Although the Social Democratic Government elected in September 1994 repealed the 'anti-union' changes to labour law, introduced by the previous conservative coalition, it has not prohibited temporary help agencies. Mahon (1996) argues that, although most atypical jobs in Sweden are not precarious, there is no guarantee that this will continue, especially as job growth is likely to be in the private service sector. The LO is now campaigning for rights for 'atypical' workers in a way that it previously failed to do.

Debate on relaxation of job security legislation is currently under way. Proposals include increased temporary working and a system whereby sectoral collective agreements can adjust employment security legislation to conditions in each industry. However, unions fear that employers will put pressure on local unions by threatening workforce reductions if disagreements arise. National unions will therefore be involved in plant level negotiations (EIRR, 276:13).

It is widely agreed that employment protection diminished faster in the UK than other EC countries during the 1980s and 1990s. There was a refusal by Conservative governments to sign the Social Chapter of the Maastricht Treaty in 1993. It also opposed a range of draft Directives which would have enhanced employment rights of workers. However, the UK government has had to increase employment rights in some areas to meet European Directive obligations (for example, Sex Discrimination Act 1986, Employment Act 1989, and the Trade Union and Employment Rights Act 1993) (see Dickens and Hall, 1995). More recently (February 1995) regulations have been brought in to give part-time workers the same protection as those working full-time, following a House of Lords ruling with respect to European Union equal pay and equal treatment law. Employment protection now covers all employees with two or more years of job tenure, so that the number of hours worked per week is no longer the qualifying condition.

Dickens and Hall (1995) list 15 key Acts between 1979 and 1993 in many of which 'the scope of employment protection rights was narrowed, access to rights was made more difficult and some protections were abolished' (Dickens and Hall, 1995:272). Other policies have been directed towards enhancing the discipline exercised by the labour market on workers, for example, through changes to social security and unemployment benefits. Notable changes also include the removal of minimum wage levels as a result of the abolition of Wages Councils and the scrapping of the Fair Wages Clause. For many writers, the most significant changes have been the weakening of the collective institutions of labour, the impact of changes in industrial relations legislation, the reduction in trade union members, and the reduction of those now covered by collective agreements which have been the most significant changes (for example, Gregg and Machin, 1994; Nolan, 1994).

Debate on non-standard work in the UK has focused on the flexible-firm thesis, employer's labour strategies and the extent to which increases in non-standard work reflect new departures or are innovative. Studies have refuted the strong version of the flexible-firm thesis, that is, the proposition that employers have systematically organised their workforce in terms of a core and periphery. Instead, it has been argued that traditional rationales for the use of non-standard workers have remained important (for example, Hunter *et al.*, 1993; Heather *et al.*, 1996). There is, however, more evidence for a weaker version of the flexible-firm thesis. When employers' strategies are conceptualised not as 'plans' but as 'patterns' of decision making (Procter *et al.*, 1994), changes in the 1990s, including restructuring in the public sector, provide supporting evidence.

Evaluation

Among the aims of policies encouraging labour market flexibility and non-standard work has been the promotion of employment growth and a wider distribution of employment. The debate on deregulation policies and removal of 'rigidities' in European labour markets has not abated after more than a decade. Nevertheless, as O'Reilly (1996) reports, the results of employment creation by means of increased non-standard working have often been disappointing. Moreover, in many cases it has generated undesired consequences, such as the creation of ghettos of disadvantaged forms of employment or, in the case of involuntary non-standard work, double jobbing or 'moonlighting'. Other consequences can also be discerned in the four countries discussed here.

The standard employment relationship has been of particular importance in Germany, resulting in high levels of wages and employment protection dependent on length of service and continuity. However, as Deakin and Mückenberger (1992) argue, the eligibility is inherently selective as it is based on the use of threshold criteria to delimit this protection. The standard employment relationship therefore privileges those workers who pursue continuous employment. Those who lack continuous employment, are unemployed or who fall below the number of hours for employment protection are, therefore, denied the insurance-related social security and have to fall back on means-tested benefits.

As we have seen, although the institutional and legal framework for deregulation of labour markets remains very different to that in Britain and the extent of non-standard employment is not as high – mainly because of lower levels of part-time work for women – non-standard employment is on the increase in Germany in the context of declining full-time employment for men. The impact of the increase in non-standard employment is, as Deakin and Mückenberger (1992) have argued paradoxically, to limit the extent of standard employment while heightening its social and economic significance as the privileged form of wage labour. The livelihoods of families are predominantly dependent on the male's lifetime earnings and access to his social security benefits. Women's opportunities to work are curtailed. Such a strategy produces a society of 'insiders' and 'outsiders' within segmented labour markets.

In Spain, too, core workers are also privileged within the labour market, although the core is smaller than Germany and labour markets more segmented. With very high levels of unemployment and precarious work, the family is the key to the stability of society, characterised by the pooling of a variety of sources of income from different labour markets, pensions and unemployment benefits being pooled (Perez-Diaz and Rodriguez, 1995). The ideal is to have one family member located within the core labour market. Families are then dependent on the main wage earner, not only for earnings but also for social security benefits. Gregg and Wadsworth (1997) further note that employment in Spain is concentrated on those with dependent families, normally men aged between 20 and 40. This is clearly shown in Figure 6.1. Compared with other European countries, Spanish heads of households have low levels and durations of unemployment (Greece, Italy and Portugal show a similar picture to Spain). While this eases the burden of unemployment for members of the family the result is that young people and women find it difficult to enter the labour market, also reflected in Figure 6.1. The greater difficulty for women in gaining access to jobs perpetuates the traditional family structure and division of labour within it.

The widespread use of fixed-term contracts does not appear to have promoted the growth of permanent jobs in Spain. Only a small proportion of workers hired on fixed-term contracts (15–17 per cent) succeed in obtaining an indefinite contract at the end of their period of employment (Milner *et al.*, 1995; Jimeno and Toharia, 1994). Further, neither the extensive informal economy nor widespread use of fixed-term contracts have substantially modified the problem of mass unemployment which reached 25 per cent of the working population in 1994 and was still 22.9 per cent in 1995. Unemployment has become increasingly feminised and women form the major part of the worst forms of unemployment, those out of work for long periods and first-time job seekers (see Table 6.4). Fixed-term contracts do not appear to have had the effect of shortening the length of unemployment spells for first-job seekers, which remain at the same level as in 1983 (Milner *et al.*, 1995).

The findings of Bentolila and Dolado (1994) suggest that the existence of workers on fixed-term contracts has had the effect of increasing the bargained real wages of those on permanent contracts. That is, fixed-term contracts have exacerbated insider–outsider problems in Spain by internalis-

Table 6.4   Unemployment rates in Germany, Spain, Sweden and UK, 1995

	Unemployment		*Long-Term Unemployment*		*% Unemployed Seeking First Job*	
	% labour force		% unemployed			
	Male	Female	Male	Female	Male	Female
Germany	7.1	9.8	41.2	47.2	4.2	3.9
Spain	18.2	30.5	49.0	60.0	14.8	25.8
Sweden	10.1	8.2	23.4	18.1	5.8	7.2
UK	10.1	7.0	49.6	32.3	8.7	12.2

Source: Eurostat, 1996.

ing such divisions within firms. Milner *et al.* (1995:29) summarise these findings as follows:

> Now the outsiders comprise both the unemployed and the temporary workers inside the firm. Neither group's interests have much bearing on the wage bargaining behaviour of the insiders – the permanent workers. The consequences of excessive wage demands (job losses) can now be accommodated by the buffer of temporary workers in the firm – whose firing costs are significantly lower for the employers.

The conclusions of the above writers is that the Spanish experience seems to represent a strong case against deregulation:

> On most of the crucial labour outcomes, the new permissive policy on fixed term contracts has exacerbated the segmented labour market problem with higher wage unresponsiveness to unemployment, greater precariousness of employment, and recently, the highest unemployment level ever recorded with more than a quarter of the workforce out of work (Milner *et al.*, 1995:38).

In Sweden, unemployment has increased in the 1990s. In 1996 it reached 8 per cent of 'open' unemployment and nearly 13 per cent if workers in labour market schemes are included. Indeed, one estimate suggests that some 25 per cent of the labour force are outside 'normal' full-time employment if the count includes workers forced to retire early, those who have involuntary part-time jobs and otherwise discouraged workers (EIRR, 270:27). Although unemployment is higher for men, due to the loss of jobs in manufacturing and construction in the early 1990s, more recently (1995–96) two-thirds of job losses have been among caring jobs funded by local authorities particularly affecting women workers (EIRR, 270:27). The decline of the Swedish model has encompassed the decentralisation of collective bargaining, increasing inequality of wages, increased unemployment, public sector privatisation and the growth of the private service sector. These processes suggest that pressures for a lessening of employment protection accompanied by an increase in non-standard work may be hard to resist. Developments in the internationalisation of the economy have changed the balance of power between employers and trade unions. Employers have become less interested in a compromise with Swedish labour. Nevertheless, the legacies of policies of the Swedish model have meant that a secondary labour force has not arisen to the same extent as in other countries. At present, both the trade unions and the social democratic government are resisting the lessening of employment protection.

In the UK, despite claims that labour market deregulation would enhance employment growth, unemployment and especially long-term unemployment has persisted (see Table 6.4). The UK did not do better than other countries in the proportion of the unemployed who have been out of work for long periods. In addition, the transition from unemployment to employment worsened for men (Blanchflower and Freeman, 1994). In the UK, women's lower unemployment rate (Table 6.4) may reflect a substantial under-recording of unemployment among women. Policies have not created jobs for the unemployed. Rather, the vast majority of part-time jobs are taken up by women married to men who are employed. Dependants of the unemployed or the unemployed themselves are effectively prevented from doing such jobs by loss of benefit or the 'poverty trap' (Deakin and Wilkinson, 1991–92).

The picture which emerges is therefore one of polarisation between households in the distribution of jobs. Dual-income households now constitute about two-thirds (62 per cent) of all households, with women's income on average representing a third of household income (Harkness *et al.*, 1995; Gregg and Wadsworth, 1997). The proportion of 'no-earner' working-age households has risen from 16 per cent in 1983 to 19 per cent in 1994 (Gregg and Wadsworth, 1997). As Gregg and Wadsworth (1997) note, the UK is less successful than other European countries in distributing jobs to the unemployed. This is reflected in Figure 6.1 which shows the persistence of unemployment for heads of households in the UK. The duration of unemployment for heads of households (male and female) is the highest in the EU, with 71 per cent of unemployed heads of households unemployed for 2 years or more in 1995.

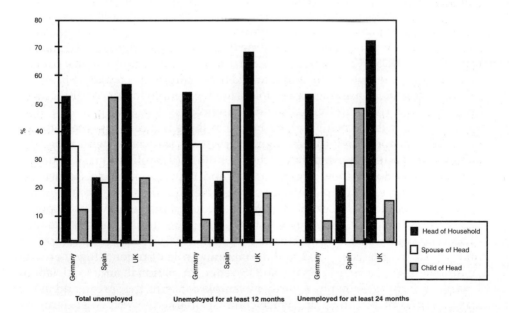

Figure 6.1   Relation to head of household of the unemployed and duration of unemployment in Germany, Spain and UK
Source: Eurostat 1996.
Note – data not available for Sweden.

The findings for the UK on non-standard employment can be put in the context of increasing polarisation of employment conditions for both men and women. Breugel and Perrons (1996) found an increasing polarisation between women's earnings. At the bottom of the income distribution however, men and women's earnings have converged as men's relative position to the median has declined. However, with so many women in part-time work they remain disadvantaged in terms of hourly pay, training, promotion prospects, social security entitlements and pensions (Breugel and Perrons, 1996; Osborne, 1996; Dex and McCulloch, 1995).

Conclusion

In conclusion, the use of non-standard employment increased across the European member states during the 1990s, especially during the years of recession but also in the first year of employment growth in 1995. Even in Sweden and Germany, where non-standard employment remains highly protected (except for marginal part-time workers in Germany), non-standard employment is increasing together with pressures for lessening job security and employment protection. It was noted that the increase in non-standard employment in Germany was undermining the principal of insurance-related social security based on wage earners' continuous life-long employment. The Spanish experiments with labour reform suggest a case against deregulation with increasing polarisation and segmentation of labour markets. The majority of the workforce are now in some form of non-standard work, in a context of very high unemployment and a considerable informal economy. Studies in the UK indicate also an increased polarisation of employment conditions and experiences for both individuals and households.

However, it is not being argued here that there is a convergence between countries in non-standard employment patterns associated with economic change. International competition, the operations of multinational companies and the diffusion of new organisational and managerial models constitute similar pressures and directions for change. Nevertheless, as this chapter has demonstrated, these forces for change are mediated through the social, political and institutional structures within each country. In the UK, for example there has been a lack of participation by national trade unions in proposals for labour reform, compared to the continuing role of unions, together with employers, in Germany, Spain and Sweden in national and local labour market reform agreements. A further example concerns the spread and use of fixed-term contracts in Spain, which contrasts markedly with West Germany where new laws permitting fixed-term contracts were introduced at the same time. Finally, there are clear differences between the countries in the extent to which non-standard employment is precarious or stable. Women in Sweden benefit from 'socially acceptable' part-time work which gives them lifelong continuous labour market participation. This contrasts with the precarious nature of much part-time work for women in the UK, marginal part-time workers in Germany and fixed-term contract workers in Spain. These differences have implications not only for the gender 'contract' in each country but also household coping strategies and opportunities.

References

Bentolila, S. and Dolado, J. (1994) 'Spanish Labour Markets', *Economic Policy*, April: 53–99.

Blanchflower, D.G. and Freeman, R.B. (1994) 'Did the Thatcher Reforms Change British Labour Market Performance?', in Barrell, R. (ed.) *The UK Labour Market: Comparative and Institutional Developments*, Cambridge: Cambridge University Press.

Boletin Mensual de Estadistica (1996) Madrid: Instituto Nacional de Estadistica.

Bruegel, I. and Perrons, D. (1996) *Deregulation and Women's Employment: The Diverse Experience of Women in Britain*, London: Gender Institute, London School of Economics.

Cousins, C. (1994) 'A Comparison of the Labour Market Position of Women in Spain and the UK with Reference to the "Flexible" Labour Debate', *Work, Employment and Society*, 8: 1, 45–67.

Deakin, S. and Mückenberger, U. (1992) 'Deregulation and European Labour Markets', in Castro, A., Mehaut, P. and Rubery, J. (eds) *International Integration and Labour Market Organisation*, London: Academic Press.

Deakin, S. and Wilkinson, F. (1991–92) 'Social Policy and Economic Efficiency: The Deregulation of the Labour Market in Britain', *Critical Social Policy*, Winter, 33: 40–61.

Dex, S. and McCulloch, A. (1995) *Flexible Employment in Britain: A Statistical Analysis*, London: Equal Opportunities Commission.

Dickens, L. and Hall, M. (1995) 'The State, Labour Law and Industrial Relations', in Edwards, P. (ed.) *Industrial Relations: Theory and Practice in Britain*, Oxford: Blackwell.

Due, J., Madsen, J.S. and Jensen, C.S. (1991) 'The Social Dimension: Convergence or Divergence in the Single European Market?', *Industrial Relations Journal*, 22: 2, 85–102.

European Industrial Relations Review (EIRR) monthly.

Esping-Andersen, G. (1990) *The Three Worlds of Welfare Capitalism*, Cambridge: Polity Press.

Esping-Anderson, G. (1996) *Welfare States in Transition: National Adaptations in Global Economies*, London: Sage.

European Commission (1996) *Employment in Europe 1995* DG for Employment, Industrial Relations and Social Affairs, Luxemberg: Office for Official Publications of the European Communities.

Eurostat (1996) *Labour Force Survey*, Luxembourg, Office for Official Publications of the European Communities.

Gregg, P. and Machin, S. (1994) 'Is the UK Rise in Inequality Different?', in Barrell, R. (ed.) *The UK Labour Market: Comparative and Institutional Developments*, Cambridge: Cambridge University Press.

Gregg, P. and Wadsworth, J. (1995) 'A Short History of Labour Turnover, Job Tenure and Job Security 1975–93', *Oxford Review of Economic Policy*, 11: 1, 73–90.

Gregg, P. and Wadsworth, J. (1997) 'Prosperity Begins at Home', *Financial Times*, 8 January 1997.

Gregory, A. and O'Reilly, J. (1996) 'Checking out and Cashing up: The Prospects and Paradoxes of Regulating Part-Time Work in Europe', in Crompton, R., Gallie, D. and Purcell, K. (eds) *Changing Forms of Employment: Organisations, Skills and Gender*, London: Routledge.

Hakim, C. (1990) 'Workforce Restructuring in Europe in the 1980s', *The International Journal of Comparative Labour Law and Industrial Relations*, 5: 4, 167–203.

Harkness, S., Machin, S. and Waldfogel, J. (1995) *Evaluating the Pin Money Hypothesis: The Relationship Between Women's Labour Market Activity, Family Income and Poverty in Britain*, STICERD Welfare State programme Discussion Paper WSP/108, London: London School of Economics.

Heather, J., Rick, J., Atkinson, J. and Morris, S. (1996) 'Employers' Use of Temporary Workers', *Labour Market Trends*, September: 403–11.

Hunter, L., McGregor, A., MacInnes, J. and Sproull, A. (1993) 'The "Flexible" Firm': Strategy and Segmentation', *British Journal of Industrial Relations*, 31: 3, 383–407.

Income Data Services (IDS) (1997) 'Spain: Will Labour Reform Dent Unemployment?', *Employment Europe*, Issue 425, May: 27–28.

Jimeno, J. and Toharia, L. (1994) *Unemployment and Labour Market Flexibility: Spain*, Geneva: ILO.

Kjellberg, A. (1992) 'Sweden: Can the Model Survive?', in Ferner, A. and Hyman, R. (eds.) *Industrial Relations in the New Europe*, Oxford: Blackwell.

Kravaritou-Manitakis, Y. (1988) *New Forms of Work: Labour Law and Social Security aspects in the European Community*, Luxembourg: European Foundation for the Improvement of Living and Working Conditions.

Lane, C. (1993) 'Gender and the Labour Market in Europe: Britain, Germany and France Compared', *The Sociological Review*, 14: 2, 274–301.

Lewis, J. and Astrom, G. (1992) 'Equality, Difference and State Welfare: The Case of Labour Market and Family Policies in Sweden', *Feminist Studies*, 18: 1, 59–87.

Mahnkopf, B. (1992) 'The "Skill-Oriented" Strategies of German Trade Unions: Their Impact on Efficiency and Equality Objectives', *British Journal of Industrial Relations*, 30: 1, 61–81.

Mahon, R. (1996) 'Women Wage Earners and the Future of Swedish Unions', *Economic and Industrial Democracy*, 17: 545–86.

Martinez Lucio, M. and Blyton, P. (1995) 'Constructing the Post-Fordist State?: The Politics of Labour Market Flexibility in Spain', *West European Politics*, 18: 2, 340–60.

Marullo, S. (1995) *Comparison of Regulations on Part-time and Temporary Employment in Europe*, Income Data Services, Research series No. 52.

Meulders, D., Plasman, O. and Plasman, R. (1994) *Atypical Employment in the EC*, Aldershot: Dartmouth.

Miguelez Lobo, F.M. (1988) 'Irregular Work in Spain', in *EEC Survey Underground Economy and Irregular Forms of Employment, Final Report*, Brussels.

Milner, S., Metcalf, D. and Nombela, G. (1995) *Employment Protection Legislation and Labour Market Outcomes in Spain*, London: Centre for Economic Performance, London School of Economics.

Moss, P. (1996) 'Parental Employment in the European Union 1985–1993', *Labour Market Trends*, December: 517–22.

Nätti, J. (1995) 'Part-Time Work in the Nordic Countries: A Trap for Women?' *Labour*, 9: 2, 343–57.

Nolan, P. (1994) 'Labour Market Institutions, Industrial Restructuring and Unemployment in Europe', in Michie, J. and Grieve Smith, J.G. (eds) *Unemployment in Europe*, London: Academic Press.

Organisation for Economic Co-operation and Development (OECD) (1991/2, 1994) *Economic Survey: Spain*, Paris: OECD.

O'Reilly, J. (1996) 'Labour Adjustments through Part-Time Work' in Schmid, G. and O'Reilly, J. (eds) *International Handbook of Labour Market Policy and Evaluation*, Cheltenham: Edward Elgar.

Osborne, K. (1996) 'Earnings of Part-Time Workers: Data from the 1995 New Earnings Survey,' *Labour Market Trends*, May: 227–35.

Perez Amoros, F. and Rojo, E. (1991) 'Implications of the Single Market for Labour and Social Policy in Spain', *International Labour Review*, 130: 3, 359–72.

Perez-Diaz, V. and Rodriguez, J.C. (1995) 'Inertial Choices: An Overview of Spanish Human Resources, Practices and Policies', in Locke, R., Kochan, T. and Piore, M. (eds) *Employment Relations in a Changing World Economy*, Cambridge, MA: The MIT Press,

Procter, S.J., Rowlinson, M., McArdle, L., Hassard, J. and Forrester, P. (1994) 'Flexibility, Politics and Strategy: In Defence of the Model of the Flexible Firm', *Work, Employment and Society*, 8: 2, 221–42.

Recio, A. (1992) 'Economic Internationalisation and the Labour Market in Spain', in Castro, A., Mehaut, P. and Rubery, J. (eds) *International Integration and Labour Market Organisation*, London: Academic Press.

Rhodes, M. (1989) 'Whither Regulation? Disorganized Capitalism and the West European Labour Market', in Hancher, L. and Moran, M. (eds) *Capitalism, Culture and Economic Regulation*, Oxford: Clarendon Press.

Rogowski, R. and Schömann, K. (1996) 'Legal Regulation and Flexibility of Employment Contracts', in Schmid, G. and O'Reilly, J. (eds) *International Handbook of Labour Market Policy and Evaluation*, Cheltenham: Edward Elgar.

Rubery, J. (1992) 'Pay, Gender and the Social Dimension in Europe', *British Journal of Industrial Relations*, 30: 4, 605–21.

Rubery, J. and Fagan, C. (1994) 'Does Feminization Mean a Flexible Labour Force?', in Hyman, R. and Ferner, A. (eds) *New Frontiers in European Industrial Relations*, Oxford: Blackwell.

Rubery, J. and Tarling, R. (1988) 'Women's Employment in Declining Britain', in Rubery, J. (ed.) *Women and Recession*, London: Routledge and Kegan Paul.

Sly, F. (1996) 'Women in the Labour Market: Results from the Spring 1995 Labour Force Survey', *Labour Market Trends*, March: 91–113.

Streeck, W. (1992) *Social Institutions and Economic Performance: Studies of Industrial Relations in Advanced Capitalist Economies*, London: Sage.

Notes

1   The statistics used in this chapter are taken from the Eurostat Labour Force Survey. The definition of part-time workers relies on how workers interviewed classified themselves. A self-employed worker is defined as in business on her or his own account. Eurostat figures appear to include in this category, employers with one or more employees as well as self-employed with no employees.

2   The use of fixed-term workers varies by size of firm with small and newly started firms having the highest proportions and large firms the lowest. Sectors in which fixed-term workers constitute more than a third of the workforce include agriculture, construction, shoe and leather industries, hotels and restaurants (Milner *et al.*, 1995). Extensive use of fixed-term contracts are also to be found in the secondary sector of multinational firms, retailing firms, contracted-out work in the public sector and small local firms (Recio, 1992).

3   However, EIRR 270 reports that in the year to May 1996 temporary employment fell by 18 000 jobs as local authorities cut their workforces and failed to renew temporary contracts.

4   Temporary work in the UK can be fixed-term contracts, interim work, seasonal work, and casual work. In 1994, 3 per cent of the male workforce and 4 per cent of the female workforce were on fixed-term contracts. The use of fixed-term contracts has been increasing, especially in the public sector, and such workers are often relatively highly qualified (Dex and McCulloch, 1995).

5   Labour market reform in 1994 accelerated the process of repealing the labour ordinances, many of which date back to the Franco period and which regulate a wide range of employment conditions. The unions and employers' confederation signed an agreement in 1994 to replace the existing labour ordinances. At the same time, negotiation of a variety of employment conditions passes to collective bargaining at sectoral or company levels. The union UGT is reported to have found that on the whole collective bargaining in 1995 was effective in maintaining employment rights and minimising the possible deregulatory effects of the labour reforms (EIRR, 268).

6   Employers and unions have agreed to create a new type of open-ended employment contract, especially aimed at workers who are finding it difficult to gain access to the labour market; for example, young unemployed people aged 18–29, long-term unemployed people, unemployed workers over 45 years and people with disabilities (EIRR, 280:25).

7 The Expansion in Non-Standard Employment in Australia and the Extension of Employers' Control

John Burgess and Glenda Strachan

Introduction

Employment insecurity is hardly a new phenomenon, nor is it a new means for extending employer control over the labour process. What is new, in Australia at least, is the extent and speed associated with the deregulation of employment conditions and the associated erosion of standard employment arrangements. The centralised employment regulatory regime, based on industry/occupational awards, so long a characteristic of Australian industrial relations, is being dismantled. In conjunction with this deregulatory process the security of employment is also diminishing rapidly through the growth in non-standard employment arrangements together with the decline in trade union presence at the workplace. More workers find themselves located outside of the employment regulatory regime, outside of trade union representation and in forms of marginal and insecure employment.

There are a number of stories to tell here. First, there is the deregulatory stance of the Federal Labor Government over the term of its office, 1983–96. Second, there are the support and compliance of the Australian trade union movement, notably the Australian Council of Trade Unions (ACTU), in this process, especially through a mechanism known as the Prices and Incomes Accord. Third, there is the acceptance of a deregulatory imperative alongside high and persistent rates of unemployment. The story we wish to concentrate on is the impact of these developments on the labour process, in particular through the growth in non-standard employment arrangements. Over the past decade the spread of non-standard employment arrangements has decreased employment security and allowed employers to extend their indirect and direct control over the labour process. In turn, and as a consequence, the profits share in GDP increased continuously over the past 15 years while the dispersion of earnings has widened (Gregory, 1997).

121

This chapter outlines the trends in non-standard employment in Australia and discusses the characteristics of the non-standard workforce in terms of age, gender, industry and occupation. The forces that are driving non-standard employment growth in Australia are analysed and the intersections between non-standard employment growth, trade union policies and changes in the regulatory regime governing employment, including the likely impact of recent legislative changes, are examined. This is followed by a discussion of the growing insecurity of employment and the process of employment deregulation. The impact of these developments on the labour process is examined and it is asserted that growing employment insecurity and growing non-standard employment are a lever for extending employers' control and exacting an ever-growing surplus. The final section of the chapter considers whether these employment developments together with the associated reshaping of the labour process will continue into the future.

Non-Standard Employment in Australia

The exact nature of standard employment is imprecise, often being prescribed through employment law, collective agreements, custom and practice, and trade union policy. Standard employment is associated with a normal employment contract involving continuity and regularity of employment, mutuality and security in employment and access to defined fringe employment benefits (Leighton, 1986:504). A widespread perception of work is that it is of full-time duration, has employee status, has ongoing tenure, is at an establishment owned by the employer and is unionised. This perception is one that is historically specific and dominates conventional post-1945 economic analyses of the labour market. The 'worker' has long been represented in fiction and nonfiction as a male, full-time employee, unionised, performing a craft occupation and working at an organised workplace generally located in the manufacturing sector.[1] Fevre (1991:58) argues that full-time paid employment, which dominated post-1945 working arrangements, has achieved the status of a stereotype. The exact nature and context of standard employment has only been considered, Mückenberger (1989:381) argues, when it could no longer be taken for granted due to the growth of employment forms which diverged from the standard employment model.

According to Hepple (1992:287) there are numerous departures from the standard employment model including the degree of subordination to an employer, the duration of employment, the organisation of working time, the location of employment and the method of recruitment. As a consequence, non-standard employment embodies a variety of employment arrangements that deviate from the standard employment form, but in themselves are disparate.

This inclusive concept embraces part-time employment, self-employment, fixed-term employment, working unsociable hours and temporary employment. It also includes several ambiguous employment forms such as homeworking and agency working. These employment types differ in many respects such as income, status and security. They are grouped together because they share, to differing degrees, a departure from standard employment. Such departures include combinations of the following: less than full-time employment duration, non-permanent employment status, non-employee status (for example, employment on a contract basis) or a non-regulated workplace.

The standard/non-standard employment classification is based on a regulatory and entitlement norm. Standard workers have the rights of employees: they can belong to a trade union, can expect minimum award entitlements[2] and employment continuity, are in receipt of specified minimum non-wage entitlements, can expect rudimentary protection from unfair dismissal and discriminatory employment practices, and receive a minimum (living) income associated with full-time waged employment. An approximation for the non-standard workforce in Australia can be gained by summing non-employees, part-time employees and full-time casual employees (see Table 7.1).

Table 7.1 demonstrates the relative growth in non-standard employment arrangements and the related relative decline in standard employment over the period 1982 to 1996. Estimates are not available prior to 1982. The standard workforce share is the percentage of full-time, permanent employees in the workforce. The non-standard workforce percentage is equal to the sum of the percentages for part-time casual employees, full-time casual employees, part-time permanent employees and non-employees. The non-employee category is an aggregation of a number of distinct employment arrangements (employer, the self-employed and unpaid workers in family businesses) that lie outside the regulations and entitlements for employees. The largest non-employee component is the self-employed, or own-account workers, who make up about two-thirds of the non-employee total (Burgess, 1990).

For purposes of international comparison the concept of casual employment in Australia can be equated with the more widely used concept of temporary employment. Casual employment in Australia is defined, for statistical purposes, as employment that does not attract entitlements for either holiday or sickness benefits. This largely conforms to the award system in Australia which prescribes minimum legal entitlements for employees. In general those employees with on-going, or permanent, employment have an entitlement to a range of benefits including sickness and holiday benefits. Those without such benefits are classified as casuals by the Australian Bureau of Statistics. Under the award system casuals are also excluded from many of the other entitlements and protections associated with permanent employ-

Table 7.1   The standard and non-standard workforce in Australia, 1982–1996 (percentage of total workforce)

Year	Standard Work-Force	Non-Standard Work-Force	Part-Time Permanent Employees	Full-Time Casual Employees	Part-Time Casual Employees	Non-Employees
1982	67	33	–	–	–	16
1986	63	37	–	–	–	17
1988	64	36	5	4	11	16
1989	63	37	5	4	12	16
1990	62	38	5	4	12	17
1991	60	40	6	5	12	17
1992	59	41	7	5	12	17
1993	58	42	7	5	14	16
1994	56	44	7	6	14	17
1995	56	44	7	6	15	16
1996	55	45	7	7	15	16

Key: standard workforce is full-time, permanent employees; non-standard workforce is all other workers: part-time permanent employees, full-time casual employees, part-time casual employees and all non-employees (employers, the self-employed, unpaid workers in family businesses). Estimates for total casual and permanent employment are available in 1982 and 1986. To derive the number of full-time permanent employees, the OECD (1993:22) division is used for 1986 and an estimate of 92 per cent of full-time employees is applied to the 1982 data.

Sources: Australian Bureau of Statistics (Catalogue 6203, The Labour Force; Catalogue 6334, Employment Benefits; Catalogue 6325, Trade Union Members) and unpublished data.

ment including prior notice of employment termination and protection from unfair dismissal. In practice the casual classification covers a large number of different employment arrangements including seasonal employment, fixed-term employment, irregular employment and at-call employment. The conceptual and measurement difficulties associated with the casual employment category in Australia are discussed in Burgess (1997). The OECD (1993; 1996) in its international survey of temporary employment arrangements equates casual employment in Australia with temporary employment elsewhere in the OECD. On this basis Australia ranks second behind Spain in terms of the workforce share of temporary employment and its relative growth over the past decade (OECD, 1996). The term 'temporary' will be used in the remainder of this chapter to refer to casual employment in Australia.

The relative growth in the non-standard workforce is largely attributable to the related growth in part-time and temporary employees. The share of non-employees in the workforce has remained stable. Over the 1982–96 period the non-standard employment share increased by more than a third from 33 per cent to 45 per cent. If multiple job holdings, employment experience over the year, external workers, seasonal workers, temporary workers, fixed-term workers, incorporated and salaried business owners, and unrecorded work are included, the non-standard workforce would exceed 50 per cent of the workforce. Table 7.1 is indicative of the trend towards non-standard employment and the intensity of the transformation taking place in the Australian workforce.[3] Increasingly Australian workers find themselves in unprotected, unregulated forms of employment, often receiving less than a full-time income and outside the regime of standard non-wage benefits. Employment regulations, awards and standard employment conditions have less application now than at any time in the last 50 years.

Characteristics of the Non-Standard Workforce

The standard workforce in Australia has declined across all industries (Campbell, 1996; Campbell and Burgess, 1997; Brosnan and Campbell, 1995; Romeyn, 1992). While structural developments in Australian industry account for part of this change (especially the decline in manufacturing and the growth in personal/recreation services), the decline affects all industries. Information services based industries such as banking and finance are increasing their share of the non-standard workforce, and with the exception of public administration, these are sectors with relatively low standard workforce ratios. Despite discontinuity problems with occupational data, the trends are clear-cut. For all occupations the standard workforce accounts for a declining share of the total workforce. Occupations with traditionally high ratios of standard workers, such as those associated with the trades, account for a decreasing share of the total workforce. Occupations with post-secondary education training and entry requirements account for a growing share of the standard workforce.

Men account for a declining share of the standard workforce, despite the fact that males traditionally had a very high ratio of standard workers. Despite much of the growth in female participation rates being in part-time employment, women nevertheless account for a growing share of the standard workforce. However, for both males and females the share of standard workers to total workers is declining. On an age basis the emerging trend is that younger and older age workers account for a declining share of the standard workforce. Those in the 25 to 54 years age group have increased their share of the standard workforce. Across all age groups the share of the standard workforce in the total workforce has declined. On the basis of longer-term workforce experience, those with continuous full-time employment of more than 12 months account for approximately 55 per cent of all workforce experiences and less than a half of all labour force experiences.

A number of observations can be made about non-standard employment by analysing the published evidence (summarised in Table 7.2). Younger and older workers are more likely than others to be in some form of non-standard employment. Women dominate part-time permanent employment, part-time temporary employment and unpaid family business workers, while men dominate self-employment, full-time temporary employment and the em-

Table 7.2   The characteristics of the non-standard workforce

Characteristic	Non-Standard Employment
Gender	Females dominate part-time employment, temporary employment and unpaid family business workers. Males dominate self-employment and employers.
Age	High incidence of part-time and temporary work for workers aged 15–24 years and 60–64 years.
Industry	Agriculture, retail trade and construction (self-employment); retail trade, finance and business services, community services, recreation (part-time employment); retail trade, community services and recreation (temporary employment).
Occupation	Salesworker (part-time, temporary and self-employment); trades worker and farmer (self-employment); labourer and related unskilled occupations (part-time, temporary employment).
Sector	Overwhelmingly private sector; non-standard employment share increasing in public sector.
Firm Size	Inverse relationship: extent of part-time and temporary employment declines with increasing firm size.
Other	Relatively low trade union densities and award coverage for part-time and temporary employees. Relatively low levels of training for temporary employees. Non-employees outside employment regulations.

ployer category. The industry and occupational patterns for non-standard employment are diverse. Agriculture and construction have high representation from non-employees and temporary employees. The retail trade, community services and recreation/personal services have high part-time and temporary employee representation. Farmers, trades workers and salespersons have relatively large numbers of self-employed workers. Labourers and related workers have relatively large numbers of part-time and temporary employees. The private sector has significantly higher ratios of non-standard to total employment than the public sector. Even if non-employees are netted out, this observation still applies for part-time and temporary employees. Moreover, there is an inverse relationship between firm size and part-time and temporary employment.

The emerging scene in Australian employment is one in which non-standard employment arrangements are widespread. Virtually no industry, occupation or demographic category has been immune from the spread of non-standard employment arrangements. Between 1982 and 1995 there were 1.839 m additional jobs generated in Australia; 1.510 m, or more than 80 per cent, were non-standard jobs. The vast majority of all new jobs now involve some form of non-standard employment arrangement. It is clear that employers have adopted the non-standard employment model with gusto in Australia and that standard employment arrangements are rapidly disappearing.

Forces for Change

There has been a clear retreat from standard employment in the post-1974 period in Australia and across many OECD economies. One factor contributing to this retreat in standard employment, and concomitantly to the growth in non-standard employment, is the persistence of high unemployment. This provides employers with potential power to vary the terms and conditions of employment given that workers are in a diminished position to bargain or to resist through quitting their job. High unemployment also assists in establishing political pressure on unions and on labour to accept variations in their terms of employment, notably though the imperative of 'labour flexibility' (Campbell, 1993). In addition, the diminished prospects for finding employment may force many workers to seek forms of employment outside standard employment as a refuge from unemployment or as an opportune measure until the labour market improves (Stricker and Sheehan, 1981). Average unemployment rates, and average unemployment duration, have successively increased since 1970 in Australia.

Growth in female participation rates has been directed away from standard employment, with most of the new jobs for women involving some form of non-standard employment arrangement (Strachan and Burgess, 1997). Many women, because of domestic responsibilities, may desire more flexible working time arrangements than occur with standard employment. In turn they are prepared to accept part-time work, employment under temporary conditions, or forms of external work such as homeworking. The growth in female participation rates and its impact on employment patterns interacts with the depressed labour market conditions. Given the segregation of females into low-paying and often part-time occupations, the shift towards employment in information services based industries has itself supported female and part-time job growth. The two fastest growing areas of employment are part-time and temporary employment, both interact and are dominated by women, many of whom may be additional workers, forced into employment to augment family income when their spouse has been made redundant or overtime has been eliminated. The preference of many married women for 'flexible' working time arrangements together with stagnation allows employers to place pressure on existing employment conditions (Lewis, 1990; Henry and Franzway, 1993).

The industrial shift in employment composition has also been important in undermining the standard employment regime. The decline in manufacturing employment is one factor contributing to the decline in male, full-time and unionised employment. The growth in employment in information services based industries has been conducive to less regulated and non-standard employment growth. In general, service industries such as retailing, and banking and finance, directly provide the end consumer while manufacturing output is distributed through a chain of intermediaries before reaching the end consumer. Service sector employment can be less continuous, organised on a needs basis and less regulated than manufacturing employment. Service sector growth has generated a large number of low paying, semi-skilled jobs filled by women along typical lines of gender segregation. Traditionally the private service sector has been less unionised than other sectors, largely as a consequence of its strong female presence and partly as a consequence of trade union policies (Lever-Tracy, 1988).

The institutional balance of power in labour markets has shifted to employers who have been able to strengthen their position relative to organised labour. The persistence of high unemployment rates places employers in a better position to negotiate with both trade unions and governments. The internationalisation of markets and production, and the deregulatory pressure of the globalisation rhetoric (Macdonald and Burgess, 1996), allows employers to use the threat of offshore or national relocation to strengthen their bargaining position with trade unions and government. Employers have been politically more active in directly lobbying governments and in directly pushing for labour market deregulation. In Australia this has involved the formation of well-funded 'think tanks' and the use of common law action or trade practices legislation against striking workers and their unions (Dabscheck, 1989: ch. 6). In addition, some employers are actively pursuing labour flexibility strategies that encompass a declining core of full-time, permanent workers, and a growing periphery of supporting part-time, temporary and contracted workers (Probert, 1995). In Australia some employers such as Conzinc Rio Tinto Ltd (a subsidiary of Rio Tinto Zinc Ltd) have been at the vanguard of a concerted plan to deregulate and de-unionise employment through the conversion of employees into contractors (McDonald and Timmo, 1996). The common rules and regulations governing employment have been systematically eroded (Kane and Marsden, 1988:112). Collectively and politically, labour has been in a very weak position to resist these challenges.

The State has demonstrated an inability to come to terms with a new international trading regime and a regime of low growth. The political reaction has been towards an embracing of market liberalism and a retreat from the dictums of Keynesian discretionary demand management. This retreat has encompassed different policy responses (Lipietz, 1992: ch. 1) ranging from supply side policies in the USA to monetarist policies in Britain and corporatist policies in Australia. Some forms of the liberal response actually assist in the destruction of standard employment, for example, the privatisation and corporatisation of government business enterprises and the contracting out of government services. In countries such as Britain the government has led the way in the contraction in standard employment through privatization, corporatisation and contracting out (Casey, 1989). In Australia the effects of fiscal restraint, monetary austerity and public sector rationalization such as corporatisation and contracting out have been just as devastating to public sector employment and employment conditions (Campbell, 1996).

Centralised, equity-based wage determination arrangements have given way to decentralised, efficiency-based wage determination processes in Australia. In part these reforms promote and institutionalise fragmented working arrangements. The process of enterprise bargaining has left many workers outside the bargaining domain and directly vulnerable to managerial prerogatives, while at the same time it has intensified wage inequality and increased employment insecurity (Strachan and Burgess, 1997).

In a sense, the shape of the workforce is returning to that of an earlier era, the 1920s and 1930s, characterised by economic stagnation, considerable international uncertainty and significant economic and political pressure on employment conditions and trade unions. The challenges facing labour and unions in the 1990s in Australia are remarkably similar to those of the 1930s (Rawson, 1992). Many of the new employment forms are insecure, non-unionised, unregulated and exhibit similarities with the putting-out and piecework regime of the nineteenth century (Frances, 1993). The economic, political and institutional regime supporting full-time, permanent or standard employment has been systematically eroded. While this erosion of supporting conditions for standard employment has in general applied right across the OECD, the Australian experience represents one of the more spectacular departures from the standard employment model. It is within this context of extensive labour market restructuring combined with an associated institutional and political shift away from the post-1945 wage regime that the growth in non-standard employment can be comprehended.

Trade Unions, Regulation and Industrial Relations

In Australia the award system has provided support and protection for full-time, permanent, waged employees. Other work forms have been assumed to be unimportant or evaded regulation, and frequently trade union policy has been ambiguous and indifferent towards the growth in non-standard employment. Since the early 1990s the Australian system of industrial relations has been transformed from centralised intervention towards decentralised enterprise bargaining arrangements. This development has provided a further stimulus for non-standard employment arrangements. Over the later term of the Prices and Incomes Accord (1983–96) between the Federal Labor Government and the ACTU the regulatory system was successively decentralised in the name of modernisation, efficiency and international competitiveness (Dabscheck, 1995). While this suited many full-time (mainly male) employees who had had their real wages constrained by the centralised wage controls, it meant that 'trade-offs' became the norm for achieving wage increases in all sectors, including those in which productivity growth was difficult to measure directly (Rimmer, 1994).

At the same time many of the state governments, especially Victoria and Western Australia, introduced a far-reaching program of industrial relations deregulation that reduced the application of the award system, led the way for individual contracts and directly attacked the legal status of trade unions (Dabscheck, 1995:100). Workers who had their conditions guaranteed and regulated soon found themselves subject to strong employer pressure to trade-off conditions and to sign individual contracts. This was a three-pronged attack on employment conditions. Non-standard employment growth gave employers greater temporal and wage flexibility and acted as a lever against those standard workers who remained within a collective and protective arrangement (Campbell, 1996). The Prices and Incomes Accord gave more power and discretion to workplace managers to use enterprise bargaining as a framework that eroded working conditions and increased employment insecurity (Henry and Franzway, 1993). The direct legislative attack by a number of state governments on trade unions and collective employment security increased management power (Dabscheck, 1995:100–4). These developments reinforce each other to undermine the regulatory framework governing employment and to strengthen the position of employers in the labour process.

Trade unions, largely by indifference or hostility to non-standard employment, allowed non-standard employment to flourish and thus indirectly undermined standard employment conditions. Non-standard employment growth is one reason why trade union densities have fallen rapidly from 51 per cent in 1976 to 31 per cent in 1995 in Australia (Burgess and Ryan, 1996). If the share of the non-standard workforce continues to increase, and in the absence of any significant institutional or policy changes, the density of trade unions will continue to fall. These issues have been addressed by Bray (1991:199–201) who identified four potential responses from trade unions to non-standard workers: ignore them; exclude and oppose them; limit their numbers and regulate them; recruit and integrate them. In the past the traditional trade union response has been to see non-standard employment as a potential threat to standard employment conditions, and strategies which ignored, excluded or limited the number of non-standard jobs were undertaken (Lever-Tracy, 1988). However, the magnitude of the numbers in non-standard employment and the increasing political and legislative attacks on trade unions have forced unions to move increasingly towards schemes which recruit these workers, even though such strategies are costly and face opposition both within trade unions and from employers (Crosby, 1992).

Two aspects of non-standard employment deserve emphasis in the context of any discussion about trade unionism in Australia. First, the majority of non-standard employees are female, and trade unions have been extensively criticised for ignoring the needs and the vulnerability of female employees, especially those employed on a part-time and/or temporary basis (Henry and Franzway, 1993; Bennett, 1994). Second, a large number of part-time/temporary employees are workers less than 24 years of age. For this group of workers such employment constitutes their introduction to the workplace and to trade unions. If they are unrepresented, ignored by trade unions or see trade union membership as irrelevant, this can establish an attitude towards trade unions that persists into subsequent spells of employment (Plowman, 1992:272).

There are strategies available for trade unions to organise the non-standard workforce (Campbell, 1996). The Prices and Incomes Accord had a male, standard workforce focus, and as a consequence non-standard workers (and many women workers) were excluded from the centralised incomes policy (Henry and Franzway, 1993). Subsequent regulatory changes have significantly strengthened the position of employers and undermined the employment conditions of the standard workforce. The ACTU is in part responsible for the unregulated growth in non-standard employment and for the subverting of employment conditions. Both have strengthened managerial prerogatives and encouraged state governments to push ahead with direct legislative attacks on employment conditions and trade unions. At the same time a compliant Labor Government and opportunistic employers have contributed to the successive undermining of employment conditions in Australia. All these policies have combined to increase employment insecurity and to validate non-standard employment arrangements. In this process non-standard employment both places pressure on standard employment conditions, and enables employers to push further to reduce the proportion of permanent workers and externalise their workforce.

Extending Labour Control through Increasing Employment Insecurity

In addition to the growth in non-standard working arrangements, these developments allow employers to extend labour 'flexibility' strategies into standard employment. Increasingly full-time, permanent employees are finding that their employment conditions are under threat and their conditions are being traded off for what amounts to more insecure employment arrangements. 'Flexibility' is both a set of loosely defined practices and an ideology (Campbell, 1993) and in terms of work practices 'flexibility' denotes the increased ease with which management can utilise labour. Thus 'flexibility' has been introduced into workplace or enterprise agreements through an abolition of penalty rates, an increase in the span of ordinary working hours (even to 24 hours a day, 7 days a week, 52 weeks a year), a reduction in overtime or overtime payments, the introduction of broken shifts and so on. This means that employers can call on staff without payment for what was regarded as unsocial working times, frequently at short notice. Despite the widespread rhetoric of both Labor and conservative governments relating to policies which create a 'family friendly' workplace which allows both women and men to combine effectively their responsibilities for their family as well as paid employment, there is little evidence of changes in enterprise agreements which enhance a worker's abilities to combine these parts of their lives. Worker's control over their working lives is declining. In a survey of more than ten thousand employees, one-quarter to one-third of workers (depending on the type of agreement they were covered by) reported that they were less satisfied with the balance of work and family in the previous 12 months, while between 56 per cent to 60 per cent reported no change. Significant factors in declining job satisfaction were perceptions of reduced opportunities for employees to use their skills, decreased career opportunities, diminished job security, curtailed information flows from management, reduced employee say in decision making, and deteriorating work and family balance (Department of Industrial Relations, 1995: ch. 5).

While part of the rhetoric surrounding the introduction of decentralised wage bargaining arrangements was that enterprise agreements could respond to localised conditions, they have come to contain a few standard clauses focusing on wages and the arrangement of working hours. Hours of work were included in 72 per cent of pre-1995 agreements examined by the Australian Centre for Industrial Relations Research and Training (ACIRRT) and were present in 100 per cent of 1995 agreements. A majority of these agreements (58 per cent) provided for a working week greater than 37.5 hours. Annualised salaries, overtime paid at ordinary time rates, averaging ordinary hours over a number of weeks, increasing the days on which work can be performed were commonplace and 'provide significant cost benefits to employers' (ACIRRT, August 1995:6–7).

The changes in industrial relations legislation have hastened the introduction by employers of various strategies to increase numerical flexibility. Banks have adopted specific internal labour market strategies which rely on a pool of female part-time staff, in excess of 20 per cent, who have little chance of advancement beyond the lowest grades of employment (Strachan and Winter, 1995; Romeyn, 1992; Women's Bureau, 1989). Analysis of five enterprise agreements (concluded with Finance Sector Union involvement) in small to medium sized banks showed that the most likely changes were those which increased the daily spread of hours, increased the span of ordinary hours to include Saturday and placed little restriction on part-time workers' hours. Lloyds, Deutsche and the Bank of Melbourne deregulated hours almost completely, with the agreements allowing the bank to determine the hours worked, in some cases with the employee's agreement.

The Labour Deregulation Imperative and the End of Employment Security

The federal conservative (Liberal-National Party Coalition) government, elected in 1996, has introduced industrial relations reforms that will assist in the process of reducing employment security and strengthening managerial prerogatives. The major thrust is to deregulate employment arrangements and to remove the potential intrusion over workplace arrangements provided by the award system and trade unions. In the past 15 years Australia has moved from a highly centralised system of regulation of labour which relied on decisions and awards from state and federal industrial relations commissions, towards a more fragmented and individualised system. This process was set in place by the federal Labor Government (1983–96) as centralised arbitration was dismantled and collective bargaining at separate workplaces encouraged. The rhetoric which drove these changes emphasised that wage increases were linked to increased productivity, although there was no check on changes in productivity before an agreement was ratified through the Industrial Relations Acts. Since 1993 there has been a large increase in the number of workers whose conditions are governed principally by an enterprise agreement specifying key working conditions and an award relating to their industry which covers additional conditions. The *Industrial Relations*

Reform Act 1993 allowed non-union agreements, but these were used in only a few cases.

The *Workplace Relations Act 1996* (operative from 1997) introduced by the conservative government builds on the foundation of collective bargaining at the level of the enterprise introduced in the past decade but contains some quite different emphases. It introduces the individualisation of workplace agreements and severely limits union powers. While the new Act alters incrementally some aspects of industrial relations, it also fundamentally changes industrial relations in Australia. The 1996 Act is based on the policy of 'Better Pay for Better Work' which the conservative parties propounded in their election campaign: 'A more flexible industrial relations system will increase productivity, achieve faster real growth in wages and profits and, most importantly, create more real jobs.' The policy stated that an industrial relations system 'where employers and employees work as a team' was needed 'at the level of the individual enterprise where employers and employees can see most clearly that they have a common interest in the success of the enterprise' (Reith, 1996a:1). The government's rationale is that 'the new framework supports a more direct relationship between employers and employees, with a much reduced role for third party intervention and greater labour market flexibility' (Department of Industrial Relations, 1996).

Flexibility is a feature of the *Workplace Relations Act* and its first objective is 'encouraging the pursuit of high employment, improved living standards, low inflation and international competitiveness through higher productivity and a flexible and fair labour market'. The individualisation of industrial relations is encompassed in the second object: 'ensuring that the primary responsibility for determining matters affecting the relationship between employers and employees rests with the employer and employees at the workplace or enterprise level'. The rhetoric of 'more effective choice and flexibility for parties in reaching agreements' is administered through the introduction of two types of enterprise agreements – Australian Workplace Agreements (AWAs) and Certified Agreements (CAs). AWAs are essentially individual documents (the first time such agreements have been incorporated into a federal industrial relations act), signed by each individual, while CAs retain a collective element and are targeted at larger employers.

AWAs may be reached individually or collectively but are required to be signed individually. Employees and employers may appoint a bargaining agent but uninvited union involvement will be excluded. Bargaining over agreements need not occur. The Act merely states that the employer must provide existing employees with a copy of the proposed agreement at least 14 days before signing it (5 days for new employees) and must explain the effect of the AWA to the employee who must genuinely consent to it. The agreement has to be approved by the Employment Advocate (a new position) who must be satisfied that it meets a no-disadvantage test; that is, that the agreement when considered as a whole is no less favourable to the employee than the relevant award or legislation, 'with respect to the overall package' (Department of Industrial Relations, 1996). The Australian Industrial Relations Commission (AIRC), however, can approve an agreement which results in an overall reduction if it is judged not to be contrary to the public interest: for example, where the agreement is part of a strategy to deal with a short-term business crisis. Nothing in the legislation prevents employers from offering new employees pay and conditions inferior to that of existing employees (Catanzariti and Baragwanath, 1997:27). Certified Agreements can be made between employers and unions (if they have a member at the enterprise) or employers and employees. The agreement must be explained to employees and CAs must meet the no-disadvantage test. A majority of employees to whom the agreement applies must have genuinely made, or genuinely approved, the agreement (this does not apply to greenfield sites). Once again, bargaining is not a necessity. The CA may expressly allow the employer to enter into AWAs with employees covered by a CA so a multiplicity of different arrangements could emerge in the one workplace.

In its efforts to reduce the role of central regulation, the award system, which has been the foundation of wage determination since the first decade of the twentieth century, is to be circumscribed. Awards, which still cover 35 per cent of the workforce, will be reduced to a system of minimum wages and conditions, with matters allowed in awards reduced to 20, principally covering wages, hours and leave. This 'award simplification' process as it is called, is to be completed by mid-1998 and conditions other than those specified will be deemed not to exist. Already the Australian Chamber of Commerce and Industry is coordinating a push by employers in the retail, hospitality, health and printing industries to pare back their awards (Davis and Long, 1997:3). When this occurs, this section of the workforce will lose certain entitlements and safeguards. One important part of this process is that regular part-time work (defined as less than full-time hours, reasonably predictable hours of work and providing the same award conditions as full time employees on a pro rata basis) cannot be restricted, that is, quotas and minimum and maximum weekly hours' provisions will be removed from the award system.

In addition to non-union and individual agreements, union's activities have been circumscribed in other ways. One of the fundamental principles underlying the conservative government's industrial relations policy is 'the principle of freedom of association – including the choice whether or not to be in a union or employer organisation' (Reith, 1996b). Compulsory unionism (imposed in any way) and preference to unionists is outlawed: 'Greater choice will encourage the development of registered organisations that are more competitive, providing a higher level of service to members' (Department of Industrial Relations, 1996); and new unions with a minimum of 50 members can be formed. Enterprise unions covering a majority of employees in an enterprise can be registered if the majority of people eligible support its registration, and one is already trying to establish in a finance sector company. In addition, unions' right of entry to workplaces has been restricted: they must have a member at the workplace, obtain a permit from the Registrar and provide the employer with at least 24 hours' notice of the visit.

Penalties for industrial action have been increased and it will be more difficult for unions to take such action. There is a right to take industrial action or to lock out employees (immunity from civil liability) during the negotiation of an AWA provided three days' notice is given. However, as these agreements are 'negotiated' on an individual or group basis and signed on an individual basis this right would be difficult for employees to exercise and may not have much impact. The notice period required plus the fact that only a small group of employees are involved would mean that employers would have no difficulty in getting other employees to cover the work (Catanzariti and Baragwanath, 1997:32). There is a limited right to take industrial action or lock out during the bargaining period for a CA provided certain conditions are met and three days' notice given. If a solution cannot be reached, the AIRC can cancel the bargaining period and conciliate on the matter, and, failing this, arbitrate on the matter. Industrial action is illegal outside the bargaining period and the AIRC's powers in relation to unlawful industrial action have been strengthened. The definition of industrial action has been widened in the Act: 'the performance of work in a manner different from that in which it is customarily performed, or the adoption of a practice in relation to work, the result of which is a restriction or limitation on, or a delay in, the performance of the work'. It is unlawful for an employer to pay strike pay or an employee to accept it (except in instances of reasonable concern over health and safety) and the AIRC no longer has jurisdiction over claims for strike pay. In addition, secondary boycott provisions have been restored to the Trade Practices Act 1974. Thus, workers' ability to influence changes in working practices and conditions has been curtailed.

Implications for the Future

The growth in non-standard employment arrangements together with the growing insecurity of standard employment continues at a startling pace in Australia. These developments occurred during the period of a federal Labor Government with centralised employment regulations. The Australian experience demonstrates that labour regulation, a relatively strong trade union movement and a sympathetic government were not sufficient to abate the trend of non-standard employment growth, the growing insecurity of employment and the strengthening position of employers in the labour process. High rates of unemployment, growth in female participation in the labour market in jobs which frequently involve some form of non-standard working

conditions, the decline in manufacturing and the growth in service and information based industries have assisted this change. Employers have been able
to strengthen their position relative to that of labour and there has been an
erosion in conditions of employment for standard workers as well as growth
in the numbers employed under non-standard conditions. A centralised system of wage determination has given way to one of collective bargaining at
individual enterprises and this has resulted in a wider variety of wages and
working conditions.

This development has profound implications for trade unions. They are
faced with a radically altered workforce structure, a hostile political context
and a growing non-standard workforce which we anticipate will include at
least 80 per cent of all new jobs in the next decade. As conservative state and
federal governments implement industrial relations legislation which emphasises individual agreements, with fewer minimum standards, this makes
taking industrial action more difficult and dramatically reduces the role of
trade unions, standard as well as non-standard workers facing increased
managerial control of the labour process.

References

Australian Centre for Industrial Relations Research and Teaching (ACIRRT) (1995)
    ADAM: *Agreements Data Base and Monitor*, Sydney: ACIRRT, University of Sydney.
Bennett, L. (1994) 'Women and Enterprise Bargaining: The Legal and Institutional
    framework', *Journal of Industrial Relations*, 36: 2, 191–212.
Benyon, H. (1975) *Working for Ford*, Wakefield: EP Publishing.
Bray, M. (1991) 'Conclusions', in Bray, M. and Taylor, M. (eds) *The Other Side of
    Flexibility: Unions and Marginal Workers in Australia*, Sydney: ACIRRT, University of
    Sydney.
Brosnan, P. and Campbell, I. (1995) 'Labour Market Regulation in Australia: Towards
    New Forms of Workforce Division', paper presented at Conference of the Interna-
    tional Working Party on Labour Market Segmentation, Sienna.
Burgess, J. (1990) 'Non-Employee Status in Australia: Trends and Issues', *Australian
    Bulletin of Labour*, 17: 4, 233–53.
Burgess, J. (1997) 'Workforce Casualisation in Australia', in Mortimer, D., Leece, P. and
    Morris, R. (eds) *Readings in Contemporary Employment Relations*, Sydney: Harcourt,
    Brace and Co.
Burgess, J. and Ryan, S. (1996) 'Non-Standard Employment: The Growing Challenge
    for Trade Unions', in Griffin, G. (ed.) *Contemporary Research on Trade Unions: Theory,
    Membership, Organisation and Non-standard Employment*, 1: 152–72, Melbourne: Na-
    tional Key Centre for Industrial Relations, Melbourne.
Campbell, I. (1993) 'Labour Market Flexibility in Australia: Enhancing Managerial
    Prerogatives?', *Labour and Industry*, 5: 3, 1–32.
Campbell, I. (1996) 'Casual Employment, Labour Regulation and Australian Trade
    Unions', *Journal of Industrial Relations*, 38: 4, 571–99.
Campbell, I. and Burgess, J. (1996) 'Precarious Employment: Concept and Applica-
    tion', paper presented at Conference on Precarious Employment in Australia, Cen-
    tre for Research on Employment and Work, Griffith University, Brisbane.

Campbell, I. and Burgess, J. (1997) 'National Patterns of Temporary Employment: The Distinctive Care of Casual Employment in Australia', paper presented at 19th Conference of the International Working Party on Labour Market Segmentation, Porto, Portugal, July.

Casey, B. (1989) 'The Extent and Nature of Temporary Employment in Britain', *Cambridge Journal of Economics*, 12: 487–509.

Catanzariti, J. and Baragwanath, M. (1997) *The Workplace Relations Act*, Sydney: Newsletter Information Services.

Crosby, M. (1992) 'Organising a Mobile Workforce', in Crosby, M. and Easson, M. (eds) *What Should Unions Do?*, Sydney: Pluto.

Dabscheck, B. (1989) *Australian Industrial Relations in the 1980s*, Melbourne: Oxford University Press.

Dabscheck, B. (1995) *The Struggle for Australian Industrial Relations*, Melbourne: Oxford University Press.

Davis, M. and Long, S. (1997) 'Employers Seek Fast Action on Awards', *Australian Financial Review*, 20 February.

Department of Industrial Relations (1995) *Enterprise Bargaining in Australia: 1994. Annual Report*, Canberra: Australian Government Publishing Service.

Department of Industrial Relations (1996) 'Changes in Federal Workplace Relations Law-Legislation Guide', http://www.nla.gov.au/dir/faq/faq.htm#technical.

Fevre, R. (1991) 'Emerging Alternatives to Full-Time and Permanent Employment', in Brown, P. and Scase, R. (eds) *Poor Work: Disadvantage and the Division of Labour*, Milton Keynes: Open University Press: 56–70.

Frances, R. (1993) *The Politics of Work: Gender and Labour in Victoria, 1880–1939*, Melbourne: Cambridge University Press.

Gregory, R. (1997) 'Wage Deregulation, Low-Paid Workers and Unemployment', in Sheehan, P., Grewal, B. and Kumnick, M. (eds) *Dialogues on Australia's Future*, Melbourne: Centre for Strategic Economic Studies, Victoria University.

Henry, M. and Franzway, S. (1993) 'Gender, Unions and the New Workplace: Realising the Promise?', in Probert, B. and Wilson, B. (eds) *Pink Collar Blues: Work, Gender and Technology*, Melbourne: Melbourne University: 126–53.

Hepple, R. (1992) 'Labour Law and the New Labour Force', in Gladstone, A. (ed.) *Labour Relations in a Changing Environment*, Berlin: Walter de Gruyter: 287–96.

Ireland, D. (1973) *The Unknown Industrial Prisoner*, Sydney: Angus and Robertson.

Kane, E. and Marsden, D. (1988) 'The Future of Trade Unions in Industrialised Market Economies', *Labour and Society*, 13: 2, 109–24.

Leighton, P. (1986) 'Marginal Workers', in Lewis, R. (ed.) *Labour Law in Britain*, Oxford: Basil Blackwell: 501–27.

Lever-Tracy, C. (1988) 'The Flexibility Debate: Part-Time Work', *Labour and Industry*, 1: 2, 210–41.

Lewis, H. (1990) *Part-time Work: Trends and Issues*, Canberra: Department of Industrial Relations.

Lipietz, A. (1992) *Towards a New Economic Order: Post-Fordism, Ecology and Democracy*, London: Polity Press.

Macdonald, D. and Burgess, J. (1996) 'Globalisation, Restructuring and Industrial Relations in the Hunter Region of Australia', paper presented at Conference on Globalisation of Production and the Regulation of Labour, University of Warwick.

McDonald, J. and Timmo, N. (1996) 'Killing the Union? Individualised Contracts and CRA', in Griffin, G. (ed.) *Contemporary Research on Trade Unions: Theory, Membership, Organisation and Non-standard Employment*, Melbourne: National Key Centre for Industrial Relations: 422–59.

Mückenberger, U. (1989) 'Non-Standard Forms of Work and the Role of Changes in Labour and Social Security', *International Journal of the Sociology of the Law*, 17: 381–402.

Organization for Economic Co-operation and Development (OECD) (1993) *Employment Outlook*, Paris: OECD.

OECD (1996) *Employment Outlook*, Paris: OECD.

Plowman, D. (1992) 'Arresting Union Decline: Membership Retention and Recruitment Strategies', in Crosby, M. and Easson, M. (eds) *What Should Unions Do?*, Sydney: Pluto: 266–88.

Probert, B. (1995) *Part-time Work and Managerial Strategy: Flexibility in the New Industrial Relations Framework*, Canberra: Department of Education, Employment and Training.

Rawson, D. (1992) 'Has Unionism a Future?' in Crosby, M. and Easson, M. (eds) *What Should Unions Do?*, Sydney: Pluto, pp. 2–15.

Reith, P. (1996a) *Better Pay for Better Work: The Coalition's Industrial Relations Policy*, np.

Reith, P. (1996b) *Workplace and other Legislation Amendment Bill*: Second Reading Speech.

Rimmer, S. (1994) *The Australian Labour Market and Microeconomic Reform*, Melbourne: La Trobe University Press.

Romeyn, J. (1992) *Flexible Working Time: Part-time and Casual Employment*, Canberra: Department of Industrial Relations.

Strachan, G. and Burgess, J. (1997) 'Employment Restructuring, Enterprise Bargaining and Employment Conditions for Women Workers', in Bramble, T., Harley, W., Hall, R. and Whitehouse, G. (eds) *Current Research in Industrial Relations*, Brisbane: Association of Industrial Relations Academics of Australia and New Zealand: 321–29.

Strachan, G. and Winter, M. (1995) *Overcoming Barriers to Women's Employment and Advancement in Information Technology Intensive Industries in Queensland*, Brisbane: Department of Business, Industry and Regional Development.

Stricker, P. and Sheehan, P. (1981) *Hidden Unemployment: The Australian Experience*, Melbourne: Melbourne University.

Women's Bureau, Department of Employment, Education and Training (1989) *New Brooms: Restructuring and Training Issues for Women in the Service Sector*, Canberra: Australian Government Publishing Service.

Notes

1 See, for example, David Ireland's fictional account of Australian workplace industrial relations in an oil refinery (Ireland, 1973). In the non-fictional arena see the account by Huw Benyon (1975) of working on the assembly line for the Ford motor company in Britain.

2 In Australia an award sets out minimum conditions of employment including rates of pay, hours and non-wage entitlements which are registered with industrial tribunals and are legally enforceable. Award coverage is not dependent upon trade union membership.

3 The static estimates of non-standard employment understate the degree of workforce insecurity in a number of ways. First, the employment count is of primary jobs, not all jobs. Nearly all second jobs, around 500000 in total, are non-standard. Second, many short-term jobs such as full-time fixed-term and seasonal jobs do receive sickness and holiday entitlements, so they are classified as being permanent under the Australian classification system. Third, data on employment

experience over the year indicates high employment turnover for part-time and casual workers, with employment interspersed with spells of unemployment or outside of the labour force. Thus, the numbers experiencing insecure employment over the year exceeds the numbers in insecure employment as at any one point in time (Campbell, 1996).

8 Gender Contracts, Welfare Systems and Non-Standard Working: Diversity and Change in Denmark, France, Germany, Italy and the UK

Sue Yeandle

Introduction

This chapter reviews evidence relating to the extent and type of non-standard, or atypical, work being done in five European countries – Denmark, Germany, France, Italy and the UK, during the period 1985–95. Five countries were selected as the largest number which could be considered in one chapter, and to represent both a variety of labour market situations and a geographical spread. 'Non-standard' work is paid work which is neither full-time according to national definitions (usually 35+ hours per week) nor permanent in that the employee has a contract of employment for an indefinite period (see Fevre, 1991; Pollert, 1991 for a discussion). The chapter seeks to locate the trends observed in their wider social context.

In the first section, key demographic indicators are outlined, and the ideological and political framework within which welfare and other social policies operate is noted. Although all belong to the European Union (EU), there are significant differences between them, notably differences in their history of labour relations and in gender arrangements, which mean that changes in employment practice occur in very different contexts.

The second section summarises[1] an analysis of Eurostat (and other) data (based on the European Labour Force Survey[2]). Data are for 1985–95 only: earlier data were patchy and the samples used posed problems of comparability. The analysis explores trends in the five countries by age group and sex and by employment sector, and offers a picture of significant and quite rapid change in each case, with important variations.

The final section offers analysis and discussion of this data. It argues that there are some trends observable in all five countries towards polarisation between secure and comfortable employment conditions and lifestyles for some workers and job insecurity and risk in relation to the labour market for others. However, the polarisation emerging is not a simple one, between workers with standard employment contracts at the positive pole and workers with non-standard patterns at the negative one. Rather, a more complex relationship between individuals and labour markets is emerging across the life course. This is one which is fraught with risk and requires skilful negotiation, but which can produce both major opportunities to prosper in terms of economic status and security, and the danger of labour market marginalisation and social exclusion for those who lack qualifications, skills, personal flexibility (which is often a gendered characteristic related to parenthood) or luck.

Context

The demographic context

All five countries have ageing populations, with increased longevity, reduced rates of mortality and declining birth rates. In Denmark, France and the UK a very large minority of births occur outside marriage, and here as well as in Germany a significant minority of children experience family life in households which are not headed by a couple. Table 8.1 summarises the relevant evidence. Italy, which has recently witnessed a rapid decline in its birth rate, has a low divorce rate and a smaller proportion of children born outside marriage. In all five countries, female labour force participation has been influenced by changing family patterns and fertility rates across the twentieth century. Ability to control fertility, increased lifespans, and latterly the trend towards delaying and in some cases rejecting marriage and motherhood, has reduced the constraints imposed on women by the work of childrearing. This development is itself fed by changes in opportunities for education and vocational qualifications which have made an especially marked impact on women's lives.

Welfare arrangements and institutional support for education and training

Esping-Andersen *et al.* have argued that it is the welfare state, the industrial relations system and the education system which 'emerge as key institutional filters for employment structuration. These are the main forces that dictate the family-work nexus' (1993:33). This type of analysis is helpful insofar as it enables the relationship between these elements to be delineated, although the direction in which any causal factors operate does not necessarily become clear. Other commentators emphasise the possibility of a two-way relation-

Table 8.1 Key demographic indicators, 1983–1993, selected European countries

	Denmark 1983	Denmark 1993	France 1983	France 1993	Germany 1983	Germany 1993	Italy 1983	Italy 1993	UK 1983	UK 1993
Proportion of population aged over 65	15	16	13	15	15	15	13	16	15	16
Proportion of population aged under 15	19	17	22	20	17	16	21	16	20	19
Total fertility	1.38	1.75	1.78	1.65	1.43	1.30	1.49	1.21	1.77	1.82
Completed fertility – women born 1945/55	2.06	1.83	2.24	2.13	1.79	1.67	2.07	1.77	2.17	2.01
Live births outside marriage as percentage of all births	41	46[92]	16	33[92]	15	15	5	7	15	31[92]
Couples with children as a percentage of all families with children	81[81]	78[91]	90[81]	84[91]	85[81]	81[91]	n.a.	n.a.	81[81]	78[91]
Lone parents as per cent of families with at least 1 child <18 (early 1990s)*	n.a.	19	n.a.	12	n.a.	19	n.a.	6	n.a.	21
Age at first birth – women (early 1990s) (rounded)*	n.a.	27	n.a.	27	n.a.	27	n.a.	27	n.a.	26
Divorces per 1000 people per annum	2.9	2.4	1.8	1.9[91]	2.2	1.7[92]	0.2	0.4	2.9	3.0[91]
Marriages per 1000 people per annum	5.3	5.9	5.5	4.4	6.3	5.5	5.4	5.1	6.9	6.1
Living alone: percentage of all households that are single-person households (1991)*	n.a.	34	n.a.	27	n.a.	34	n.a.	21	n.a.	26

Figures are for 1983 and 1993 except where indicated in the cells in superscript.
Main source: Eurostat, 1995. *Source: Millar and Warman 1996:12, 22.
1 Total Fertility indicates the average final family size implied by childbearing in the year.
2 Completed fertility is the average number of children born to women in the birth cohort by 1983 (women born in 1945) and 1993 (women born in 1955).

ship between these institutions and gender relations rooted in family structures. The concept of a 'gender order' (Connell, 1987) may help to capture the
complex interrelationships between individual biography and personality,
life-course experience of changing family structures, educational and vocational choice and opportunity, and the labour process and employment relations. Others (see Siim, 1993:47 n. 1) have found it useful to conceptualise
family and gender relations in terms of a 'gender contract' which forms a
backdrop to the development of institutionalised welfare arrangements.
These ideas are discussed further later in the chapter.

The idea that welfare states fall into three principal types has also been
widely discussed, in a debate stimulated by Esping-Andersen's *Three Worlds
of Welfare Capitalism* (1990). Orloff (1993) engages with this debate in a discussion which brings gender relations into the centre of welfare state analysis,
working with the typology of 'liberal', 'conservative-corporatist' and 'social
democratic' welfare state regimes. Briefly (and focusing only on the work/
family interface), in the 'liberal' welfare state (including the UK), there is a
laissez faire approach to aspects of concern to working parents – childcare
provision, maternity/paternity leaves and pensions. In 'conservative-
corporatist' systems (including France, Germany and Italy), there is an ideological attachment to family and gender arrangements which construe
women as carers and men as providers, and it is these private arrangements
which the welfare system is designed to support. In 'social democratic' systems (e.g. Denmark), policy is directed more strongly towards achieving
individual autonomy, underpinned by ideological commitments to equality
of opportunity and to individual responsibility. Here the welfare system is
less concerned with achieving stable family arrangements based around marriage and couple-headed households, than with offering education and training arrangements and social supports which permit individuals to achieve
their potential within a highly institutionalised labour market dominated by
a publicly funded service sector.

European family relationships and policies have recently been reviewed by
Millar and Warman (1996). They show that Denmark and France have the
most extensive state support, extending to widespread assistance with the
care of pre-school children, whereas in Italy, Germany and the UK the state
plays a more minor role (1996:30–31). Denmark, France and Italy offer high
levels of nursery/kindergarten provision (over 80 per cent), with Germany in
a middle category (50–80 per cent) and the UK with lower coverage. However, only Denmark targets its support for infants and very young children at
all parents, while in France this form of support is aimed specifically at
working parents. In Italy pre-school provision is intended to support parental
care, rather than to replace it, and in Germany and the UK there is more
limited state provision for young children. In the UK especially, this assistance is aimed principally at families where children are deemed to be at risk
or in need of special provision.

The Danish and French social systems thus provide rather good support for working parents (see Hantrais [1993:116] for a discussion of policy shifts in France in the second half of the twentieth century), enabling many parents to participate in full-time standard employment. By contrast, German and Italian families are expected to provide care for young children within the family setting, with a strong social expectation that this care will be provided by women. In the UK there is minimal state support for families with young children, but increasing pressures towards dual earning driven by housing patterns (a trend towards mortgage-based home ownership), by relatively low wages, and by a growth in the demand for and the supply of part-time labour.

The extent to which state benefit arrangements encourage part-time employment has also been identified as an important factor in encouraging or discouraging part-time employment (OECD, 1996:48–51). For example, there is a markedly stronger financial incentive for unemployed parents to take part-time work in Germany than in either Denmark or the UK (OECD, 1996:51). The balance between encouraging part-time working (in ways which make full-time employment less attractive) and discouraging it through tighter benefit regimes is one with which several of the countries are currently grappling, and is an aspect which brings values relating to family life and to the marketplace into conflict.

Patterns of education and vocational training also vary markedly (OECD, 1996:151). The five countries have all seen a decline in the labour force participation rates of young people over the decade, but not in equal measure. There has also been a trend towards prolonging full-time education in all five, again with significant variability. Denmark has a particularly high proportion of its young people in schooling or apprenticeships, while the UK has the lowest education/apprenticeship participation rate. Youth unemployment figures are especially high in Italy and in France. These variations between countries are again consistent with the welfare state types indicated above.

Family structures and ideology

Analysing patterns of family obligations in Europe, Millar and Warman have suggested that European countries can usefully be categorised into three broad groupings which do not map neatly onto welfare state categories. The groupings are: 'individual autonomy', where societal expectations of family obligations are low and welfare policies are addressed mainly to individuals (e.g. Denmark); 'nuclear family' where expectations are mainly directed at kin groups consisting of spouses and their children (e.g. France, Germany, the UK); and 'extended family' where the obligations of the nuclear family are 'embedded within a much wider set of familial obligations which bring in grandparents, siblings, uncles and aunts' (1996:46–8) and where state policy is expected to be non-interventionist (e.g. Italy). Millar and Warman's approach takes forward the debate about welfare state types by incorporating insights from feminist critiques of Esping-Andersen and others. These critiques have argued that by giving scant attention to the family dimension, and concentrating on the state–labour market relationship, gender relations have been excluded from analysis.

In order to capture the significance of changing patterns of employment, and notably the emergence of non-standard forms of work, it is essential that the family and gender dimension is drawn in. This enables the importance of the implicit 'gender contract' to be recognised. The social democratic and individual autonomy status of Denmark in these analyses is consonant with high female participation rates and a widespread commitment of public resources to supporting parents. The much lower participation rates and very different rationale for the provision of childcare in Italy is similarly consistent with the conservative-corporatist state and extended family system of obligations observed there. Millar and Warman's analysis gives significant purchase on the differences between the three conservative-corporatist states considered here (Italy, France, Germany), while the distinction between liberal and conservative-corporatist regimes helps to explain differences between the 'nuclear family' states (UK, France, Germany). There are particularly interesting differences here with respect to differences in values and attitudes towards responsibility for childcare. In France, for example, these help to explain the emphasis on state responsibility for the care of young children, while in Germany and the UK, their care is viewed as a familial, and specifically maternal, responsibility which the state has a duty to support rather than to erode.

Variability in the status of women

While the focus on family arrangements helps to explain variability in the status of women, it tells only part of the story. The status of women in each society is also related to other aspects of the 'gender contract': their representation in political structures; their occupation of positions of power and authority in the labour market; their autonomy; and the esteem in which they are held in cultural life, including in family and religious structures.

In Italy, the Catholic Church exercised an important influence on family policy and thus on the status of women until at least the 1960s. Divorce became possible only in 1970, with the 1974 referendum signalling 'a change in the political orientation of Italian women (and paving) the way for the legalisation of abortion' (Lovenduski, 1986:267). The wider kin group still plays an important role in the establishment and enactment of obligations within the family (Millar and Warman, 1996), much more so than in any of the other countries. This is reflected in the importance of family working in Italy, although it is also related to other factors such as the sectoral distribution of employment.

Of the five countries, Denmark has established the most secure basis for the development of gender equality. In the 1970s and 1980s far-reaching changes in gender relations and politics have produced a situation in which it is 'usual' for both parents to have paid work and where 'gender equality has become one of the core values of the political culture' (Siim, 1993:44–5). Family arrangements have become relatively flexible, with alternatives to the marriage-based nuclear family widely accepted, and many Danish adults experiencing a variety of family and household arrangements, including se- rial monogamy, across the life course. Although the family, and women's unpaid domestic work within it, continues to underpin wider social arrange- ments and to be valued, the emphasis on individual autonomy results in more extensive state provision for the care needs of aged persons and people with disabilities than is the case in any of the other countries. Furthermore, Danish women have taken on wider political roles to complement their increased participation in the labour market: 'they participate in trade unions, in social movements such as the peace and ecology movements, in formal organisa- tions, in political parties and in social welfare institutions to almost the same extent as men' (Siim, 1993:41).

In France, women's labour force participation has been facilitated by com- prehensive childcare provision and their social position has been significantly affected by policies affecting women in national political life, in part a result of influential French feminists (Chamberlayne, 1993) and of a leftward shift in national political life in the 1980s. Progress on rights at work was particularly impressive in the 1980s (Hantrais, 1993).

The 'institutional conservatism' of German social policy (Rerrich, 1996) in the former West can be contrasted with the widespread incorporation of women into the labour force, with childcare supports, in the former German Democratic Republic (DDR). In the Federal Republic the strong link between labour market position, citizenship and welfare rights (benefiting men and offering women security through lifelong marriage) encouraged women to select a housewife role and discouraged the development of maternal and part-time employment, denoting a 'gender contract' which emphasised women's economic dependency.

The UK saw significant legislative change directed at achieving sex equality during the 1970s. Women's participation in formal politics remained at a low level (Lovenduski, 1986; Snyder, 1992) during the decade,[3] although more equality of educational opportunity has been achieved, and women have secured more positions in professional and managerial jobs. By 1995, approxi- mately 30 per cent of women workers were in relatively high-status jobs (Yeandle, 1996), and there is now much more widespread acceptance of women's right to enter and sustain a career alongside a family life and motherhood. Young women enter higher education in numbers which match those of young men, and their educational achievements at school have now surpassed those of their male counterparts. There is continued occupational segregation in the UK labour force, with significant differentiation between boys' and girls' subject choices in education. Fewer girls than boys leave school unqualified, but those that do have poor employment prospects, and a higher chance of becoming lone parents than their qualified sisters. UK women have high risks of poverty if they are lone parents, and most find it practically impossible to secure paid employment which can cover childcare and living costs. Here, too, the underlying 'gender contract' remains one of female reliance upon male support.

Trends in Non-Standard Work

Part-time employment

Between 1985 and 1995 there has been significant variation in patterns of part-time working in all five countries, with changes in virtually all age groups and both sexes. The detailed picture is shown in Figures 8.1 and 8.2. Although part-time work is one of a range of flexible working time arrangements (Di Martino, 1995) including flexi-time, staggered hours, compressed work weeks, job-sharing and hours-averaging, only part-time is considered here because of the variability of these other types of arrangement, and the difficulty of identifying comparable data on the five countries.

One in ten Danish males was employed part-time by 1995, although there was a marked decline in part-time working among Danish women.[4] The upward trend for men was marked in all age groups under 65, and particularly strong among men aged 25 to 49 and the young, many of whom were financing their studies – in 1994 about 50 per cent of Danish males aged 18 (16 per cent aged 22) were both employed and attending school (OECD, 1996:132). By contrast, among Danish women, part-time increased only for young women (over 60 per cent of Danish females aged 18 [10 per cent aged 22] were both working and studying in 1994), while part-time working declined for all older women, across all sectors. Jonung and Persson (1993) have suggested that such evidence requires careful interpretation, citing the Swedish case where relatively generous parental benefits for full-time workers enable many women to have periods away from work while re-corded as in full-time employment. While parental leaves are less generous in Denmark, with more emphasis on public day-care provision (Siim, 1993:35), many Danes are entitled to full income replacement maternity leave. Danish couples now share breadwinning more equally, although women still do most childcare, both unpaid, as mothers (including as lone parents), and as paid childcare workers. For example, Danish statistics show women on formal childcare leave from employment outnumbering men by a factor of 12:1 in 1995 (Lind, 1997).

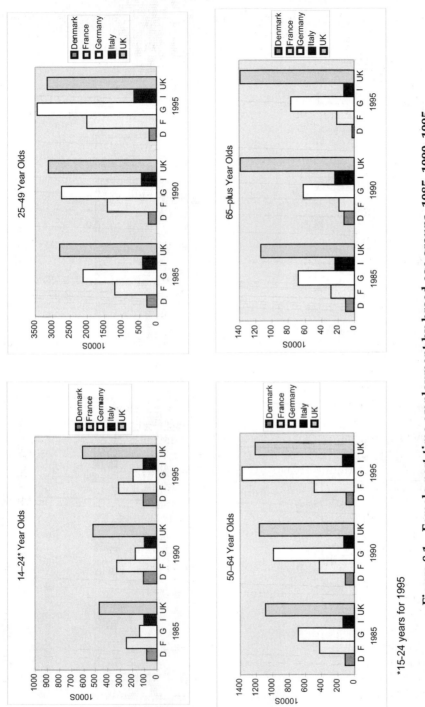

Figure 8.1   Female part-time employment by broad age groups, 1985, 1990, 1995

Source: Eurostat (1985, 1990, 1995), Labour Force Survey for the European Union.

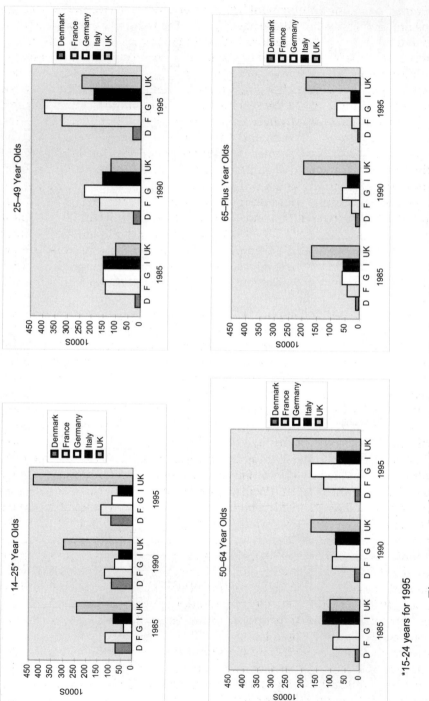

Figure 8.2   Male part-time employment by broad age groups, 1985, 1990, 1995

Source: Eurostat (1985, 1990, 1995), Labour Force Survey for the European Union.

*15-24 years for 1995

In France, part-time employment has also been increasing for men in all age groups under 65, especially those aged 25–49. The trend is especially marked in the industrial and service sectors, although part-time working is declining for men in agriculture. In a period of rising male unemployment much of this part-time working has been involuntary. Overall, by 1995, 5 per cent of French men and 29 per cent of French women were working part-time. The trend for women was most marked in the service sector (rising more than 60 per cent) although it also showed strongly in industry (up 17 per cent). Part-time working among young French men and women also increased, but the strongest trend was among women of parental age, 25–49. Hantrais has noted that the link between maternal employment and part-time working has been weaker in France than in the UK or Denmark. In France insufficient full-time employment opportunities for young labour market entrants has affected this group (1993:129). Between 1983 and 1995, female unemployment rose significantly (1.08m to 1.6m [OECD, 1996]) and much faster than in the other countries. Involuntary part-time employment may therefore be more important in France, than elsewhere, which would also be consistent with France's established pattern of continuous female employment across the childbearing years.

The German picture is complicated by the inclusion of figures covering the New Länder following unification in 1991, and 1995 figures cannot be compared with earlier figures. Among female German employees, part-time employment rose to almost 34 per cent by 1990, and it remained high in 1995. Part-time working was particularly important in the 25–49 age group, with approximately two-thirds of all part-timers in this age group, among them some 400 000 men. Compared with the other countries, part-time employment was less important among young Germans, although there was strong growth from a low base in this age group. This probably reflects prolonged full-time education into the 20-plus age group (Rainbird, 1993), and the relative affluence of (West) German families. One-third of German university students 'support themselves' (Wallace, 1994), although German service sector employment shows considerable heterogeneity among unskilled service workers and little evidence of 'youthful stop-gap jobs' (Blossfeld *et al.*, 1993). Public policies encourage German mothers of under threes to remain outside the labour market (Scheiwe, 1994), although part-time employment is a more favoured option for women with older children, and Germany now allows it, if under 19 hours per week, to be combined with flat-rate maternity benefit (Scheiwe, 1994). In addition, the organisation of the German school day makes part-time work the only option for mothers without access to forms of childcare other than their own labour.

Italy has the smallest part-time workforce by a considerable margin. Although part-time working for men and women has increased in services and for women (only) in industry, these upward trends have been offset by a decline in part-time working for both sexes in agriculture, and for men in industry. More Italian men aged 25–49 now work part-time, by contrast with the trend for other age groups, while for women there has been a strong increase in part-time working (60 per cent) in the 25–49 age group. Younger Italian women also showed a small increase in part-time employment, but this was countered by an opposite trend among older Italian women. Very few young Italians combine attendance at school/college with employment (OECD, 1996:132).

The UK has an established pattern of maternal part-time employment, with over 44 per cent of employed women working part-time in 1995. This represents over three million women aged 25–49 and over one million women aged 50–64, with further significant numbers of part-time women workers in younger and older age groups. All the increase in part-time employment was in the service sector, and this strong upward trend was partly offset by a downward trend in the industrial and agricultural sectors. The trend for UK men was also strongly upwards, especially for age groups under 65, with a particularly noticeable increase (of 145 per cent) among men aged 25–49.

In summary, a much larger proportion of female than of male workers are part-timers. While part-time figures are always difficult to interpret (e.g. one person may hold two or more part-time contracts – see Watson, 1992:543), contracting workers part-time is now a very significant employment practice, and one which has continued to rise throughout the decade in several of the countries. This trend, strongly female, but now clearly visible among men, too, is most marked in Germany and the UK. By 1995, in each of these countries, employers had made more than three million part-time employment contracts with women workers, with the totals for all age groups reaching over five million in both Germany and the UK. France and Italy occupy a middle position between these strong female-part-time employment countries and Denmark, where the importance of part-time work is declining, notably among Danish women of parental age. Figure 8.3 shows that while approximately two-thirds of French, German and Italian women working part-time are aged 25–49, the corresponding figures for Denmark and the UK are closer to 50 per cent: in Denmark there is a relatively higher concentration among younger women, while in the UK there is significant part-time employment among older women (aged 50–64). Patterns of education and training for younger women, and of support with childcare for women of parental age are influential factors, although the significance of employer demand, and its sectoral distribution, as well as the prevalence of other forms of employment, such as self-employment, considered next, also need to be taken into account.

Increases in self-employment and fixed-term contracts

Self-employment is most important, in relative terms, in Italy, where more than a quarter of economically active males, and more than 1 in 8

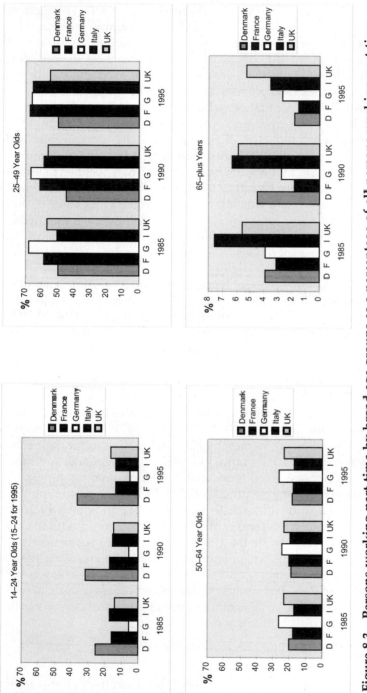

Figure 8.3   Persons working part-time by broad age groups as a percentage of all persons working part-time, 1985, 1990, 1995

Source: Eurostat (1985, 1990, 1995), Labour Force Survey for the European Union.

Note: Graph 65-plus, columns set to a different scale.

Data for Germany pre-1991 refers to the Federal Republic, any later data refers to Germany including the New Länder.

economically active females works on this basis (Figure 8.4). Trends in self-employment are related to the sectoral distribution of employment, although the significance of kin networks in Italian culture is another important influence. Therborn has noted the 'distinctively petit-bourgeois flavour to (the Italian) class structure' where 'there are four self-employed and family workers for every ten workers/employees' (1995:78). The proportion of the economically active Italian population who are self-employed has remained remarkably stable for both men and women over the 10-year period. Denmark, by contrast, has only a small proportion of its economically active population in self-employment. It is rare (less than 4 per cent) for women to work for themselves, and by 1995, the figure for men had declined to less than 8 per cent. The UK witnessed a rather marked increase in male self-employment between 1985 and 1990, which levelled off in the years to 1995, with a more muted upward trend for women. In France self-employment declined between 1990 and 1995. In all countries except Italy governments have introduced special schemes to assist the unemployed into self-employment Teague (1989).

Temporary or fixed-term contract working (Figure 8.5) affects a small proportion of workers in Italy and the UK, and has been fairly stable for the working population as a whole in these countries (OECD, 1996:10–11). In Denmark and Germany, such employment affects a larger, but again apparently stable proportion of the working population (10–12 per cent, although Beck [1992:148] asserts such work is mostly hidden in Germany) while in France, temporary working has increased rapidly – from 3 per cent in 1983 to 11 per cent in 1994. Fixed-term contracts are slightly more common for women than for men in all countries. States regulate fixed-term contracts in a variety of ways (Schömann *et al.*, 1994; Cousins, 1997): Denmark 'does not restrict the use of fixed-term contracts by prescribing reasons for their conclusion' (Schömann *et al.*, 1994:31); France has rather tight regulations requiring employers to compensate fixed-term contract employees on termination; Germany specifies closely the circumstances in which fixed-term employment is possible and limits most contracts to 18 months (Employment Promotion Act, 1985); Italy permits fixed-term contracts only if certain conditions apply (Schömann *et al.*, 1994:31); while the UK 'has no statutory restrictions . . . on entering into fixed-term contracts of employment' (Schömann *et al.*, 1994:34). Data for 1991 showed a notable concentration of fixed-term contracts in the agricultural sector in Italy, but a much wider spread across industrial sectors in the other four countries, with significant use of such contracts in services, construction and the distributive trades.

Family workers

Italy has the strongest tradition of family working, and although this form of work (in which persons work without an individual salary for a member of their kin group) has declined for women since 1985, from 9 to 6 per cent of the

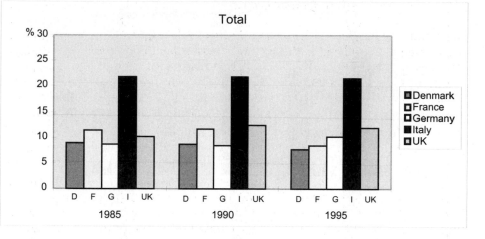

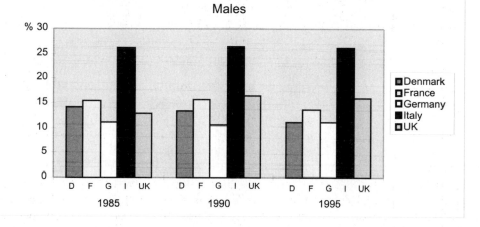

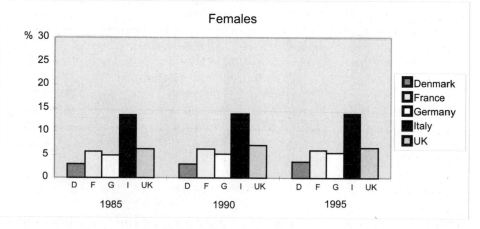

Figure 8.4 Self-employed workers as a percentage of the economically active population

Source: Eurostat (1985, 1990, 1995), Labour Force Survey for the European Union.
Note: Data for Germany pre-1991 refers to the Federal Republic, any later data refers to Germany including the New Länder.

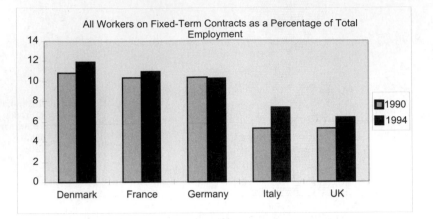

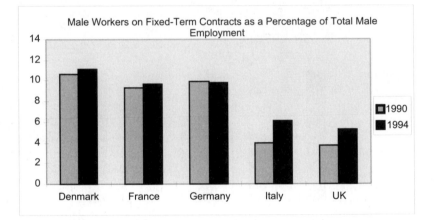

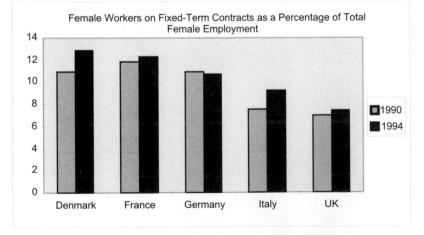

Figure 8.5   Workers on fixed-term contracts

Source: Trends; Changes in Employment, Analyses, Evaluation, No. 24 1996, series produced from the SYSDEM network.

Note: Data for Germany pre-1991 refers to the Federal Republic, any later data refers to Germany including the New Länder.

economically active female population, one in 25 of the economically active population in Italy still works on this basis (Figure 8.6). At the other extreme, in the UK, family working affects only 0.5 per cent of the economically active population, and in Denmark, Germany and France the figures are well under 2 per cent. Change here reflects declining employment in agriculture, together with trends away from family stability and towards greater female autonomy in some countries. Far more women than men are family workers, and only in Italy does family working affect significant numbers of men. Here it appears to be strongly linked to unemployment levels and to problems of insertion into the labour market for young workers. In Denmark, France and Germany, female family working has declined, and although only 1995 figures are available for the UK, there it is very low (although some is undoubtedly statistically invisible [Adkins, 1995:68–91]).

Technological and other changes affecting the organisation of employment

This chapter cannot outline the way all technological developments have affected patterns of employment, and debates about homeworking, teleworking and home-based working are not entered into. It can be observed, however, that while the potential for change in the organisation of employment is large, relatively little use has been made of technology to shift production to the home, notwithstanding important changes in the organisation of work in parts of the service sector and in manufacturing. The potential to break down barriers between male and female employment or between paid work and domestic work has not been fully exploited, and there is acknowledged difficulty in establishing reliable figures in this field.

Another notable development is the re-emergence of private domestic work (Yeandle, 1996). This has been documented for parts of the UK (Gregson and Lowe, 1994) and has been noted also in Germany (Rerrich, 1996). The use of the paid labour of women outside the family for childcare, cleaning and other domestic services by dual-earner families is a source of polarisation between women in societies where the state has not accepted responsibility for enabling parents to participate in the labour force. For Germany, Rerrich suggests that it is non-German women who are private domestic workers; in the UK they are often poor women in families in receipt of state benefit, or young women without other employment opportunities, including some non-EU nationals working as au pairs (Gregson and Lowe, 1994).

Discussion

Important changes are occurring in the labour markets of the selected countries in the final decades of the twentieth century. These are not temporary

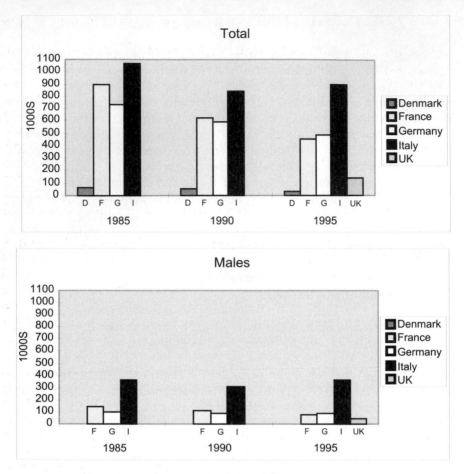

Data not available for UK 1985,1990 and Denmark Males 1985,1990

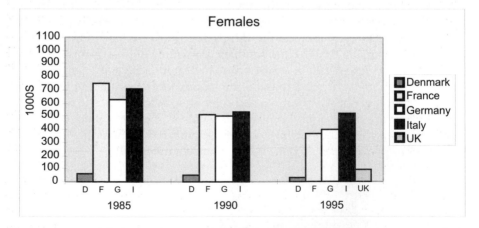

Figure 8.6   Total numbers employed in family work
Source: Eurostat (1985, 1990, 1995), Labour Force Survey for the European Union.

changes but major shifts in the social division and organisation of labour, likely to increase in complexity in the twenty-first century, despite probable continuities in occupational segregation by sex. Therborn has noted a trend towards 'deproletarianisation', that is, increasing non-agricultural self-employment (affecting Italy and in Britain) (Therborn, 1995:78), while Beck has argued that 'the new system of flexible pluralised underemployment and decentralised forms of work' is 'revolutionary', creating 'completely new *disequilibria of power* between the parties in the labour market and their interest organisations' (Beck, 1992:148). Feminist analysis also notes polarisation tendencies which fragment the categories 'male' and 'female', with some of the differences between women becoming at least as important as those between women and men.

Shifts towards more diversity in employment arrangements, and the consequent fragmentation of employees' and other workers' experience of that diversity, contributes to growing divisions between groups which have until relatively recently been mostly treated as homogeneous. This is particularly true of women. The study of women as a social group took off in the middle of the twentieth century as the focus of mainstream sociological work. Prior to this – particularly in the field of industrial sociology – research seemed to be directed almost exclusively to the social situation of men. At the same time, opportunities for women to determine some aspects of their own fate, or at least to be less subject to dominant ideological definitions of a woman's place, created new sources of differentiation between women. Developments in labour markets in the last quarter of the twentieth century both reflect and influence that differentiation. At the same time, new sources of variability in men's experience of work have come into view. Changes stemming from the economic crisis of the 1970s – 'the watershed in industrial history' (Therborn, 1995:71) – have created new divisions of social status and economic security between men. These new sources of differentiation overlay the divisions of class, status and power which dominated the preceding century. They are likely to mean changes in social experience at the personal, familial and societal level for everyone. They touch on individual autonomy and choice, on the domestic division of labour and the negotiation of household strategies as well as on the social distribution of labour, reward and opportunity.

Historically, the gender contract in the countries studied has centred on the allocation of a breadwinning role to men and a care-giving role to women. For most men, full adult status has been attained and socially validated through securing a secure, regular, income from employment or from family/self-employment. For women, marriage and motherhood, with the support of a husband, have been key goals for girls seeking to attain adult status. Pfau-Effinger has discussed the importance of 'housewife marriage' in the German case (1993), and all modern welfare regimes have been linked to the male breadwinner ideal: an ideal whose 'persistence, to varying extents, cuts across established typologies of welfare regimes' (Lewis, 1992:162). Lewis conceptualises 'strong' 'modified' and 'weak' male breadwinner countries, offering Britain, France and Sweden respectively as examples. Germany and Italy fit in the 'strong male breadwinner' category, too, with Denmark somewhere between the 'modified' and 'weak' models. If this analysis is supplemented with work on patterns of family obligation (conceptually indebted to Finch [1989] but carried forward by Millar and Warman's comparative study [1996]) it becomes possible to conceptualise sources of influence on the development of non-standard working, as in Table 8.2. This summarises conceptual developments in theorising the family/labour market/welfare state nexus, and incorporates the 'gender arrangement' (Pfau-Effinger, 1996), which draws on Connell's approach to gender relations. Connell sees the gender order in a given society as fluid, structured through the division of labour, but also through political and other forms of power and through the structure of interpersonal relations.

The key idea of this chapter is that non-standard working both stimulates and is stimulated by a complex of relations between labour markets, welfare systems, gender contracts (in both the family and the society) and the class system. Non-standard working is more than a dismantling of established employment relations in organised workforces in certain Western economies. It is an indicator of complex social change, and of change within the organisation of domestic life and relationships, with shifts in gender relations no less important than shifts in the sectoral distribution of employment or in employee–employer relations.

In the late twentieth century, Denmark and the Nordic countries, especially Sweden, have led the way from a family/marriage-based gendered division of labour and status towards the social validation of individual autonomy, with strong institutional support in the form of the welfare state. Gender divisions have not been eliminated in Denmark – indeed there is a very high level of occupational sex segregation in the Danish labour force, and Danish women continue to provide the majority of personal care for those in need of it. But the lifelong economic dependence of Danish women on an individual man – upon the status of wife – has been reduced. A large minority of Danish women now organise their family lives without a husband, sometimes for prolonged periods without a man at all. Their support, should it be needed, comes not so much from the family as from the state, but with an emphasis on self-maintenance, which favours a shift away from part-time employment (also affected by legal and unemployment benefit changes [Lind, 1997]), and towards equalisation in the labour market participation patterns of men and women.

This shift in family behaviour and in the supports offered to the 'individual autonomy' arrangement meshes with changes in the patterns of labour force participation in Denmark. These include a strong public sector offering support for working parents through the employment of mainly female labour,

Table 8.2 Factors relevant to the development of non-standard working arrangements

Country	Type of Male Breadwinner Regime	Type of Welfare State	Gender Arrangement	Patterning of Family Obligations	Sectoral Distribution (per cent) of Employment	1973	1994
Denmark	weak/modified	social-democratic	dual breadwinner/dual carer	individual autonomy	Agriculture Industry Services	10 34 57	5 27 68
France	modified	conservative-corporatist	[family economic] towards dual breadwinner/state carer	nuclear family	Agriculture Industry Services	11 40 49	5 27 68
Germany	strong	conservative-corporatist	male breadwinner/female carer	nuclear family	Agriculture Industry Services	7 47 45	3 38 59
Italy	strong	conservative-corporatist	[family economic] towards male breadwinner/female carer	extended family	Agriculture Industry Services	18 39 42	7 33 60
UK	strong	liberal/residual	male breadwinner/female carer	nuclear family	Agriculture Industry Services	3 42 55	2 26 72

Sources: OECD, 1996; Lewis, 1992; Esping-Anderson, 1990; Pfau-Effinger, 1993 and 1996; Millar and Warman, 1996.

an ideology of gender equality enshrined in educational practice and in legislation, and the emergence of a service sector based economy in which standardised employment patterns have become less advantageous to employers. These trends reinforce one another and promote a shift towards more fragmented labour market experience for Danish men and more integrated, albeit segregated, employment for Danish women. Indications that there is the beginning of a corresponding gender shift in the division of unpaid caring work reinforce the view that gender may be becoming a less important marker of labour market status difference. Paradoxically, it is divisions between women which seem likely to open up, notwithstanding the increased political resources which Danish women now command (Siim, 1993:46).

By contrast, the Italian situation is one of the continued invisibility and informality of much of women's work, recorded in 'family working', but disguised in agriculture, behind self-employment and in unpaid work within extended family networks. The social and political progress of Italian women has provided a push towards greater labour market participation by women, but it is still among the lowest of the OECD countries. Non-standard working is important in Italy partly because standard, Fordist, employment arrangements have never dominated the Italian labour market, due to the influence of Italian agricultural and family systems, and partly because new sources of flexibility have come into play in the late twentieth century.

The sources of non-standard employment in the UK and in Germany are rather different. There are differences between the two, but there are also important and shared sources of differentiation between female workers, which are stimulating growing demand for non-standard employment. Without comprehensive state support for dual career partnerships or for women's full-time employment, recourse has to be made to private solutions to the problem of how to deliver domestic labour. Whereas Denmark has found it crucial to respond to demand through public sector provision, financed primarily from local taxes (Andersen, 1993:119), creating many 'standard jobs' for women in the process, in the UK and in Germany,[5] private solutions have increasingly to be found. These involve the employment of non-standard workers who perform tasks of childcare, household cleaning and laundry, usually on a part-time basis, sometimes in the employ of private companies. In the UK, especially, the rapid expansion of part-time working in retail (Reeves, 1996), and the deregulation of shopping hours, has also been a response to women's reduced availability to shop during 'normal working hours'.

In France, the shift towards part-time employment but away from self-employment and family working, with increased fixed-term and temporary employment, reflects the difficult economic situation and high unemployment experienced, particularly in younger age groups. The history of state support for parents, with its roots in pro-natalist policy, and the long record of childcare provision (Hantrais, 1993) has led more mothers to choose full-time employment, contributing to breadwinning, while non-standard working arrangements have become familiar to those finding entry to the labour market difficult, or being eased out in the later years of their working life.

Non-standard working, then, is changing the face of labour force participation in Europe, although there are both old (agriculture, family systems) and new (financing of education, moves towards gender equality, restructuring of major industries, technological change, responses to dual career families) sources of these developments. Increasing social polarisation is a likely result of these changes, for they offer both opportunities and risks to the individuals and families concerned. There is a complex relationship between demographic change, industrial restructuring, new patterns of labour force participation and shifts in the relative power and autonomy of women. Both European policy and individual state measures need to be responsive to the risks of widening divisions between those able to capitalise on the opportunities which non-standard working affords, and those constrained by the limitations which labour market marginalisation imposes. There are important implications here for common policy approaches to non-standard employment within the EU, which will not produce uniform effects because of the differences in the contextual factors discussed in this chapter.

References

Adkins, L. (1995) *Gendered Work: Sexuality, Family and the Labour Market*, Buckingham: Open University Press.

Andersen, B.R. (1993) 'The Nordic Welfare State under Pressure: The Case of Denmark', *Policy and Politics*, 21: 2, 109–20.

Beck, U. (1992) *Risk Society: Towards a New Modernity*, London: Sage.

Benson, E. (1993) 'Employment Protection', in Gold, M. (ed.) *The Social Dimension: Employment Policy in the European Community*, Basingstoke: Macmillan.

Bielenski, H. (1994) *New Forms of Work Activity: Survey of Experience at Establishment Level in Eight European Countries*, Dublin: European Foundation for the Improvement of Living and Working Conditions.

Bimbi, F. (1993) 'Gender and the "Gift Relationship" and Welfare State Cultures in Italy', in Lewis, J. (ed.) *Women and State Policies in Europe*, Aldershot: Edward Elgar.

Blossfeld, H.-P., Giannelli, G. and Mayer, K.U. (1993) 'Is There a New Service Proletariat? The Tertiary Sector and Social Inequality in Germany', in Esping-Andersen, G. (ed.) *Changing Classes: Stratification and Mobility in Post-Industrial Societies*, London: Sage.

Chamberlayne, P. (1991) 'New Directions in Welfare? France, West Germany, Italy and Britain in the 1980s', in *Critical Social Policy*, 33: 5–21.

Chamberlayne, P. (1992) 'Income Maintenance and Institutional Forms: A Comparison of France, West Germany, Italy and Britain', *Policy and Politics*, 20: 4, 299–318.

Chamberlayne, P. (1993) 'Women and the State: Changes in Roles and Rights in France, West Germany, Italy and Britain, 1970–1990', in Lewis, J. (ed.) *Women and Social Policies in Europe*, Aldershot: Edward Elgar.

Connell, R.W. (1987) *Gender and Power: Society, the Person and Sexual Politics*, Cambridge: Polity Press.

Cousins, C. (1997) 'Non-Standard Employment in Europe: A Comparison of Recent Trends in the UK, Sweden, Germany and Spain', Paper presented to the Fifteenth Annual International Labour Process Conference, University of Edinburgh.

Cox, S. (1993) 'Equal Opportunities', in Gold, M. (ed.) *The Social Dimension: Employment Policy in the European Community*, Basingstoke: Macmillan.

Di Martino, V. (1995) 'Megatrends in Working Time', *Journal of European Social Policy*, 5: 3, 235–49.

Esping-Andersen, G. (1990) *The Three Worlds of Welfare Capitalism*, Cambridge: Polity Press.

Esping-Andersen, G., Assimakopoulou, Z. and van Kersbergen, K. (1993) 'Trends in Contemporary Class Structuration: A Six-Nation Comparison', in Esping Andersen, G. (ed.) *Changing Classes: Stratification and Mobility in Post-Industrial Societies*, London: Sage.

European Commission (1996) *Employment in Europe 1996*, Directorate General for Employment, Industrial Relations and Social Affairs, Luxembourg: Office for Official Publications of the European communities.

Eurostat (1985, 1990, 1995) *Labour Force Survey for the European Union*.

Eurostat (1995) *Eurostat Yearbook '95: A Statistical Eye on Europe 1983–1993*, Luxembourg: Office for Official Publications of the European Communities.

Fevre, R. (1991) 'Emerging "Alternatives" to Full-Time and Permanent Employment', in Brown, P. and Scase, R. (eds.) *Poor Work: Disadvantage and the Division of Labour*, Milton Keynes: Open University Press.

Finch, J. (1989) *Family Obligations and Social Change*, Cambridge: Polity.

Gregson, M. and Lowe, N. (1994) *Servicing the Middle Classes*, London: Routledge.

Jonung, C. and Persson, I. (1993) 'Women and Market Work: The Misleading Tale of Participation Rates in International Comparisons', *Work, Employment and Society*, 7: 2, 259–74.

Hantrais, L. (1993) 'Women, Work and Welfare in France', in Lewis, J. (ed.) *Women and State Policies in Europe*, Aldershot: Edward Elgar.

Lewis, J. (1992) 'Gender and the Development of Welfare Regimes', *Journal of European Social Policy*, 2: 3, 159–73.

Lind, J. (1997) 'The Social Benefits and Deficits of Flexibility: Unemployment and Non-Standard Work', paper presented to the Conference on *Work and Social Integration: Perspectives on Unemployment and Non-Standard Employment* (Organisers: Dept. of Sociology, University of Lund and Centre for Integration and Differentiation, University of Copenhagen), University of Lund, Sweden, May 1997.

Lovenduski, J. (1986) *Women and European Politics: Contemporary Feminism and Public Policy*, Brighton: Wheatsheaf.

Millar, J. and Warman, A. (1996) *Family Obligations in Europe*, London: Family Policy Studies Centre.

OECD (1996) *Employment Outlook: July 1996*, Paris: Organisation for Economic Co-operation and Development.

Orloff, A.S. (1993) 'Gender and the Social Rights of Citizenship: The Comparative Analysis of Gender Relations and Welfare States', *American Sociological Review*, 58: 303–28.

Ostner, I. (1993) 'Slow Motion: Women, Work and the Family in Germany', in Lewis, J. (ed.) *Women and Social Policies in Europe: Work, Family and the State*, Aldershot: Edward Elgar.

Pfau-Effinger, B. (1993) 'Modernisation, Culture and Part-Time Employment: The Example of Finland and West Germany', *Work, Employment and Society*, 3: 7, 383–410.

Pfau-Effinger, B. (1996) 'Theorising Cross-National Differences in the Labour Force Participation of Women', paper presented at the Seminar on Gender Relations, Employment and Occupational Segregation: a Cross-National Study, University of Leicester.

Pollert, A. (ed.) (1991) *Farewell to Flexibility?*, Oxford: Basil Blackwell.

Rainbird, H. (1993) 'Vocational Education and Training', in Gold, M. (ed.) *The Social Dimension: Employment Policy in the European Community*, Basingstoke: Macmillan.

Reeves, D. (1996) 'Women Shopping', in Booth, C., Darke, J. and Yeandle, S. (eds) *Changing Places: Women's Lives in the City*, London: Paul Chapman.

Rerrich, M. (1996) 'Modernizing the Patriarchal Family in West Germany', *European Journal of Women's Studies*, 3: 1, 27–37.

Scheiwe, K. (1994) 'Labour Market, Welfare State and Family Institutions: The Links to Mothers' Poverty Risks. A Comparison between Belgium, Germany and the United Kingdom', *European Journal of Social Policy*, 4: 3, 201–24.

Schömann, K., Rogowski, R. and Kruppe, T. (1994) 'Fixed Term Contracts in the European Union', *European Observatory Policies*, No. 24, inforMISEP, European Commission.

Siim, B. (1993) 'The Gendered Scandinavian Welfare States: The Interplay between Women's Roles as Mothers, Workers and Citizens in Denmark', in Lewis, J. (ed.) *Women and State Policies in Europe*, Aldershot: Edward Elgar.

Snyder, P. (1992) *The European Women's Almanac*, London: Scarlet Press.

SYSDEM *Trends*, Employment Observatory Trends: The Bulletin of the European System of Documentation on Employment, No. 24.

Teague, P. (1989) *The European Community: the Social Dimension. Labour Market Policies for 1992*, London: Kogan Page.

Therborn, G. (1995) *European Modernity and Beyond: the Trajectory of European Societies 1945–2000*, London: Sage.

Titmuss, R. (1958) *Essays on the Welfare State*, London: Allen and Unwin.

Wallace, C. (1994) 'Education and Training', in Clasen, J. and Freeman, R. (eds) *Social Policy in Germany*, New York, London: Harvester Wheatsheaf.

Watson, G. (1992) 'Hours of Work in Great Britain and Europe: Evidence from the UK and European Labour Force Surveys', *Employment Gazette*, 11: 539–58.

Yeandle, S. (1996) 'Change in the Gender Composition of the Labour Force: Recent Analyses and their Significance for Social Theory', Centre for Regional, Economic and Social Research, Sheffield Hallan University, Paper GW7.

Notes

1   My thanks to Alison Herrington who analysed the statistical data.
2   The ELFS is 'the only source of data on employment, unemployment and related variables which is comparable and complete for all Member States . . . based on a survey of households . . . uses a common set of questions . . .' (European Commission, 1996:163). ELFS data may differ from national data.
3   The UK 1997 General Election produced a marked increase in women Members of Parliament.
4   Lind's (1997) figures differ, but trends are in the same direction.
5   Ostner notes the rapid erosion of ' "Errungenschaften" – child and mother centred policies [of the former DDR]' (1993:93).

9   Global Restructuring and Non-Standard Work in Newly Industrialised Economies: The Organisation of Flexible Production in Hong Kong and Taiwan

Tai-lok Lui and Tony Man-yiu Chiu

Introduction

The post-war economic performance of the East Asian newly industrialised economies – Hong Kong, Singapore, South Korea and Taiwan – has been remarkable. This so-called 'East Asian miracle' has sparked off a race among observers – academic and journalist – to find the winning formula behind their success. Many different accounts have been offered, including macro-level analysis of global economic restructuring, micro-level discussion of economic culture, the role of the capitalist developmental state and the forces of the market.[1] Yet, despite the fact that research on East Asian development has come to constitute a growing industry of its own incorporating a wide array of research areas, few attempts have been made to look at the organisation of production in these societies.[2] This neglect is problematic and reflects the lacunae in the existing literature on East Asian development. Very often, the focus of discussion is placed on mechanisms external to the organisation of economic activity, such as the developmental state, economic culture, global division of labour or the market. The implication is that one can unravel the secrets of economic success in the East Asian economies without knowing the organisational basis of the economic activities on which competitiveness rests. Differently put, most of the existing studies of East Asian development focus on various structural, institutional and cultural dimensions of the economic environment and tend to neglect the basic organising processes of economic activity. Failure to develop an analysis of the 'East Asian miracle' from below raises basic questions about our understanding of economic development and encourages an uncritical perspective on the state, Asian management, economic culture and the market. Much has been said about the structural and institutional configurations of rapid industrialisation in terms of state intervention, the role of the family in managing economic transactions and organisational development, entrepreneurial drive and so on. Few studies, however, really take a serious look at interactions between the structuring of the global economy and local economic organisations; patriarchy and capitalism at the workplace; and family and work in the structuring of business and labour supply. Indeed, more attention is given to the conditions facilitating industrial development than to the actual organisation of industry and work.

This chapter is an attempt to fill in this gap in the literature. It is based upon a review of current research on the 'satellite factory system' and the practice of non-standard work in Hong Kong and Taiwan. The expression 'satellite factory system' (*weixing gongchang*) is used in Taiwan to denote 'a hierarchical subcontracting manufacturing that consists of numerous small-scale, family-centred, and export-oriented factories' (Hsiung, 1996:1; see also Hamilton, 1997:284–5). It serves to capture the interconnectedness among the subcontractors and their links to the wider world market. We argue that the use of flexible, non-standard work has played an important part in the facilitation of rapid industrialisation on the basis of labour-intensive, export-led manufacturing. Like other contributors to this volume, our discussion of 'atypical' or non-standard work covers a wide range of forms of employment, such as casual and part-time work, homeworking, unpaid labour of family members, contract labour and self-employment (see also Michon, 1981; Rodgers, 1989). First, we shall analyse the practice of various flexible production strategies in Hong Kong and Taiwan in the context of their articulation with the global economy. Second, we look at the hidden inequalities in the social organisation of flexible work in these economies. Third, we discuss the limitations of such flexible production strategies in the facilitation of industrial upgrading and their implications for industrial restructuring. In the context of this discussion we conclude that ongoing restructuring processes in Hong Kong and Taiwan, reflected in the increase in offshore production, exemplifies the precarious position of flexible workers.

Global Commodity Chains and Non-Standard Work

The success stories of the economies of Hong Kong and Taiwan are well documented. Given the limits of this short chapter, we shall not dwell upon the details of economic development in Hong Kong and Taiwan (see Chiu, Ho and Lui, 1997; Hamilton, 1997). Suffice to say, Hong Kong was primarily an entrepôt prior to its industrialisation, whereas Taiwan's economic development started with import-substitution and subsequently export-led industrialisation. Despite their differences, manufacturing industries in Hong Kong and Taiwan are similar. They are export-oriented, run by small local capitals and connected with the global economy through the intermediaries of international buyers, sourcing agents and local import-export houses. In the early stage of development, manufacturers in these two economies capitalised on supplies of cheap labour and relatively low production costs to break into global markets of consumer non-durables. Since then they have developed their strengths in manufacturing production and have been able to sustain industrial growth by being flexible and responsive to changes in the world economy.

Our discussion of the practice of non-standard work needs to be understood in the context of the interface between the organisation of production and the political, economic and institutional circumstances of East Asian development. The growing literature on the organisation of commodity chains in the global economy is useful here (see, especially, Gereffi and Korzeniewicz, 1994). In Gereffi's (1994) analysis of global commodity chains, two distinct types of governance structures have been identified; namely 'producer-driven' and 'buyer-driven' commodity chains. The former is best exemplified by direct investments carried out by multinational corporations in developing countries, with transnational corporations retaining a centralised control of the production process including backward and forward linkages. This type of governance structure is commonly found among capital- and technology-intensive industries, such as automobiles, electrical machinery and aircraft. The latter refers to those industries co-ordinated by large retailers, brand-named merchandisers and trading firms. These commercial intermediaries link up manufacturers in developing countries with the global market. The key feature of this type of governance structure is that production is decentralised. Local manufacturers are original equipment manufacturing (OEM) producers. That is, their main task lies in handling assembly processes according to the specifications provided by trading companies, overseas retail chains or sourcing agents, who also take care of distribution and marketing of finished products produced by the OEM manufacturers. Such a form of trade-led arrangement is common in labour-intensive, consumer-goods industries like footwear, garments, toys and consumer electronics. Nowadays, many of the leading companies in sports footwear and fashion garments 'are not "manufacturers" because they have no factories. Rather, these companies are "merchandisers" that design and/or market, but not make, the branded products they sell' (Gereffi, 1994:99).

In Hong Kong and Taiwan, many of the local manufacturers – particularly those in the manufacturing of garments, shoes and toys – are connected to the global economy along 'buyer-driven' commodity chains via global buyers and local trading houses. This characteristic is manifested in the predominance of small, local industrial capitals. Thus, in Hong Kong in 1995, 88.5 per cent of all manufacturing establishments employed less than 20 persons. In the same year there were only 430 manufacturing companies either wholly or partly owned by foreign interests (see Industry Department, 1996). In Taiwan in 1987, 98.7 per cent of all manufacturing establishments were classified as small and medium enterprises and, in the same year, 89.9 per cent of all investments in manufacturing were of local origin (see Chung-Hua Institution for Economic Research, 1993:43, 95). A further feature of both economies is the role of traders and buyers as intermediaries connecting local manufacturers to the global economy. In their study of 294 small and medium manufacturing establishments in Hong Kong in 1987, survey findings suggested that less than 10 per cent (8.9 per cent) of the respondents had orders direct from overseas (Sit and Wong, 1989:150; for more on commercial subcontracting, see Chiu and Lui, 1995). In Taiwan, Skoggard's study of shoemaking factories in 1986 reported that only 7.2 per cent of shoe manufacturers had their own sales arrangements directly with overseas retailers (1996:74–5; see also Hsing, 1997). Both Hong Kong's and Taiwan's manufacturers have little control over the marketing of their outputs. They primarily serve the role of subcontractors in the 'buyer-driven' global commodity chains.

Such a mode of incorporation into the global economy has its effect on the structuring of production in Hong Kong and Taiwan (Poon, 1993). 'Buyer-driven' commodity chains entail a governance structure characterised by 'decentralised industrialisation'. These provide local manufacturers with more room for manoeuvre to develop their own production. The limited role of multinational corporations in the local economy means that local manufacturers are less directly subordinated to the centralised control of foreign investments over production and are given more opportunities to shape the structure of their industries. In addition, their concentration on labour-intensive production facilitates their entry into manufacturing. As a result, petty entrepreneurship is vibrant and interfirm linkages among small firms constitute a significant feature of the organisational ecology of the manufacturing sector.

However, at the same time, 'buyer-driven' global commodity chains have the effect of confining local manufacturers to the role of OEM producers. The major production processes handled by local manufacturers are those of assembly and cosmetic product design. 'Buyer-driven' global commodity chains facilitate the growth of subcontracting activity among local manufacturers, including specialised and capacity subcontractors. While the tasks they handle may vary according to the requirements of the technical division of labour, subcontractors are primarily manufacturers assigned to work on the assembly process. Few would be asked to provide innovative or technologically sophisticated inputs. Indeed, this mode of governance structure of global production is developed upon the basis that the core economies and their leading firms retain control over higher value-added processes of commodity production and circulation (i.e. product design, research and development, and marketing). Those in the semi-periphery and the periphery are locked into the role of manufacturer and are dependent on the former to gain access to the global market. Since most of the local manufacturers are OEM producers handling the assembly processes, the principal firms in the local economy can benefit from subcontracting production to the secondary firms. By these means, they are able to expand their production capacity, cope with seasonal fluctuations and spread the risk of producing in volatile product markets. In short, although there are various kinds of constraints imposed upon the local manufacturers, in general they have the opportunity of developing a relatively autonomous structure of industrial production in their own economies. It is true that local manufacturers are unlikely to assume the role of supplier to dominant multinational corporations operating in their economies and subject to tight controls by foreign investors. Nevertheless, there are ample opportunities for small local industrial capital to look for orders from abroad, mediated through local import-export houses and subcontracted by larger local firms. The result is a proliferation of small local firms in manufacturing.

In Hong Kong and Taiwan, there are a number of tiers of subcontracting activity in manufacturing production. In the case of garment making, various kinds of non-standard work have been used for production (see Lui, 1994). These include internal contracting (mainly for cutting, buttoning and ironing), capacity subcontracting (for finishing an entire garment to the handling of some processes of assembly), part-time work (for assembly) and homeworking (mainly for assembly). In the earlier period of industrial development, the use of non-standard work offered employers the opportunity to reduce production costs, including evasion of payments to labour as required by employment regulations. More recently, the use of non-standard work has been adopted for the purposes of coping with labour shortages and enhancing the flexibility of production (Ka, 1993; Hsiung, 1996; Lui and Chiu, 1993). As a result of global restructuring in garment and fashion retailing and the pace of change in fashion consumption, garment manufacturers are required to be responsive to rapid changes in the retail market (Ward, 1991). In other words, they have to be flexible producers, capable of dealing with seasonal – and now, more often, subseasonal – fluctuations in the flow of orders and production scheduling in order to maintain their ability to secure orders from global sourcing agents and buyers.

Networking among local manufacturers, contractors (*bao gong*) and homeworkers is built upon trust and repetitive exchange. There is no need here to romanticise business networking in Chinese societies. As noted in various studies of subcontracting activity in Hong Kong (Sit, 1983) and Taiwan (Hsiung, 1996): 'There is no long-term relationship among local producers, trading companies, and international buyers. While international buyers are constantly searching around the globe for comparable products made by the cheapest available labor, trading companies form only fragile bonds with local producers' (Hsiung, 1996:67). Flux and uncertainty in product markets are crucial to the shaping of economic relationships among overseas buyers, trading houses and local manufacturers.

While *guanxi* (social relations) and trust do matter and can be effective lubricants for the facilitation of economic exchange, the division of labour among OEM producers constitutes an effective mechanism for the development of repeated exchanges among subcontractors. Two points are worthy of note. First, networks consist of large numbers of subcontractors competing for orders, each of whom has to prove him/herself reliable. Information on subcontractors is easily available and the use of subcontracting is based on insiders' knowledge of their own trade which constitutes a kind of folk wisdom. Second, without invoking the notions of trust and *guanxi*, there are plentiful supplies of reliable contractors, subcontracting firms and homeworkers. In this regard, it is interesting to note that the cultivation of relational contracting is always selective (Hsiung, 1996; Lui, 1994; Zhao, 1993). Many manufacturers have chosen a group of reliable contractors, subcontractors and homeworkers to handle production on a regular basis. The latter constitute what might be described as the 'core flexible workforce', that is, labour which the employing firms can rely upon in urgent and contingent situations which is available on a long-term basis. At the same time, there is a highly 'casualised flexible workforce' that employing firms would use only when required. Irrespective of their status, contractors, subcontractors and homeworkers are all in a dependent position and need to prove themselves reliable in order to maintain adequate orders to support their production.

Thus, among these labour-intensive OEM producers, there exist many interdependencies and interlinkages surrounding non-standard work. The essential character of this form of flexible production is that of numerical (or quantitative) flexibility. Given the limited range of tasks to be handled by these OEM producers, functional division of labour is relatively restricted. In this context, flexibility is primarily about the assembly of products and the use of labour to deal with volatile markets. It is also about spreading risks, and evading labour protection of legislation, for the purposes of handling changes in fashion and fluctuations in the flow of orders. Homeworkers stand at the end of these chains of non-standard work. Larger firms spread their risks of production by subcontracting. Subcontractors, in turn, pass on the risk by contracting out to homeworkers. The latter, under the existing legislation, are not considered as employees and thus fall outside the scope of labour protection.

Hidden Inequalities under Flexible Production

As we have noted earlier, quantitative flexibility is an important strategy for local manufacturers in coping with flux and uncertainty in the global market.

Subcontracting and the use of various forms of non-standard work are essential components of this strategy. In Hong Kong and Taiwan, the practice of informal work has created opportunities for petty entrepreneurship. Many manufacturers start as subcontractors or gang leaders involved in internal contracting. In Taiwan, there is a notion of 'black hands becoming their own bosses', originally referring to motorcycle or other mechanics who set up their own workshops in order subsequently to become petty entrepreneurs (Shieh, 1992). In Hong Kong, there are numerous cases of 'briefcase entrepreneurs' who start their manufacturing businesses by getting an order from abroad or from a local firm and carry out their project without factories of their own. They are completely reliant upon subcontractors and homeworkers for production. Such 'briefcase entrepreneurs' more resemble agents from trading companies than either manufacturers (see, for example, Vong, 1993) or industrial workers who seek to become small manufacturers in their own right (for survey findings, see Sit and Wong, 1989). The reality behind these dreams of business success is that, while firms grow rapidly in a booming market, they are also vulnerable to market changes. Also, perhaps more importantly, such petty entrepreneurship is buttressed by the exploitation of a flexible workforce, family labour and gender inequalities. Current research on the 'satellite factory system' in Taiwan, as well as on small workshops and homeworking in Hong Kong, shows that the dynamism of petty entrepreneurship and the practice of non-standard work are built upon gender inequalities and power differentials in the labour market and in the family.

In the period of industrial take-off, local manufacturers in Hong Kong and Taiwan drew upon young daughters from working class and/or rural peasant families as the main source of cheap labour (Salaff, 1981; Kung, 1983). Women workers were recruited as unskilled and semi-skilled labour in large factories run by multinational corporations or small local workshops. For instance, between 1961 and 1971 the number of women production workers in Hong Kong increased by 87.8 per cent, a figure significantly higher than the rate of increase of all production workers (39.3 per cent) in the same period. Most of these new recruits to factory work were young single women who, primarily in order to finance the family economy, had to look for jobs in the growing manufacturing sector. It has been observed that many of these working daughters started employment at an early age because their parents were eager to raise money to support the education of their sons. The main channel through which these factory girls could study in evening schools was by becoming economically independent (Salaff, 1981; Kung, 1983). Many employers found them to be disciplined workers, capable of overtime, handling rush jobs and providing a source of casual or contract labour to cope with seasonal fluctuations. In short, they provided the labour supply for flexible workshop production.[3]

Studies of women workers in Hong Kong and Taiwan in the 1970s largely concentrated on the first cohort of factory girls, prior to their reaching the age of marriage (Hsiung, 1996:4). Further research on women working in the manufacturing sector has led researchers to explore very different work milieu. Hsiung went to Taiwan's 'small factories in rice fields, sweatshops on the back streets and alleys, and families' living rooms' (1996:12), while Lui (1994) visited women homeworkers and those who organised home-based work in high-rise government housing blocks. Of course, it is wrong to assume that homeworking in Hong Kong and Taiwan only emerged in the 1980s. Homeworking has long been an integral part of the manufacturing system in these newly industrialised economies (Lui, 1994:53). What these studies of female workers in the 1980s shows is that hidden home-based work has been unduly neglected in discussions of industrial development and the situation of women workers in the East Asian economies. Furthermore, because most of these married women homeworkers were factory workers prior to their withdrawal from the labour market, they constitute an important source of experienced labour for the manufacturing sector. Studies of homeworking in Hong Kong and Taiwan show that most female homeworkers are recruited to handle jobs such as garment machining or assembling the components of toys or electronic products. Nevertheless, some are employed as skilled workers to produce an entire fashion garment or to produce samples and prototypes (on different types of jobs and job-ladders in the homeworking labour market (see Ka, 1993:108–9; Lui, 1994:162–3). Some employers regard these women homeworkers, especially those handling jobs of a higher skill level, as part of their regular workforce. However, that said, it should be noted that the majority of the women homeworkers are employed as flexible workers to cope with flux and uncertainty in the process of production. Furthermore, women homeworkers can be flexibly employed because they are not covered by the labour legislation (Hsiung, 1996; Lui, 1994).

Most female homeworkers come from working-class backgrounds with the objective of earning more money to finance their family economy. Since many have to stay at home to take care of their children, they shoulder the responsibilities of housework, childcare, and paid employment (Hsiung, 1996; Lui, 1994). Such a family-based strategy is used by many working-class households to tackle the demands of housework and childcare, on the one hand, and finance, on the other. There are also cases of women homeworkers moving from homeworking to become middle-persons in the labour contracting processes – and subsequently becoming petty entrepreneurs in collaboration with their husbands (Lui, 1994; Shieh, 1992). In these cases, however, they have to continue to shoulder both domestic responsibilities and responsibilities for paid work. Moreover, their role is subordinated to the larger project of the family, which is often defined in patriarchal terms.

The employment of homeworkers is one of the strategies used by small manufacturers to enhance their production capacity and at the same time to maintain their flexibility in dealing with instability in securing orders from larger factories or local trading companies. In addition to the employment of homeworkers, many local small manufacturers run their businesses by mobilising their family members to assist in management and production. While it is true to say that husbands, wives, sons and daughters are all often mobilised in the family business project, the use of unpaid family workers is gender-specific. Hsiung (1996:41) shows that in 1986 women comprised 69.3 per cent of all unpaid family workers in the manufacturing sector of Taiwan. In Hong Kong, women constituted 74.0 per cent of the pool of unpaid family workers in 1996 (Census and Statistics Department, 1997:98). It is essential to recognise that the family in Chinese societies still is patrilineal. The father plays a critical role in organising the family business. On his death/retirement, this role is passed down to his sons. Even when wives and daughters go out to take up paid work in the labour market or become unpaid family workers in the family firm, they are expected to contribute to the family economy and to support various family plans. Their role is to support the larger family project – for example, educating their brothers or financing and supporting the family business. As pointed out by Hsiung, 'Taiwan's export-led economy has created many opportunities for men to become employers, while the new opportunities open to women are mainly as wage workers' (1996:42). When the wives and the daughters participate in their family business and take up homework as unpaid family workers, their own personal careers are subordinated to other commitments.

The same situation characterises the role of the wife (*lao ban liang* or *tou jia liang*) in Chinese family firms. While wives are often active participants in the family business and quite often co-manage workshops (see Shieh, 1992:195–6; Ka, 1993:90–91), the division of labour between husbands and wives within the workshop reflects their roles at home: 'Most of the internal affairs of the workshop are handled by me [the *lao ban liang*]. External affairs like delivery, storage, and finance are handled by my husband' (Ka, 1993:91).

The authority of the *lao ban liang* derives from her status as the spouse of the boss and she is the boss's most trusted partner in business. Nevertheless, her role is essentially managing the family business project – it belongs to the boss's family.

In short, whether they take up overtime work, contract labour or homework commissioned by local factories – or whether they assist management and production of their family businesses – women workers are dedicated to work for larger family projects rather than their own personal careers.

Industrial Restructuring and the Precariousness of Non-Standard Work

Labour-intensive OEM production in Hong Kong and Taiwan is difficult to upgrade, both in terms of enhancing its technological sophistication and of shifting its focus towards the higher end of the commodity chain (i.e. to product design and marketing). This difficulty is best understood in the light of the above discussion of global commodity chains, petty entrepreneurship, quantitative flexibility strategy and the perpetuation of labour-intensive production. The 'satellite factory system' offers local manufacturers the advantages of flexibility and maintaining low-cost production in the context of labour-intensive manufacturing. However, due to a continuous rise in production costs (mainly labour and land), local manufacturers find it difficult to maintain their competitiveness. Other newly industrialised economies with lower production costs are catching up, particularly those in Southeast Asia such as Thailand, Malaysia and Vietnam. In consequence, manufacturing in Hong Kong and Taiwan has undergone a restructuring process. Increasingly, labour-intensive manufacturers have adopted a strategy of plant relocation (for Hong Kong, see Chiu, Ho and Lui, 1997; for Taiwan, see Hsiung, 1996). In the case of Hong Kong, plant relocation has brought about a drastic decline in manufacturing employment. Between 1987 and 1995 there was a displacement of some 489000 employees from the manufacturing sector, a drop of more than a half of the manufacturing workforce (see Chiu and Lui, 1995; Industry Department, 1996). Meanwhile, in Taiwan employment in manufacturing dropped from 2635000 in 1986 to 2449000 in 1995. While this represents a mere 7.1 per cent decrease in the overall manufacturing labour force (Executive Yuan, 1996:217), when we look at employment figures for the labour-intensive industries the restructuring effect is evident. In 1986 the number of persons engaged in labour-intensive industries was 1469000. By 1995 the figure had fallen to 1049000, representing a drop of 28.6 per cent (Executive Yuan, 217).

> The pace of workers' displacement increased significantly in 1995, reflecting a new trend of development that under the pressure of labour shortage and soaring wages manufacturers of labour-intensive industries either reduce their scale of business, close their production, or move offshore and such industries are undergoing contraction. The employment figures in labour-intensive industries dropped from 57.5 per cent in 1978 to 42.8 per cent in 1995, a decrease of 14.7 per cent. Meanwhile, the employment figures in more technologically sophisticated capital-intensive industries grew from 42.5 per cent in 1978 to 57.2 per cent in 1995 (Executive Yuan, 1996:218).

In Hong Kong, de-industrialisation has driven many production workers out of the manufacturing sector and massive plant relocation has reshaped the interfirm networks of subcontracting and other forms of informal work. In the process of labour market restructuring, it is interesting to observe that, despite a reduction in the employment of production operatives (a decrease of 43 per cent between 1981 and 1991), most manufacturing industries have experienced an increase in their employment of non-operative employees (a growth of 11 per cent in the period 1981–91 for the manufacturing sector) (Census and Statistics Department, 1993:119). These non-operative employees are engaged in 'supporting services such as sourcing of raw materials, product design, production management and engineering, marketing and so on' (Census and Statistics Department, 1993:120). Such a change in employment mix shows the general trend of production reorganisation in the face of changes in the business environment. Particularly, '[f]or industries where outward processing activities are prominent, this also reflects the increasing role of local industries in providing technical support to the production processes relocated to China' (Census and Statistics Department, 1993:120).

At present, given the dearth of research on relocated firms, it is difficult to estimate the impact of relocation on the structure of local production. Tentatively, we see that relocation of larger firms has forced many subcontractors to follow and to move their plants to South China (Vong, 1993). Currently available information does not allow us to talk firmly about a relocation of subcontracting networks across the border. However, Vong's (1993) exploratory study of relocated firms shows that there are, at least, two options for Hong Kong's manufacturers. One is to relocate and increase the extent of their production integration (vertical and/or horizontal). The other is to reproduce a subcontracting network with original subcontractors or local Chinese factories in the Pearl River Delta. However, in both options, Hong Kong will function as a strategic centre for the co-ordination of production and, more importantly, for business networking with global buyers. Hence, the role of Hong Kong as a production base is weakened. Based upon such observations, it is not unreasonable for us to assume that the established chains of non-standard work have been reshaped, making contractors, subcontractors and particularly homeworkers very vulnerable to market changes. Indeed, in her study of the restructuring strategies of garment manufacturers, Lai (1997) found that those factories which have not relocated are seeking support from subcontractors in the Pearl River Delta. In other words, given the extent of relocation and the availability of cheap labour in South China, when Hong Kong manufacturers have to look for new sources of flexible labour, they are likely to move across the border rather than recruit locally.

The transformation of Hong Kong into a business networking centre has differential impacts on the local labour market. As noted earlier, production relocation has brought about a displacement of some 489 000 manual workers from manufacturing. Further reduction of the size of manufacturing employment is projected because of massive relocation of industrial plants to Mainland China. Workers displaced by industrial restructuring tend to be female, older, less-educated and less-skilled (cf. Census and Statistics Department, 1996). The impact of industrial restructuring on the local labour market is mediated by existing social divisions. Local labour organisations have expressed concerns about rising unemployment among marginalised workers. Given their lack of formal educational credentials and restricted experience of working outside the manufacturing sector, displaced industrial workers experience great difficulties in finding new jobs. At the time of writing, there are no official statistics that allow us to comment on the pattern of job shift in the context of recent restructuring processes in the manufacturing sector, although some tentative findings do exist (see, for example, Chiu and Lee, 1997; Ngo, 1994). These suggest that many retrenched women workers can only find new jobs in the lower tiers of the labour market in the service sector. Quite a number of them have become part-timers in fast-food chain stores or janitors. Their experiences of transition from manufacturing to services often means moving down to lower-paying and insecure jobs in a casualised labour market.

Gender differences in life chances after displacement are also significant. In 1995 a telephone survey of 1145 workers, all of whom were employed in manufacturing five years prior to interview, showed that male production workers were more likely to keep their jobs in the manufacturing sector (Chiu and Lee, 1997:758). Whereas 55.7 per cent of the male respondents suggested that they had stayed in manufacturing, only 28.5 per cent of women respondents had been able to do so. Not only do they have difficulty in keeping their manufacturing jobs, female respondents are also more likely to exit from full-time employment (30.9 per cent compared with 5.6 per cent of male respondents) and to have problems in finding full-time work (26.7 per cent compared with 12.8 per cent of male respondents). Given such a process of labour market adjustment in Hong Kong, women workers in general, and women homeworkers in particular, are pushed towards disadvantaged positions in the labour market.

Labour-intensive industries in Taiwan have also undergone a restructuring process. Unlike Hong Kong, Taiwan is still able to develop new and competitive local manufacturing industries. However, similar to the situation in Hong Kong, many labour-intensive manufacturers have relocated their plants offshore (on relocation to China, see Hsing, 1996). Their new role is one of 'triangular manufacturing', that is, they receive orders from abroad and the production is done offshore (see Gereffi, 1994:113–14). Upon her revisit to Taiwan in 1992, Hsiung found that the satellite factories she once researched had become 'sunset' factories (1996:148–56). She looked for the six factories where she had interviewed in 1989–92 and found only four were still in the same line of production. Hsiung also revisited several homeworker informants and reported that most had experienced difficulties in maintaining their working lives. Official statistics inform us that in 1995 among a total population of 118 000 unemployed people, 50 000 had previously been production and manual workers (Executive Yuan, 1995:145). Generally speaking, those who have worked in manufacturing as production workers were found to be vulnerable to unemployment (Executive Yuan, 1995:142–5). The impacts of industrial restructuring and relocation are perhaps well described by Hsiung (1996:151). In her revisit to Taiwan, mentioned above, she found 'the massive flourishing of the sex industry' in the community. The social and economic environment of the community had changed drastically and her informants worked in providing services to young women involved in the growing sex business. What was once a growing area for small factories and family business had been transformed by this restructuring process. Not only had the economic structure undergone rapid change, but also the outlook of the community had been affected.

Conclusion

This chapter has sought to unravel the hidden aspects of economic success in the East Asian newly industrialised economies. We have tried to locate the 'satellite factory system' in Hong Kong and Taiwan in the context of 'buyer-driven global commodity chains'. We have suggested that this, in turn, provides local manufacturers with a flexible production system which facilitated rapid economic development. Being confined to the role of OEM producers, manufacturers in Hong Kong and Taiwan find it difficult to get onto a 'high road' of upgraded industrial production. As a result of being locked into labour-intensive production, when subject to competitive pressures they are driven to relocate factories and businesses in offshore locations. We have also sought to demonstrate some of the ways in which such a system of flexible production rests upon the exploitation of family – and in particular female – labour. The failure of such labour-intensive industries to upgrade themselves poses further problems for women employees and homeworkers. The case of Hong Kong best illustrates the precarious position of flexible workers. When employers find new sources of cheap labour and different production options – such as subcontractors across the border – they quickly move offshore and abandon the local flexible workforce.

References

Applebaum, R. and Henderson, J. (eds) (1992) *States and Development in the Asian Pacific Rim*, Newbury Park: Sage Publications.

Balassa, B. (1988) 'Lessons of East Asian Development: An Overview', *Economic Development and Cultural Change*, 36: 273–90.

Census and Statistics Department (1993) 'Structural Changes in Manufacturing Industries 1981–1991', in *Hong Kong Monthly Digest of Statistics*, September: 113–23.

Census and Statistics Department (1996) 'Worker Displacement', in *Social Data Collected by the General Household Survey: Special Topics Report No. 13*, Hong Kong: Government Printer.

Census and Statistics Department (1997) *1996 Population By-Census: Main Tables*, Hong Kong: Government Printer.

Chen, C.H. (1994) *Cooperative Networks and the Structure of Everyday Life*, Taipei: Luen Chin Publications (in Chinese).

Cheng, L. and Gereffi, G. (1994) 'The Informal Economy in East Asian Development', *International Journal of Urban and Regional Research*, 18: 2, 194–219.

Chiu, S., Ho, K.C. and Lui, T.L. (1997) *City-States in the Global Economy: Industrial Restructuring in Hong Kong and Singapore*, Boulder: Westview Press.

Chiu, S. and Lee, K.C. (1997) 'After the Hong Kong Miracle: Women Workers under Industrial Restructuring', *Asian Survey*, 37: 8, 752–70.

Chiu, S. and Lui, T.L. (1995) 'Hong Kong: Unorganized Industrialism', in Clark, G. and Kim, W.B. (eds) *Asian NIEs and the Global Economy*, Baltimore: Johns Hopkins University Press.

Cho, U. and Koo, H. (1983) 'Capital Accumulation, Women's Work, and Informal Economies in Korea', *Working Papers on Women in International Development No. 21*, Michigan State University.

Chu, Y.W. (1992) 'Informal Work in Hong Kong', *International Journal of Urban and Regional Research*, 16: 3, 420–41.

Chung-Hua Institution for Economic Research (1993) *The Overall Environment and the Development of Taiwan's Small and Medium Enterprises*, Taipei: Bo Hai Tang (in Chinese).

Deyo, F. (1989) *Beneath the Miracle*, Berkeley: University of California Press.

Executive Yuan (1996) *Economic Annual Report: Changes and Adjustments in the Economic Structure*, Taipei: Executive Yuan (in Chinese).

Gereffi, G. (1994) 'The Organization of Buyer-driven Global Commodity Chains: how US retailers shape overseas production networks', in Gereffi, G. and Korzeniewicz, M. (eds).

Gereffi, G. and Korzeniewicz, M. (eds) (1994) *Commodity Chains and Global Capitalism*, Westport: Praeger.

Hamilton, G. (1997) 'Organization and Market Processes in Taiwan's Capitalist Economy', in Orru, M., Biggart, N.W. and Hamilton, G. (eds) *The Economic Organization of East Asian Capitalism*, Thousand Oaks: Sage Publications.

Henderson, J. (1989) *The Globalisation of High Technology Production*, London: Routledge.

Hsing, Y.T. (1996) 'Blood Thicker than Water: Interpersonal Relations and Taiwanese Investment in Southern China', *Environment and Planning A*, 28: 2241–61.

Hsing, Y.T. (1997) 'Traders, Managers, and Flexibility of Enterprise Networks: Taiwanese Fashion Shoe Industry in Southern China', paper presented at the conference on 'Economic Governance and Flexible Production in East Asia', National Tsinghua University, Taiwan, 4–6 October.

Hsiung, P.C. (1996) *Living Rooms as Factories: Class, Gender, and the Satellite Factory System in Taiwan*, Philadelphia: Temple University Press.

Industry Department (1996) *Hong Kong's Manufacturing Industries: 1996*, Hong Kong: Government Printer.

Ka, C.M. (1993) *Market, Social Networks, and the Production Organization of Small-Scale Industry in Taiwan*, Taipei: Academia Sinica (in Chinese).

Kung, L. (1983) *Factory Women in Taiwan*, Ann Arbor: UMI Research Press.

Lai, Y.M. (1997) 'Restructuring strategies and organization of work in Hong Kong's garment industry', unpublished MPhil thesis, Sociology Department, The Chinese University of Hong Kong.

Lui, T.L. (1994) *Waged Work at Home: The Social Organization of Industrial Outwork in Hong Kong*, Aldershot: Avebury.

Lui, T.L. and Chiu, S. (1993) 'Industrial Restructuring and Labour Market Adjustment under Positive Non-Interventionism', *Environment and Planning A*, 25: 1, 63–79.

Michon, F. (1981) 'Dualism and the French Labour Market: Business Strategy, Non-Standard Job Forms and Secondary Job', in Wilkinson, F. (ed.) *The Dynamics of Labour Market Segmentation*, London: Academic Press.

Ng, S.H., Lui, T.L. and Chan, F.T. (1987) *Report on the Survey on the Conditions of Work for female Workers in Tsuen Wan*, Hong Kong: Government Printer.

Ngo, H.Y. (1994) 'Economic Development and Labour Market Conditions in Hong Kong', mimeograph (in Chinese).

Poon, T. (1993) 'Comparing the Subcontracting System: Towards a Synthesis in Explaining Industrial Development in Hong Kong and Taiwan', paper presented at the 5th Asian Pacific Researchers on Organizational Studies International Colloquium, East-West Center, Hawaii, 13–15 December.

Redding, S.G. (1990) *The Spirit of Chinese Capitalism*, Berlin: Walter de Gruyter.

Rodgers, G. (1989) 'Precarious Work in Western Europe', in Rodgers, G. and Rodgers, J. (eds) *Precarious Jobs in Labour Market Regulation*, Geneva: International Institute for Labour Studies.

Salaff, J. (1981) *Working Daughters of Hong Kong*, Cambridge: Cambridge University Press.

Shieh, G.S. (1992) *'Boss' Island: The Subcontracting Network and Micro-Entrepreneurship in Taiwan's Development*, New York: Peter Lang.

Sit, V.F.S. (1983) *Made In Hong Kong: A Study of Factories in Domestic Premises*, Hong Kong: Summerson Eastern Publishers Ltd.

Sit, V.F.S. and Wong, S.L. (1989) *Small and Medium Industries in an Export-oriented Economy: The Case of Hong Kong*, Hong Kong: Centre of Asian Studies, University of Hong Kong.

Skoggard, I.A. (1996) *The Indigenous Dynamic in Taiwan's Postwar Development*, Armonk: M.E. Sharpe.

Vong, T. (1993) 'Form of organizing in context: local entrepreneurs under the relocation process', unpublished MPhil thesis, Sociology Department, The Chinese University of Hong Kong.

Ward, M. (1991) 'Fashioning the Future: Fashion, Clothing, and the Manufacturing of Post-Fordist culture', *Cultural Studies*, 5: 1, 61–76.

Zhao, H.L. (1993) 'An analysis of the co-operative networks of small and medium enterprises in Taiwan', unpublished MPhil thesis, Institute of East Asian Societies and Economies, Tunghai University (in Chinese).

Notes

1 Some useful references on these topics include the following: on global economic restructuring, Henderson (1989); on economic culture, Chinese entrepreneurship and management style, Redding (1990); on the developmental state, Applebaum and Henderson (1992); and on market forces, Balassa (1988).

2 Exceptions include Chen (1994); Cheng and Gereffi (1994); Cho and Koo (1983); Chu (1992); Hsiung (1996); Ka (1993); Lui (1994); Poon (1993); Shieh (1992). See also on the subordination of labour, Deyo (1989).

3 Women's overtime work is regulated by labour legislation and has become a contentious issue between unions and business groups. On the question of overtime work, see Ng, Lui and Chan (1987).

We would like to thank the editors and Grace Wen-chi Chou for their comments on an earlier version of this chapter.

10 New Managerial Strategies of Japanese Corporations

Eiji Kyotani

Introduction

Japanese corporations became so competitive in the global market in the 1980s that their example generated the 'Japanization' of management throughout the world. However, in the 1990s they have faced serious challenges. Corporations in other Asian countries like Korea, Taiwan and China are catching up. There has been a major appreciation of the yen and corporations in North America and Europe have become fiercely competitive. Moreover, Japanese corporations are facing internal problems, such as the 'hollowing out' of Japanese industries. In the 1990s, while overseas investment by Japanese corporations has been increasing, particularly in Asian countries, the production of Japanese manufacturing industry decreased remarkably and has not yet fully recovered. This trend has a critical influence on small and medium sized enterprises which provide large corporations with intermediate products. These conditions have weakened the performance of the Japanese economy in general. In 1996, unemployment rose to its highest level since the end of the Second World War (3.4 per cent).

In order to cope with this harsh environment in the 1990s, and in order to develop further in the twenty-first century, Japanese corporations are trying to establish new managerial strategies. A major source of information about these new strategies is contained in a research project report published in May 1995 by the Japanese Federation of Employers' Associations (Nikkeiren, 1995). This chapter will draw upon material contained in this report, and other sources, in order to analyse new managerial strategies and their impact upon Japanese labour-management relations. The first section will document the development of flexible employment policies by Japanese management, including the categorisation of employees into three groups. The chapter will go on to explore changes in established personnel policies, including the seniority (*nenko*) wage, traditional promotion systems and lifelong employment (*shushin-koyo*). The implications of these new strategies for gender divisions in employment will also be considered. The chapter will

181

conclude with a discussion of growing pressures to deregulate the labour market.

Seeking More Flexibility in Employment

Japanese management is seeking more flexible ways of utilizing human resources. Its new personnel policy divides employees into three groups (Nikkeiren, 1995). The first (Group A) consists of regular employees with 'long-term employment based on the long-term accumulation of job ability' (English summary of the Nikkeiren Report, 1995:1). These not only have job security but will eventually be promoted to supervisory or managerial positions. Their wages will, in part, be increased regularly following the principle of the *nenko* wage system. The system has provided Japanese workers with a guarantee of regular wage increases based on the 'livelihood' principle, established by the militant labour movement immediately after the Second World War. They are, in this respect, equivalent to traditional core employees. However, as will be explained later, their wages and promotions will be determined more by appraisal systems than by *nenko* principles.

The second group, referred to as Group B, consists of the 'employees whose professional specialty is valued for immediate use, but without expectation of long-term employment (e.g. specialists with a fixed-term contract)' (English summary of the Nikkeiren, 1995:1). Employees of this group are professionals engaging in product design or research and development (R&D) with fixed-term contracts of three to five years. An example of this strategy is Toyota's 'Professional Contract Policy' implemented in 1994, which specified that the employment term of professionals, such as product designers, cannot be extended over five years. Although currently the number with this contract is small, Toyota is planning to hire more professionals in newly developed business fields such as communication equipment, aerospace vehicles and new transportation systems. 'In the next century', declares Toyota, 'those without long-term contracts will be increased to 30 per cent of all employees' (*Asahi Newspaper*, 14 July 1995). Nissan, another large automobile corporation, is planning to implement a similar scheme called the 'Specialist Contracts Policy'. This policy does not apply to newly hired employees but only to current employees. Employees who want to work on 'specialist contracts' instead of regular contracts will receive a 20 to 30 per cent wage increase along with a minimum guarantee of an annual salary of nearly $87000. However, they forfeit a guarantee for long-term employment and will receive only one-year contracts. If they perform badly, their contracts will not be extended. Nissan is planning to apply this policy not only to the staff in the design department and the sales promotion department but also to departments such as information and communication technology and R&D (*Nikkei News*, 20 June 1997). These professionals employed according to the new contract policy will not have the job security Group A employees hold. On the other hand, because their wages are determined solely by their efforts and results, they may possibly receive higher wages than those in Group A.

Group C, the third category, consists of 'employees with more flexible patterns of employment based on diversified personal needs and work consciousness' (English summary of the Nikkeiren, 1995:1). These employees are part-time workers and workers from staff dispatching companies (temp agencies) engaged in unskilled jobs, such as clerical work, manufacturing or sales. They are employed on fixed-term contracts and have no job security. They are paid on an hourly wage system which does not include a seniority element and will not be subject to regular increments. Wages are determined by their jobs and will not be increased regularly. Most of these individuals belong to the peripheral class of the Japanese labour market.

Other research indicates the present and future composition of Groups A, B and C. While the percentage of employees belonging to Group A will decrease from 81.3 to 70.8 per cent, those of Group B and C will increase respectively from 7.1 to 11.2 per cent and from 11.6 to 18 per cent (Nikkeiren, 1996:14). As Table 10.1 shows, 64.6 per cent of Japanese corporations plan to decrease employees belonging to Group A, whereas 72.8 per cent and 70.6 per cent expect to increase those of Groups B and C. This study also investigated the type of employees that Japanese corporations expected to reduce or increase *within* each of the three categories. It was clear that reductions in numbers of Group A employees were heavily concentrated among manufacturing workers. In contrast, the number of manufacturing workers in Group C were expected to increase markedly. It was also anticipated that R&D staff in Group B would increase sharply.

As a result of new personnel policies pursued by Japanese management, the peripheral sector of the labour market is growing. Table 10.2 shows that while there has been an increase in the *numbers* of workers of all kinds (including part-time and temp agency workers), 'non-standard' forms of employment have increased as a *proportion* of all employment.

Table 10.1   The future composition of the three groups (%)

	Increase	No Change	Decrease
Group A	3.1	32.9	64.6
Group B	72.8	21.9	6.0
Group C	70.6	26.3	3.4

Source: Nikkeiren, Follow-up Research Report on the New Japanese-Style Management System (1996:15).

Table 10.2   **Changing patterns of employment in Japan**

	'Regular' Employees			Part-Time Employees			Temp Agency Workers		
	Male	Female	Total	Male	Female	Total	Male	Female	Total
1987	24256	10309	34565	215	4462	4677	38	49	87
	(83.2)	(60.6)	(74.9)	(0.7)	(26.3)	(10.1)	(0.1)	(0.3)	(0.2)
1992	26100	11962	38062	328	5639	5967	49	114	163
	(81.4)	(58.3)	(72.4)	(1.6)	(27.5)	(11.3)	(0.2)	(0.6)	(0.3)

( ) = % of all employees.
Source: Statistics Bureau of the Japanese Government, *The 1992 Employment Status Survey*.

Figure 10.1 also illustrates that the rate of increase of employees without 'regular' contracts has been greater than that of 'regular' employees. The most rapid and consistent increase of all has been among female 'non-regular' employees.

Changing the *Nenko* Wage and Promotion System

The nenko wage system was first established around 1920. It was refashioned after World War II as a result of rising militant labour movements. In the 1960s, Japanese corporations implemented a new appraisal system known as *Noryokushugi Kanri* (the Japanese Appraisal System). In accordance with this system, wages and promotions were determined not only by the length of service (*nenko*) but by the evaluation of performance, efforts and results. Japanese management enlarged the appraisal system in the 1970s and the 1980s. For instance, in the case of NEC, one of the largest computer firms, when we compare its wage systems from 1970 and 1980 the proportion of the wages bill determined by *nenko* principles decreased from 61.4 per cent to 51.7 per cent, whereas the contribution based on evaluation principles increased from 34.6 per cent to 42 per cent. Furthermore, in 1988 large iron and steel corporations decreased the *nenko* wage from 50 per cent to 40 per cent while increasing the evaluation wage from 50 per cent to 60 per cent. They are currently planning to increase the role of evaluation still further. The Japanese Appraisal System stimulates employees to work hard, intensively and for long hours in order to achieve wage rises and promotion. Thus, intensive labour and long working hours are characteristics of the Japanese labour process (see Kyotani, 1993; 1995).

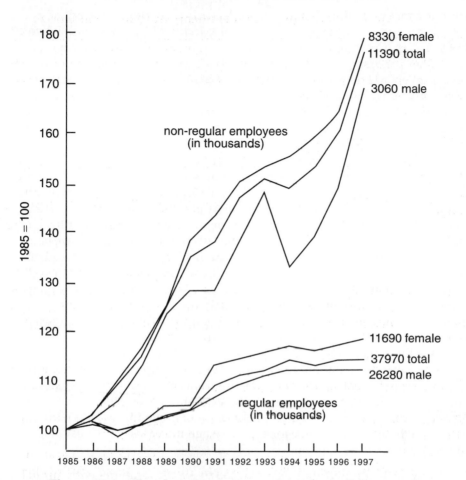

Figure 10.1   The changing pattern of regular and non-regular employment in Japan

Non-regular employees are mainly part-time workers.
Source: Statistics Bureau of the Japanese Government, *The Special Survey of the Labour Force Survey.*

In the 1990s, Japanese corporations became eager to reinforce the appraisal system by seeking to eliminate traditional personnel policies of the *nenko* system and *shushin koyo* (life-long employment) as much as possible. While in the 1960s Nikkeiren maintained that those policies would be compatible with the new appraisal system (Nikkeiren, 1969), it currently declares that they should be eliminated (Nikkeiren, 1995).

According to Nikkeiren's research, 76.4 per cent of corporations consider the wage system based on *nenko* to be an obstacle which should be removed and 81.8 per cent are planning to replace it with the wage system based on performance and effort. Indeed, in 1996, nearly a quarter increased the evaluation component of the wage (*satei*) (Nikkeiren and Kanto Keieisha Kyokai, 1996:25–26). Other research illustrates that almost all Japanese corporations are either practising, planning or considering revising the evaluation system: 45.2 per cent are revising, 41.3 per cent are planning to revise, and 8.2 per cent are considering revising. When asked about their reasons for doing so, 71.1 per cent mentioned boosting employees' morale and 64.9 per cent indicated improving their treatment of employees who perform well (Sanwa Research Institute Corporation, 1995:5–6).

These developments have brought about drastic changes in the wage system for administrative staff. Although the wages of general staff are determined by the length of service as well as performance and ability evaluation, Japanese corporations are trying to determine the wages of administrative staff solely by the latter. Accordingly, many corporations are introducing annual payment systems based on the evaluation known as *nenpo-sei*. A recent study of major corporations by the Institute of Industry and Labour demonstrates that over 10 per cent have already implemented such a system, whereas 30 per cent are planning to do so (*Asahi Newspaper*, 14 September 1996). Larger corporations more frequently utilise annual payment systems, with banks and insurance corporations to the fore. Table 10.3 illustrates how administrative staff are a major target of this policy.[1]

Once the wages of administrative staff are solely determined by performance and effort evaluation, their wages no longer necessarily increase regularly. This represents a drastic departure from the *nenko* wage system which has provided Japanese workers with a guarantee of regular wage rises. Japanese management is eagerly seeking to eliminate the tradition of regular wage increases. 'Expectation for regular wage increases every year', says the

Table 10.3   **Proportion of staff in Japanese corporations with annual payment systems (1994) (%) (includes multiple answers)**

	Admin Staff	Research Staff	Sales Staff	Professional Staff	Clerical Staff	Others
Employees						
1000+	86.8	1.3	13.0	17.9	12.7	3.1
300–999	87.9	1.7	6.7	11.7	7.8	11.0
100–299	76.0	3.7	4.3	41.8	11.1	13.1
30–99	79.4	16.1	24.8	19.1	6.7	4.7
Total	80.0	11.5	18.3	22.8	7.9	7.0

Source: The Ministry of Labour, *Comprehensive Research on Wages and Working Hours* (1996).

1995 Nikkeiren report, 'should be wiped off [eliminated]' (English summary of the Nikkeiren Report, 1995:2). The traditional wage system established after the Second World War specified a proportional raise for each employee every year, a practice commonly referred to as 'base up.' With agreements from labour unions, several corporations – such as Mitsui Metal Co. and Takeda Medical Co. – decided to abolish the system of 'base up' in 1997.

When the system of regular wage increases is eliminated, wage differentials within cohorts of employees may be expected to increase. The Japanese Appraisal System has generated a pattern of wage differentials that may be represented by the shape of a cone. Because wage differentials among employees above the managerial level will be particularly enlarged by the new system, the cone shape may be expected to become a trumpet shape. Figure 10.2 compares the outcome of the former policy with the new one.

The 1995 Nikkeiren report also declares that promotions should be determined solely by performance and effort evaluation, regardless of length of

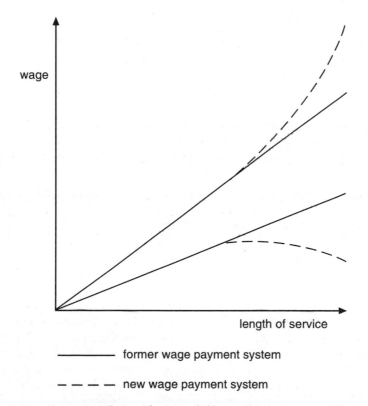

former wage payment system

– – – – new wage payment system

Figure 10.2   A comparison of wage differentials generated by former policy and new wage payment systems

Table 10.4   The job grading system and the practice of promotions (the case of Nippon Kokan Co., one of the major iron and steel corporations)

Grade	Practice of Promotion
Supervisor	The First Grade of *Shuji* (Qualified Employee) the shortest case, 5 years; the average case, 8 years; the longest case, 10 years
Subsupervisor	The Second Grade of *Shuji* the shortest case, 15 years; the average case, 22 years; the longest case, 29 years
General Production Staff	The First to the Seventh Grade of *Shain* (*General Employee*)

Source: Orii (1973:45).

service. Until recently, Japanese management has promoted workers based on evaluation as well as length of service. Table 10.4 illustrates the practice of promotion in a large Japanese iron and steel company. The length of time taken to move from subsupervisor to supervisor ranges from between 5 and 10 years, depending on performance and effort evaluation. The employers' association, Nikkeiren, in its 1995 report, argues that only the minimum number of years necessary to be promoted should be specified. When employees continually receive outstandingly high evaluations, it is suggested, they should be eligible within the minimum number of years. If employees receive bad evaluations, they may never be promoted. It follows that there will be no guarantee of promotion.

Japanese corporations, therefore, appear to be strengthening their evaluation systems. How are Japanese unions responding to this managerial strategy? A research survey which questioned 339 unions about the evaluation system found that 1.5 per cent unreservedly approved of its implementation of the evaluation system, 80.8 per cent offered conditional approval and 13.6 per cent disapproved. The conditions which the majority of unions wished to see in place included more clearly defined criteria of evaluation, minimum wage guarantees, job security and so on (Sanwa Research Institute Corporation, 1995:21–22). Unions were also asked whether the implementation of the evaluation system would strengthen or weaken their position. Nearly a third (29.2 per cent) estimated it would strengthen them, 29.5 per cent expected it would lead to no change, and 25.1 per cent anticipated it would weaken them. Those unions which painted an optimistic picture were those which expected to be able to introduce rules governing the treatment of employees with respect to matters such as wage increases and promotions or job security. Those taking a pessimistic view believed that the evaluation system would undermine the 'base up' tradition of annual wage increases, maintained and determined by collective bargaining as well as union members' solidarity.

Denki Rengo, the federation of unions in the electrical machinery industry, endorsed the reinforcement of the ability and effort evaluation system at its annual rally held in July 1997. It is planning to trade this endorsement for extending the retirement age from 60 to 65.[2] Denki Rengo claims that unions try to maintain the livelihood component of wages while simultaneously accepting reinforcement of the evaluation system (Denki Rengo, 1997). However, such a policy is contradictory because enlargement of the wage part determined by evaluation inevitably results in lessening the part determined by livelihood. Moreover, as long as the Japanese Appraisal System promotes the enlargement of wage differentials, it may undermine workers' solidarity.[3]

The End of Life-Long Employment?

Japanese corporations are also trying to undermine the traditional lifetime employment system (*shushin-koyo*). According to Nikkeiren's research, only 9.9 per cent of corporations plan to maintain the lifetime employment system (8.1 per cent in the case of those with 500 employees or over). The rest anticipate that employment will be more flexible or less stable (Nikkeiren and Kanto Keieisha Kyokai, 1996:60).

Japanese management is not only trying to diminish the number of regular employees with long-term employment (Group A described above) but is also implementing various policies for encouraging employees to leave or change their jobs. These include an early retirement policy – or a 'supporting policy for shifting gears'. Matsushita Electric Co. started a new early retirement policy which pays employees aged 50 to 58 who want to retire a premium remuneration equivalent to 2.5 times their largest potential annual salary plus ordinary retirement pay. Sony Electric Co. implemented a similar policy which pays employees over 35 with more than 10 years service a premium equivalent to 1.5 times their annual salary plus their retirement pay. Sakura Bank has established a new policy which gives special leave to employees who are planning to leave, enabling them to prepare for a new job (see Table 10.5). According to the 1997 Employment Status Survey by the Ministry of Labour, larger corporations more frequently practice these policies. Some 55.7 per cent of corporations with 5000 employees or over have early retirement programmes, 41.2 per cent have 'programmes for transferring employees to related firms' (*tenseki-shukko*), 23.7 per cent 'shifting gear programmes', and 16.3 per cent have programmes for encouraging entrepreneurship (*dokuritsu-kaigyo*) (Rodosho, 1997c:7). Transfer programmes (*tenseki-shukko*) are so popular as a means of decreasing the number of regular employees in large firms

Table 10.5   Early retirement and 'supporting shifting gears' policies

---

Matsushita Electric Co., 'The Life Plan Supporting Policy'
- applying to employees above managers between the age of 50 and 58
- premium remuneration equivalent to 2.5 times their largest potential annual salary plus ordinary retirement pay
- three-month special leave for preparing for a new job before retiring

Sony Electric Co., 'The Second Career Supporting Policy'
- applying to employees older than 35 with over 10 years of service
- premium equivalent to 1.5 times their annual salary plus their retirement pay for the purpose of starting their own businesses or new jobs

Sakura Bank, 'The New Career Supporting Policy'
- applying to employees older than 45 with over 20 years of service
- premium plus ordinary retirement pay
- special leave for preparing for a new job, the longest being 6 months and income guarantee of 80% of monthly wages and bonuses

---

Source: Nikkei News, 24 February 1996; *Asahi Newspaper,* 15 September 1996.

that 24 per cent of administrative staff working for firms with 5000 employees or over are transferred before their official retirement age of 60. The figure is 12 per cent for general staff (Rodosho, 1997c:19).

By downsizing in this way, Japanese corporations are diminishing their number of core workers. Both Hitachi and Toshiba have decreased the number of their employees by 5 to 6 per cent (*Asahi Newspaper,* 9 March 1996). At the end of 1995, the number of employees of nearly one million corporations in Japan decreased by 174765 (0.6 per cent) over the previous year (*Asahi Newspaper,* 17 July 1996).[4]

Responding to this downsizing policy, Japanese unions have demanded stable, long-term employment (Rengo, 1996; Denki Rengo, 1997). However, they have softened this position in two respects. First, they are not insisting upon job security within a single corporation but within a group of related corporations, which means they accept employee transfer programs (*tenseki-shukko*). Second, they are no longer clinging to the *nenko* wage system and are more prepared to accept the expanding evaluation system (see Denki Rengo, 1997).

By way of context, it should be noted that the postponement of the official retirement age from 60 to 65 is currently a controversial issue in Japanese industry. In the next century, Japan is expected to have a higher percentage of people over 65 than any other industrialized country. It is for this reason that in 1994 the Japanese government decided to postpone from 60 to 65 the age when people start receiving their pensions, phased in over a number of years in the early part of the twenty-first century.

At present, however, over 90 per cent of corporations have an official retirement age set at 60 and, in the near future, this is expected to rise to 97.1 per cent (Rodosho, 1997c:3). The gap between retirement age and the age when people can start receiving their pensions suggests a period of hardship for many elderly people in the future. The government is promoting a 'Working Till 65' policy in order to facilitate the postponement of the retirement age. The Japanese Ministry of Labour (Rodosho) report on this issue suggests that the redefinition of the retirement age requires the *nenko* system to be changed and the evaluation system to be expanded (Rodosho, 1997a:351–52; Rodosho, 1997b:12–14).[5]

Gender Implications of the New Strategy

Since the establishment of the *Equal Job Rights Law* in 1986, many corporations have implemented the 'Job Career Path Programme' (*Kosubetsu Koyo Seido*), which divides employees into two groups; the 'general staff group' (*ippanshoku*) and the 'executive candidates group' (*sogoshoku*). The former are engaged in unskilled or repetitive jobs under the direction of management and will never be promoted to the position of manager. However long they serve, they will always stay at the level of general staff. The latter group of employees is expected to achieve managerial or professional status after experiencing various jobs in their corporations. They may be promoted to executive positions such as chief executive officers. Large numbers of corporations have been implementing the Career Path Programme, most notably those with substantial numbers of employees. The 1995 Survey on women's employment status by the Ministry of Labour revealed that 52 per cent of corporations with 5000 or more employees had such a programme (Rodosho, 1996, *Rodojiho* 38–40). In practice, this policy is working as a means of segregating male and female employees. As Table 10.6 illustrates, in 1997 most newly hired female workers belonged to the general staff group, whereas only a few belonged to the executive candidates group. No male employees belonged to the former group.[6]

In Japan, government, management and unions are all declaring their support for the employment of more female workers. However, current policies implemented by some corporations indicate that Japanese management is trying to enhance the segregation of core and peripheral workers within the female work force. For example, Mitsubishi-Shoji, one of the largest Japanese trading companies, is planning to increase the proportion

Table 10.6   Job career path programme in major banks: newly hired employees' choice of career path in 1997 (numbers)

Banks	Sogoshoku Executive Candidates Group		Ippanshoku General Staff Group	
	Male	Female	Male	Female
Sakura	178	20	0	0
Daiichikangin	265	15	0	550
Sumimoto	173	8	0	578
Fuji	205*	–	0	385
Tokyo-Mitsubishi	145	5	0	600
Sanwa	288	4	0	625
Asahi	254	5	0	354
Tokai	251	7	0	448
Daiwa	63	0	0	25
Takugin	29	0	0	139
Total	1851	64	0	3704

* total of male and female.
Source: *Ginko Shinpo* (*The Bank News*), 2031: 5, April 1997.

of female employees among the executive candidates group to one-third. At the same time, it has decided to stop hiring female workers for the general staff group, replacing them with female temp agency workers (*Nikkei News*, 1 January 1996). Uchida Yoko, another large trading corporation, has decided to implement a similar policy. It will not only eliminate the system of hiring junior college female graduates every spring as clerical staff, but will remove all clerical employees, currently more than 400, over the next 5 years. These female employees are planned to be replaced with female workers provided by Uchida Yoko's related temp agency (*Nikkei News*, July 26 1996).

This managerial strategy for female labour is increasing the number of female workers with unstable employment contracts, such as temp agency workers and part-time workers (see Table 10.2 and Figure 10.1). Furthermore, the reinforcement of the evaluation system is expected to create harsher conditions for female workers. Masumi Mori, who has conducted research on new personnel policies in major Japanese trading companies, concluded that new policies have not only enlarged wage differentials of male and female employees but have decreased wages for a majority of female workers (Mori, 1997).

Loosening Legal Regulations

As this chapter has discussed, the new managerial strategies of Japanese corporations seek to utilise a greater number of workers in flexible employment, such as part-time workers and temp agency workers. In order to facilitate this further, employers have demanded that the government loosen labour law regulations.

First, they demand that the regulation of private job information agencies and temp agencies be weakened. Currently, the Japanese Ministry of Labour allows those agencies only to deal in designated jobs. However, employers are claiming that the Ministry should solely confine itself to listing jobs in which they are *not* allowed to deal. In other words, they insist that the 'positive list' which fundamentally limits the usage of agencies should be replaced with a 'negative list' which authorises their use. In the past, there were only 29 jobs for which private agencies could recruit (including cooks, nurses, hair dressers and administrative staff). However, regulation of recruitment to white collar jobs was completely eliminated in April 1997. Furthermore, employers are insisting that the government also eliminate regulations on blue collar jobs in the manufacturing and construction industries. Employers are also demanding the loosening of regulations surrounding temp agencies. Japanese labour law previously only allowed temp agencies to recruit workers for 15 jobs: secretaries, translators, software programmers and so on. Responding to management's demands, in December 1996 this list of jobs was increased by 11, to include R&D staff, advertisement designers, sales engineers, news reporters and so on. Employers are still demanding that temp agency workers be allowed to work in all white collar posts.

Second, legal regulations on the usage of female workers have been loosened. In June 1997 the Japanese Diet decided on this course of action at the same time as strengthening the regulations of the *Equal Job Rights Law*. Before the revision of the law, because penalties for the violators had not been specified, management could not legally be compelled to uphold it. The revised law prohibits employers from discriminating against female workers and is expected to enforce penalties by disclosing the names of deviant corporations.[7] At the same time, the Diet decided to eliminate a regulation on the use of female employees for night work. Only a few jobs – such as nurses, telephone operators, and stewardesses – used to be allowed for night labour. However, following these changes female employees working shifts in workshops are expected to engage equally with men in night work.

Finally, Japanese employers are demanding that the government weaken regulations on working hours and terms of employment contracts. As illustrated above, they are planning to increase the numbers of employees with special contracts of 3 to 5 years (Group B outlined earlier). The present legal regulation limits these terms to 1 year and they are, therefore, an obstacle to this new policy. As for a criterion of wage determination, employers are insisting that effort and result replace the number of working hours. Wages, they claim, should be determined by results not by working hours. As long as the law regulates working hours of every job evenly (for example, 40 hours a week) they cannot fully achieve this goal. Currently 11 jobs – such as R&D staff, editors, and lawyers – are exceptions to this regulation. These jobs are called *sairyo rodo*, (discretionary work), where employees have the freedom of discretion to decide on their working procedures and hours with few instructions from management. Employers have so strongly been demanding the enlargement of categories in these exceptions that the Ministry of Labour has decided to apply the 'discretionary work' system widely to white collar jobs (*Asahi Newspaper*, 3 July 1997).

Conclusion

As this chapter has shown, new managerial strategies of Japanese corporations have resulted in a reduction in the size of the core employment sector and an increase in the number of peripheral employees. Core employees are also experiencing hardship because Japanese management is trying to eliminate traditional employment systems of *nenko* and *shushin-koyo* (regular wage increases and promotions) and lifetime employment as much as possible. New strategies are having considerable implications for gender divisions in the Japanese labour market.

These changes are of great importance for Japanese labour-management relations. So far co-operative relations have been prominent in Japan, based on guarantees for regular wage increases and for job security. Because Japanese workers have enjoyed such guarantees, they have been co-operative with management in increasing productivity; for example, by participating in QC (Quality Control) or KAIZEN activities through which they voluntarily and continually improve the production process (Kyotani, 1993; 1995). However, as we have seen, new strategies are undermining these fundamental guarantees. Japanese labour-management relations may lose their stability as a result. However, it should be remembered that the membership of most Japanese unions comprises regular employees (*sei-shain*) whereas employees without regular contracts (such as part-time workers, temp agency workers and temporarily hired workers) are usually not organized. As long as new strategies decrease the number of regular employees and increase the number of non-regular employees, Japanese unions may be expected to lose membership as well as leverage. Furthermore, as long as the reinforced 'Japanese Appraisal System' is expanding wage and status differentials, employees may become more *individualized* or *atomized*. This, in turn, may undermine the foundation of labour unions' prerogatives, that is, workers' collective relationships and solidarity.

References

Abe, M. (1996) 'Kiseikanwa no motodeno Koyo Jinji System to Roshikankei' (The Influence of Deregulation Policies on Industrial Relations through the Introduction of New Employment and Personnel Management Systems), *Shakai-Seisaku Sosho (Research Series of the Study of Social Policy)*, 20: 79–101.

Asahi Newspaper 14 July 1995.

Asahi Newspaper 9 March 1996.

Asahi Newspaper 17 July 1996.

Asahi Newspaper 14 September 1996.

Asahi Newspaper 15 September 1996.

Asahi Newspaper 3 July 1997.

Denki Rengo (The Japanese Electrical, Electronic and Information Union) (1997) 'For Building the New Japanese Employment System' (Japanese), Unpublished document, 45th Conference of the DR, Tokyo: DR.

Koyo Joho Centre (The Centre of Employment Information) (1996) *A Research Report on the New Personnel Policies in the New Age* (Japanese), Tokyo: Koyo-Joho Centre.

Kyotani, E. (1993) *Flexibility towa Nanika* (What is the Flexibility of the Japanese Labour Process?), Tokyo: Madosha.

Kyotani, E. (1995) 'The Bright and Dark Sides of the Japanese Labor Process', presented at the 1995 Annual Meeting of the Society for the Study of Social Problems, Washington, DC, USA, August 18–20, 1995.

Mori, M. (1997) 'Shosha ni miru Seisabetsu Koyokanri no Konnichiteki Shoso' (Current Gender Discrimination of Employment Management in the Trading Company), *Keizai to Shakai (Economy and Society)*, 9: 111–127.

Nagai, Y. (1996) 'Rodosha Hakenho Minaoshi no Hyoka to Ronten' (An Evaluation and Discussion of the 'Revision' of the Worker Dispatching Law), *Shakai-Seisaku Gakkai Nenpo (Annals of the Society for the Study of Social Policy)*, 40: 171–202.

Nagai, Y. (1997) 'Koyo-Rodo Shijo no Danryokuka Senryaku to Nihonteki Roshi Kankei' (The Flexibility Strategy of the Labour Market and its Effects on Japanese Labour-Management Relations: A View from the Research on Temp Agency Workers) *Rodoshakai Gekkai Nenpo (Annual Review of the Japanese Association of Labour Sociology)*, 8: 37–63.

Nikkei News 1 January 1996.

Nikkei News 24 February 1996.

Nikkei News 26 July 1996.

Nikkei News 20 June 1997.

Nikkeiren (Japan Federation of Employers' Association) (1969) *Noryokushugi Kanri (The Japanese Appraisal System)*, Tokyo: Nikkeiren.

Nikkeiren (1995) *Shin Jidai no Nihonteki Keiei (The Research Project Report on the New Japanese-Style Management System)*, Tokyo: Nikkeiren.

Nikkeiren and Kanto Keieisha Kyokai (Kanto Employers' Association) (1996) *Shin Jidai no Nihonteki Keiei ni tsuiteno Follow Up Chosa Hokoku (The Follow-up Research Report on the New Japanese-Style Management System)*, Tokyo: Nikkeiren and Kanto Keieisha Kyokai.

Orii, H. (1973) *Romu Kanri Nijunen (Twenty Years of Labour Management)*, Tokyo: Toyo Keizai.

Rengo (the Japanese Trade Union Confederation) (1996) *Rengo Chingin Seisaku (Rengo's Wage Policy)*, Unpublished document, Annual Conference of JTUC, Tokyo: JTUC.

Rodosho (The Japanese Ministry of Labour) (1996) *Rodojiho*, 574 (Survey on Women's Employment Status), Tokyo: Dalichihoki Shuppan.

Rodosho (the Japanese Ministry of Labour) (1997a) *Koyo Report 1997 (The 1997 Report on Employment: How Can We Prevent Japan from being a Country with a High Unemployment Rate?)*, Tokyo: Romugyosei Kenkyujo.

Rodosho (1997b) *65sai Geneki Shakai Kenkyukai Hokokusho (A Research Report on the 'Working Till 65 Society')*, Tokyo: Rodosho.

Rodosho (1997c) *Koyo Kanri Chosa Kekka Sokuho (A Prompt Report on the 1997 Employment Status Survey)*, Tokyo: Rodosho.

Sanwa Sogo Kenkyujo (Sanwa Research Institute Corporation) (1995) *Hyoka Seido ni kansuru Chosa Kenkyu Hokokusho (A Research Report on the Evaluation System of Japanese Corporations)*, Tokyo: SRIC.

Statistics Bureau of the Japanese Government (1997), *1996 Rodoryoku Chosa Nenpo (1996 Annual Report on the Labour Force Survey)*, Tokyo: Nippon Tokei Kyokai.

Sugiura, Y. (1997) 'Nihonteki Koyokanko no Shoraizo ni tsuiteno Kosatsu' (An Analysis of the Future of the Japanese Employment System), Rodosho (the Japanese Ministry of Labour), *Rodo Tokei Chosa Geppo (Monthly Report on Labour Statistics)*, 49: 5, 6–15.

Suzuki, Y. (1996) 'Nihonteki Roshikankei no Yuragi' (Changes of Industrial Relations in Postwar Japan and Present Situation), *Keizai to Shakai (Economy and Society)*, 5: 23–44.

Takanashi, A. (1994) *Kawaru Nihongata Koyo (Japan's Changing Employment System)*, Tokyo: Nihon Keizai Shinbunsha.

Takanashi, A. (1996) 'Konnichi no Kiseikanwa to Rodoseisaku' (The Deregulation and Labour Policy in Recent Japan), *Shakai-Seisaku Sosho (Research Series of the Study of Social Policy)*, 20: 1–19.

Uchihashi, K. and Kumazawa, M. (1997) 'Kiseikanwa de Hatarakikata wa Donaruka (How will the Deregulation of Labour Law Change Working Life?)', *Sekai*, 637: 257–269.

Watanabe, T. (1995) *Kosubetsu Koyokanri to Joshirodo (Career Path Programmes and Female Workers)*, Tokyo: Chuo Keizaisha.

Notes

1   The 1996 Nikkeiren and Kanto Keieisha Kyokai report which surveyed 3200 corporations shows 46.6 per cent of them to have annual payment systems and 56.4 per cent of corporations with 500 employees or over to have them (Nikkeiren and Kanto Keieisha Kyokai, 1996:29).

2   This acceptance also reflects white collar employees' consciousness. They prefer the wage system based on the evaluation whereas blue-collar employees prefer the system based on livelihood (Sugiura, 1997:9).

3   As a result of managerial strategies for eliminating the *nenko* wage system, age differences have been of decreasing importance in explaining wage differentials of white collar employees (Rodosho, 1997a:342).

4   While Japanese employers are eager to eliminate lifetime employment, they are afraid it will undermine employees' commitment to management. Nearly three-quarters of corporations identify this symptom as a downside of eliminating lifetime employment (Nikkeiren and Kanto Keieisha Kyokai, 1996:11).

5   As shown above, unions are trying to trade the acceptance of the expanding evaluation system for the postponed retirement age. The elimination of the *nenko* system, the expansion of the evaluation system, and the increasing popularity of flexible employment are closely related to the ageing of the Japanese working population. In addition, unemployment rates for both young and elderly people

are higher than for other age groups. According to the 1996 *Labour Force Survey*, while the average unemployment rate is 3.4 per cent, the rates for ages 15–24 and 55–64 are 6.6 per cent and 4.2 per cent (Statistics Bureau of the Japanese Government, 1997:20).

6　While the executive candidates' group is open to both men and women, the general staff group is open only to women, however, this segregation does not violate the Equal Job Rights Law. The law prohibits jobs opened only to men but not those opened only to women.

7　However, the revised *Equal Rights Law* cannot solve the problem of the Job Career Path Program described above. Following the programme, each female employee chooses her career path. Moreover, if female wages are lower than those of males as a result of the evaluation system, these differentials do not fall foul of the law.

I would like to thank my colleague, William Puck Brecher, for his kindness in reviewing my draft and giving me important suggestions. I would also like to express my gratitude to Professor Yoritoshi Nagai at Ehime University for his permission to use his data.

Index of Authors

Note: page numbers in **bold** refer to illustrative figures or tables.

Index of Subjects

Note: page numbers in **bold** type refer to illustrative figures or tables.